The Perversion of Youth

PSYCHOLOGY AND CRIME SERIES

General Editor: Allen Kenneth Hess

The Perversion of Youth:
Controversies in the Assessment and Treatment of Juvenile Sex Offenders
Frank C. DiCataldo

The Perversion of Youth

*Controversies in the
Assessment and Treatment
of Juvenile Sex Offenders*

Frank C. DiCataldo

NEW YORK UNIVERSITY PRESS
New York and London

NEW YORK UNIVERSITY PRESS
New York and London
www.nyupress.org

Library of Congress Cataloging-in-Publication Data

DiCataldo, Frank C.
The perversion of youth : controversies in the assessment and
treatment of juvenile sex offenders / Frank C. DiCataldo.
p. cm. — (Psychology and crime series)
Includes bibliographical references and index.
ISBN-13: 978-0-8147-2001-1 (cl : alk. paper)
ISBN-10: 0-8147-2001-3 (cl : alk. paper)
ISBN-13: 978-0-8147-2002-8 (pb : alk. paper)
ISBN-10: 0-8147-2002-1 (pb : alk. paper)
1. Teenage sex offenders—Psychology. 2. Teenage sex offenders--
Rehabilitation. I. Title.
HV9067.S48D53   2009
364.15'30835—dc22   2008052995

New York University Press books are printed on acid-free paper, and
their binding materials are chosen for strength and durability. We
strive to use environmentally responsible suppliers and materials to
the greatest extent possible in publishing our books.

Manufactured in the United States of America

c   10 9 8 7 6 5 4 3 2 1
p   10 9 8 7 6 5 4 3 2 1

*In memory of Ray Silva,
whose sense of humor
was welcomed company
on long nights of work.*

Contents

Acknowledgments

The inspiration for this book emerged from the dozen or so years I have spent as the director of the Forensic Evaluation Service for the Massachusetts Department of Youth Services. It is to the Massachusetts Department of Youth Services that I owe the greatest debt of thanks for entrusting to me the responsibility of directing its psychological evaluation service these many years. This job has been far and away the most fulfilling professional experience of my career and one that I look forward to continuing in the future. Thanks to the numerous clinicians, case workers, administrators, and, mostly, the adolescents who have shared their stories with me over the years.

Thanks are also due to Dr. Joel Haycock, the executive director of the Bedford Policy Institute, an agency we, among others, founded together for the purpose of providing mental health services for adolescents committed to the Massachusetts Department of Youth Services. My years of service to the Bedford Policy Institute have been truly enriching, and I am very grateful for Joel's friendship and counsel.

I want to thank Tom Paladino and Bob Cohen from the Interior Class, Paul Nestor, and Jurgen Kern for their helpful critiques of some of the earlier, more misshapen versions of this manuscript. Their support and encouragement during the writing and rewriting were invaluable to me. Thanks for checking in and lending a hand.

Dr. Don Whitworth, the coordinator of the master of arts program in forensic psychology at Roger Williams University in Bristol, Rhode Island, has been a truly generous advocate and supporter. He encouraged me early on to pursue this idea and never wavered in his belief in its value and my ability, even when I doubted them the most. Thank you also to the Feinstein College of Arts and Sciences at Roger Williams University for its generous support that enabled me to complete the research and writing.

Thanks always to Tom Grisso, a mentor who first sparked my interest in juvenile delinquency as a graduate student. This book is a long overdue return on the commitment you invested in me.

I had the aid of a number of assistants who tracked down obscure references and helped in the design of the tables and graphs. In no particular order, I want to thank Meghan Everett, Emmalynn Angeles, and Kate Provencher, my graduate student research assistant, for their dedicated service and assistance.

I am especially grateful to Jennifer Hammer, my editor at NYU Press. Thank you for seeing the value in the idea and mostly thank you for your critical eye and attention to detail. This book was made significantly better by your work. I truly enjoyed working with you.

Many of the ideas behind this book were generated during many long conversations and debates I had over the years with Ray Silva, to whose memory this book is dedicated. I miss him greatly and felt the presence of his nodding endorsement through much of the writing.

Finally, thank you to Barbara and our boys, Sam and Leo. My last thoughts of the day were often about this book, but my first and best were always about you.

1

The Birth of a Moral Panic

Delinquency has always been with us. Adolescents have always fought, stolen, run away, abused substances, been truant, set fires, destroyed property, and congregated in groups that promulgate such activities. There is nothing new about adolescents engaging in these troublesome behaviors. But childhood sexuality is an idea deeply engraved in the American psyche as something altogether different: damaging, scarring, inherently harmful, traumatizing, a warping mark (Levine 1996). To borrow a phrase from Michel Foucault (1978), sex has been problematized by us moderns, and nowhere does this problematization run deeper than in the sexuality of children and adolescents.

Childhood sexuality has become a police matter, or at least a matter for the legions of child welfare and delinquency workers who police the borders of the various systems that have been devised—child welfare or dependency, education, mental health, and juvenile justice—to deal with the "troubling and troublesome children" (Weithorn 2005) who are shuttled back and forth across the porous borders of these interconnecting networks of institutions and systems. The children who are netted within the webs of these various systems often share more commonalities with each other than differences. What happens to any of these children, where they end up—in the mental health, child welfare, or juvenile justice system—often depends more on which system they happen to enter than on anything unique or distinctive about their needs (Lerman 1982). Often, where they enter depends on their race, their social class, their sex, or just plain old random misfortune. The significant question is why juvenile sex offenders have been separated out of this churning, heterogeneous mixture of "troubling and troublesome children" and set apart as separate and distinct from the rest of the children held within the vast child-saving network of systems and institutions.

Historians of childhood since Phillip Ariès (1962) have argued that children and childhood are the products of our ways of seeing. The child is not something out there in the world, a natural object, waiting to be discovered (Kincaid 1998). The child is a byproduct of the web of institutions and the systems of thought within which he or she is ensnared. And these systems of thought are historically contingent and situated. They shift and evolve, and the view of the child within their prisms shifts and changes accordingly. The idea of the child is not static, not a given or a discovery. The child is shaped by the ideational framework within which he or she is captured. Throughout history children have been trapped within discourses of romantic innocence contaminated by a vile world; discourses that portray them as a tabula rasa awaiting the imprinting of experience; discourses that depict them in a state of savagery tempered by a disciplined order; and discourses that implant within them a biological program of development that unfolds within a facilitating environment. There have been discourses upon discourses of childhood that have produced a vast gallery of distinct childhood portraitures through history.

Today the adolescent who has engaged in some form of sexual misconduct and is legally labeled a juvenile sex offender has been framed within a discourse of deviant desire. Such youth are no longer depicted as errant minors in need of some corrective guidance or instruction; rather, they have been implanted with an alien sexuality that requires exclusionary legal and mental health treatment—confinement, assessment, intervention, community surveillance—and, in most cases, the prevailing wisdom of these views argues, some of these measures need to be applied across the span of their lives. They are no longer depicted as awkward, fumbling sexual neophytes prone to impulsive and poorly judged acts that will probably smooth out with maturation and corrective experience, but instead are seen as budding sexual menaces in need of careful surveillance and control. The categories used for adolescents whose sexual experiences have drawn the attention of the legal system are often loose and amorphous. The 18-year-old victim of sexual assault is a child while the 14-year-old molester is frequently an adult (Kincaid 1998). Analyzing how these categories are constructed and maintained is the overarching task of this book. What empirical evidence exists to support the conceptualization of juvenile sex offenders in the manner that prevails today? Are there empirically sound alternatives for the treatment of juvenile sex offenders that are less potentially harmful to them and still meet the goal of protecting the community? These are the questions that occupy the chapters ahead.

• • •

"Two teens face charges of statutory rape of girl" (Schworm 2005)—a headline newsworthy enough for front page coverage in the city section of a large metropolitan newspaper. It was the third criminal case that year of underage sex in the school. Two 17-year-old boys, well-regarded athletes in a public high school of high academic standing, were arrested and charged in district court for having sex with a 15-year-old girl from the same high school. The brief newspaper report cleared up the usual questions often surrounding incidents like these. The sexual acts were not violent; they were not described as overtly coercive. The report called the acts "consensual," but legally that is impossible because the legal age of consent in this particular state begins at 16. The victim reported two separate sexual incidents with the perpetrators: the first at one of the perpetrator's homes and the second at an undisclosed location somewhere in another nearby city. The boys were also charged with disseminating obscene material to a minor, as a number of pornographic videos were confiscated from one of the perpetrator's homes. The boys allegedly viewed the videos with the girl. The newspaper article quoted the high school principal describing the case as "deeply disturbing," and in a letter sent to parents he wrote, "The behavior of these young people is unacceptable, irresponsible, and illegal." A varsity coach of one of the boys said he was stunned and "sick to his stomach."

There is no way of knowing from the story how close the victim was to the bright line for the legal age of consent—as much as a year or as little as a day—or how much the perpetrators were over that other magical transitional line—the one that divides juvenile court and adult court jurisdiction. Juvenile court jurisdiction ends after 16 years of age in this state; at 17 one is an adult. These perpetrators were suspended from school while they awaited trial in adult court for the rape of a minor child. And though they will probably be sentenced if convicted, whether by trial or by a plea, to a term of probation with community service and outpatient sex offender treatment, they will also probably have to comply with the state's mandatory sex offender registry law. They will be assigned a risk category by a classification board and will be required to inform the police within their residential community about their presence for the next twenty years.

The remaining factual ambiguities about the sexual acts themselves are easily cleared away with the description that they were engaged in willingly, if not legally consensually, by all the participants. The moral ambiguity of the story is not as easily resolved. What is this story about?

What is the warning? What makes it newsworthy? What aspect of it draws our collective attention or concern? Is it the fact that two 17-year-old boys had sex with a 15-year-old girl who was unable to provide legal consent? Or is it that two 17-year-old boys were arrested and will be charged in district court for rape of a minor—that they will be classified as sexual offenders who will be required to attend sexual offender treatment and mandated to register as sexual offenders for the next twenty years? The report itself, told with journalistic neutrality, does not betray a point of view.

The current movement to hold children equally as legally accountable for their sexual transgressions as we do adults is born out of the best of intentions. But even the best of intentions can carry coiled within them unintended negative consequences. The predominant trend that advocates dealing with most instances of sexual misconduct of children and adolescents through formal legal measures is predicated on the idea that by not doing so we enter into a sort of complicity with the offender, a subtle endorsement of the sexual act. The trend is viewed as a corrective revision of a deeply misguided historical practice that often failed to hold adolescent boys accountable for their sexual acts, when the sexually abusive behavior of juveniles was often dismissed as "an adjustment reaction," "a manifestation of stress," "sexual experimentation or curiosity," or merely "boys being boys."

Lionel Trilling (1947), the novelist and literary critic, in an essay entitled "Manners, Morals, and the Novel," advanced the idea of the novel as a form of investigation that is able to peer beneath the hidden cruelties of our most benevolent social actions. Think of the nineteenth-century novels of Charles Dickens or Henry James or the twentieth-century naturalism of Stephen Crane or Theodore Dreiser, with their stories about the carnage heaped upon the life outcomes of their protagonists, trapped like wounded animals within moral systems that foretold their ruin. Through its adherence to a perspective Trilling termed "moral realism," the novel demonstrates

> that to act against social injustice is right and noble but that to choose to act so does not settle all moral problems but on the contrary generates new ones of an especially difficult sort. . . . We have the books that point out the bad conditions, that praise us for taking progressive attitudes. We have no books that raise questions in our minds not only about

conditions but about ourselves, that lead us to refine our motives and ask what might lie behind our good impulses. There is nothing so very terrible in discovering that something does lie behind. (Trilling 1947, 116-17)

That some unspoken cruelty or, more likely, some unacknowledged fear may lie behind our "moral passions" is worth knowing. Trilling warned us about the insidious nature of our "moral passions," such as those that direct the current response to juvenile sex offenders: "We must be aware of the dangers which lie in our most generous wishes" (118). And so it is with the current trend to criminalize many forms of adolescent sexual transgressions: it solves one set of problems while generating entirely new ones that will need new solving.

Genarlow Wilson's story reads like a modern American gothic novel. He was released from a Georgia Department of Correction facility after serving two years of a ten-year sentence for the felony conviction of aggravated child molestation (CNN 2007a and b; Goodman 2007a and b). His mother and younger sister were there to greet him at the correctional facility following the Supreme Court of Georgia's decision on October 27, 2007, declaring that his sentence amounted to a violation of the Eighth Amendment's prohibition against "cruel and unusual punishment." At a 2003 New Year's Eve party, an intoxicated Wilson, 17, a star athlete and honor student, had received oral sex from an intoxicated 15-year-old girl, too young to legally consent to such an act and considered too drunk anyway to have been able to provide such consent had she been old enough. It was all right there on the videotape filmed at the party.

News of his case set off a media firestorm of controversy, capturing the support for Wilson of former president Jimmy Carter, also a former governor of Georgia, and several members of the jury that convicted Wilson, who were unaware at the time of their deliberation of the mandatory minimum sentence that a guilty verdict would require of him. A cruel twist in the case was the fact that if Wilson had had sexual intercourse with the victim rather than oral sex, he would have been spared the felony conviction and would have been convicted of a misdemeanor offense because of a "Romeo and Juliet" provision that sought to protect adolescent defendants like Wilson who engage in sexual intercourse with underage partners. The Georgia General Assembly in 2006, in response to Wilson's case, closed the oral-sex loophole, defining most sexual acts between willing but legally nonconsenting adolescent participants, no more than four years apart in age, a misdemeanor punishable by no more than a 12-month sentence without a mandatory requirement that the defendant register as a sex offender with the state. But the legislature deliberately refused to have the amended law apply retroactively. Wilson remained incarcerated until the state Supreme Court ordered his release. In the various stages of appeals, counsel for Wilson argued that the sentence was too severe for a case of two drunken teenagers at a party. The law arguably was intended to protect children from the unscrupulous predation of adult sex offenders, and was not intended to apply to an adolescent who lacked anything remotely resembling a perverted past.

The media outrage focused more on the issue of racial discrimination than the criminalization of adolescent sex. Wilson was black. His plight was largely wrapped within the larger social discourse about the entrenched racial biases in the criminal justice system. But this case at its origins may have as much to do with the collective fears of adolescent sexuality and the sexual abuse of children as it does with racial injustice. In this case the 15-year-old victim was a child and the 17-year-old perpetrator was an adult, and although they were separated by only two chronological years, more or less, they were being depicted by the criminal justice system in terms about as far apart as is possible. They existed at opposite ends of the criminal justice spectrum: victim and offender.

Wilson had refused the offer of a plea bargain from the prosecutor even though it would probably have resulted in a briefer sentence, maybe even release with time served and community registration. He refused because an admission of guilt would have affixed on him the label of sex offender, which would have trailed him for the rest of his days. As a sex offender registrant, Wilson would have to provide the state with his address, his fingerprints, his Social Security number, his date of birth, and his photograph, and he would have to update this information every year for the rest of his life. All this information would be posted in various public places and on the internet. Moreover, Wilson would be unable to live or work within one thousand feet of any child care facility, church, or area where minors congregate. What if the designation prevented him from having unsupervised contact with his younger sister or followed him into college and beyond? This was too high a price to pay, in his estimation, so he refused the plea and took his chances with the courts.

The Supreme Court of Georgia in a four to three decision concluded that "Wilson's sentence of ten years in prison for having consensual oral sex with a fifteen-year-old girl when he was only 17-years-old constitutes cruel and unusual punishment" (*Humphrey v. Wilson* 2007, 1) and was "grossly disproportionate to the offense" (11). The court further concluded that the legislative amendments to the law, reducing an adolescent defendant's sexual acts with victims not more than four years younger to a misdemeanor offense, which followed Wilson's conviction but did not retroactively apply to him, represented

> a seismic shift in the legislature's view of the gravity of oral sex between two willing teenage participants . . . [and] that the severe felony punishment and sex offender registration imposed on Wilson make no measurable contribution to acceptable goals of punishment. . . . This conclusion appears to be a recognition by our General Assembly that teenagers are engaging in oral sex in large numbers; that teenagers should not be classified among the worst offenders because they do not have the maturity to appreciate the consequences of irresponsible sexual conduct and are readily subject to peer pressure; and that teenage sexual conduct does not usually involve violence and represents a significantly more benign situation than that of adults preying on children for sex. (*Humphrey v. Wilson* 2007, 18-20)

Juvenile sexual offending is certainly a serious problem that needs to be addressed rationally. The concern now is that what started out as a solution to one social problem may have tipped over into a new problem from which new relief must be sought. It is hard to consider the story of Glenarlow Wilson and not conclude that a state of "moral panic" (Cohen 1972) presides in the current legal response to juvenile sex offenders. The current state of the legal response to juvenile sex offenders has led legal scholars like Franklin Zimring (2004) to describe it as an "American travesty" and others to lament that perhaps the pendulum has swung too far in the direction of draconian responses (Barbaree and Marshall 2006; Chaffin and Bonner 1998; Letourneau and Miner 2005).

The momentum for the current state of affairs was set off in the late 1970s and early 1980s when it was discovered that sexually dangerous adults often began their sexually deviant careers in adolescence (Abel, Becker, Mittelman et al. 1987; Abel, Osborne, and Twigg 1993; Groth 1977; Groth, Longo, and McFaddin 1982; Longo and Groth 1983). But a distorted image emerges when the life histories of such a rare and deviant group come to represent the story for the vast, heterogeneous group of adolescents who engage in sexually abusive behavior. The overwhelming majority will not repeat their sexually abusive behavior through their life course (Caldwell 2002; Letourneau and Miner 2005; Righthand and Welch 2001; Zimring 2004). Most will leave it behind, along with all their other youthful indiscretions, from driving too fast to drinking too much and all the other poorly judged and impulsive behaviors that have come to define modern adolescence. Nothing cures quite like maturation. Only a rare, dangerous few will pass through the threshold of adolescence into adulthood with their sexual deviance in tow and go on to become adult sexual offenders. Rather than an early harbinger of adult sexual deviance, most adolescent sexual offending is more properly viewed as a general sign of maladaption or emotional crisis. Rarely is adolescent sexual offending about deviant desire, perversion, or a "paraphilia," the psychiatric term for sexual deviance. It is more likely to be a nonspecific sign indicating any number of underlying problems. Unfortunately, the legal responses and clinical interventions that have evolved to address adolescent sexual offending have lacked precision and specificity. Adolescent sexual offenders are treated en masse as though the entire group harbors some silent and secret contagion that will manifest in time.

The vast majority of adolescents who are labeled juvenile sex offenders do not live up to the image that the term conjures up. They simply are not, in the aggregate, as sexually deviant as they are often made out to be. There are alternative ways to think about adolescent misconduct that are more flexible and pliable. In his book *The Changing Legal World of Adolescence*, published twenty-five years ago, Franklin Zimring (1982) lamented the social and legal foreclosure of adolescence as a time when teenagers were allowed and even expected to "muddle through" that awkward middle phase of life between the innocence of childhood and the mature rationality of adulthood, likening the stage of adolescence to a sort of "learner's permit" granted before one becomes a legally licensed and fully responsible adult:

> Part of the process of becoming mature is learning to make independent decisions. This type of liberty cannot be taught; it can only be learned. And learning to make independent judgments can be a risky process. . . . In blackjack, an ideal "career" is never to lose a hand. In the game of learning to make free choices, winning every hand is poor preparation for the modern world, just as winning every hand is a terrible way to learn to play blackjack. We want adolescents to make mistakes, but we hope they make the right kind of mistakes. (Zimring 1982, 91)

A similar perspective regarding adolescent culpability was recently taken by the U.S. Supreme Court in its decision to constitutionally ban the execution of adolescents who committed their capital offense at the age of 17 or younger (*Roper v. Simmons* 2005). The Court, echoing the position staked out in an amicus brief filed by the American Psychological Association (2005) in support of the constitutional ban, agreed that adolescents as a group are not yet mature in their decision making and are therefore less likely to consider alternative courses of action. They are more limited than adults because of their developmental immaturity. They are less likely to take into account the perspectives of others, are more vulnerable to peer pressure and group forces, have a more difficult time inhibiting impulses, and take high risks. They are simply not fully formed adults and are prone to immature judgments (Scott and Grisso 1998; Steinberg and Scott 2003).

Zimring (1982) advocated a more rational and forgiving legal jurisprudence for adolescence, arguing that most adolescents will outgrow their penchant for risk taking and their perception of invulnerability through the simple and unavoidable process of maturation. Forgiving does not mean free rides or passes, however. The task of maturation requires taking responsibility. This comes with becoming a mature adult. There must be consequences, but Zimring resoundingly rejected the notion that adolescents should shoulder the full burden we place on adults, advancing instead a continuum notion of moral and legal accountability proportional to their level of developmental immaturity. Zimring, the APA, other scholars, and even the United States Supreme Court are advocating not that adolescents be excused from punishment but simply that their responsibility be mitigated to a degree commensurate with their psychosocial immaturity. Heavy-handed retributive legal schemes not only ignore the time-limited nature of adolescent indiscretions; they also potentially interfere with adolescents' developmental progression by diverting some youth from a normal pathway of development, condemning them to a downward path through severe criminal penalties that could result in further deviant behavior. The major concern here is that the juvenile sex offender, because he is labeled a sexual deviant, may encounter some life-altering "snare" (Moffitt 1993)—a serious charge resulting in long-term incarceration, a serious record that limits future opportunity, a derailed education, or a lack of vocational opportunity—that may inhibit his ability to transition successfully to adulthood.

The legal world did not heed Zimring's warning, and if anything the 1980s and 1990s became a more punitive time for adolescents than when his book was first published. And while the assault on the rehabilitative ideal of the juvenile court had slowed substantially by the turn of the millennium (Melton, Petrila, Poythress et al. 2007, 467-68), for no group of adolescents is this more punitive legal world more real today than for the adolescent who has committed a sexual offense.

The system of legal sanctions that has been brought to bear on juvenile sex offenders over the course of the past two decades is not battling mere straw men or windmills. The problem of adolescent sexual offending is a real one that often causes real harm to its victims. Adolescents involved in serious forms of sexual offending need critical intervention, and some, unfortunately, will for the sake of public safety need to be incapacitated by means of longer-term confinement within exclusionary programs. A clear and accurate depiction of the extent of the problem of juvenile sexual offending is not easily derived, however. The various methods utilized to estimate the prevalence of the problem are fraught with imprecision, error, and bias. Often the estimates, utilizing different methodologies, are in contradiction.

The research literature has generally reported on the results of three separate methodologies for capturing the prevalence rates of various categories of sexual offenses for juveniles: official statistics, like arrest or conviction rates, self-report of sexual offending by adolescent offenders, and self-report of victims of sexual offenses committed by adolescent offenders. Each method has its own set of limitations and shortcomings. The true rate of juvenile sexual offending, like the true rate for any crime category in society, a problem often referred to as a "dark figure" by sociologists (Best 2001), is elusive. Apart from the obvious issue of the rate being contingent on how one defines "sexual offense" or "juvenile," there is simply no way to be sure if one has ever captured the true number. Not all sex offenses committed by juveniles are reported; not all reported sex offenses committed by juveniles result in an arrest. The best one can hope for is a defensible approximation of the true rate, and the best approach to determining the actual "dark figure" of sexual offense rates of juveniles will combine the three methods, off-setting the specific failings of each.

For the year 2003, of the total number of those arrested for forcible rape, including adults, about 16% were juveniles, and of the total number of those arrested for sexual offenses, excluding prostitution, about 20% were juveniles (Snyder and Sickmund 2006). There were approximately 4,155 arrests of male juveniles between the ages of 10 and 17 for the crime of forcible rape in the United States in 2003. This calculates to a prevalence rate of about .02%, or about one arrest for every four thousand male adolescents. About 98% of the juveniles arrested for rape were male and about two-thirds of those arrested for forcible rape were 16- or 17-year-olds. In the same year about 16,470 male juveniles between the ages of 10 and 17 were arrested for sexual offenses, excluding forcible rape and prostitution. The prevalence rate was about .10%, or approximately one arrest for every one thousand boys. About 90% of those arrested for a sexual offense were male and about half were 16- or 17-years-old. In total there were about 20,625 juvenile males between the ages of 10 and 17 arrested for any sexual offense in 2003, excluding prostitution. This calculates to an arrest rate of about .12%, or an arrest of one male juvenile for about every eight hundred in the population.

Most of the offenses committed by male youth are not sexual in nature. Sexual offending only makes up a small proportion of their criminality. In 2003, the crime category of forcible rape comprised only 4.6% of the total of the FBI's Violent Crime Index (Murder and Nonnegligent Manslaughter, Forcible Rape, Robbery, and Aggravated Assault) for youth. For youth, the total proportion of sexual offenses, including forcible rape, in 2003 comprised only 6.7% of the total number of arrests for person offenses, including the crime of simple assault (Snyder and Sickmund 2006). For the past twenty years, sexual offenses have amounted to about 1-2% of the juvenile indictments in juvenile court (Zimring 2004). Overall, sexual offenses make up only a small proportion of the violent crime of juvenile offenders and only a small portion of the docket of any juvenile court.

Between 1980 and 1991 the rate of arrest for rape by juveniles grew about 44%, reaching a peak in 1991, a time when the rates of most violent crime for juveniles rose dramatically. Then, as with the other crime categories for juveniles around this time, the arrest rate for forcible rape fell substantially from 1993 to 2003. In 2003 it was 22% lower than the level it had been in 1980. Between the same years, the arrests of male juveniles for violent crime, including forcible rape, decreased by about 36%. During this same time period, the arrest rate for other sexual offenses for juveniles was essentially flat. Changes in the rate of arrest for forcible rape between the years 1980 and 2003 for the ages of 10 and 17 are depicted in figure 1.1.

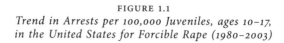

FIGURE 1.1
Trend in Arrests per 100,000 Juveniles, ages 10–17,
in the United States for Forcible Rape (1980–2003)

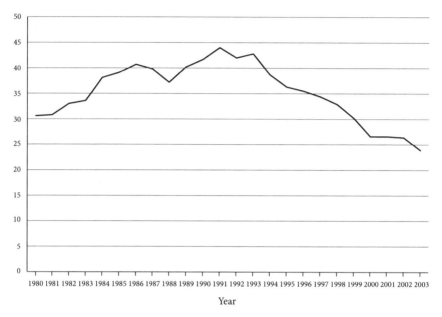

Year

Source: OJJDP, U.S. Department of Justice.

The arrest rate of juveniles for forcible rape, like the rates of arrest for all crime categories, has decreased significantly over the past fifteen years, providing little in the way of support for the current "moral panic" that currently prevails regarding juvenile sexual offending. The most telling observation from this data is that the stricter forms of legal sanctioning for juvenile sex offenders that dawned during the decade from 1993 to 2003 occurred while the arrest for rape was significantly decreasing.

A dramatically different story emerges when the arrest statistics for young male juvenile offenders under the age of 13 are examined. Between the years 1980 and 2003, this younger cohort witnessed a 116% increase in arrests for sexual offenses (Snyder and Sickmund 2006). What makes this increase all the more stunning is that it occurred during a period of time when the arrest rates for all offenses for this age group had decreased by 20%. While it is certainly possible that there was an explosive increase in the rate of sexual offending among young juveniles over this 23-year time frame, it is much more likely that the slightly more than doubling of their arrest rate was the result of changes in the way sexual offenses were officially handled for these young offenders by the police and the juvenile justice system. The police probably paid closer attention to these cases and responded through more formal processing. Sexual offending for young offenders was taken more seriously whereas in the past they may have been processed through noncriminal forms of intervention such as referral to child welfare or dependency agencies. The percentage of arrests for violent crime, forcible rape, and other sexual offenses compared to the total arrests of young juveniles aged 13 and younger, between 1980 and 2003, are depicted in figure 1.2.

While the arrest rate for rape was falling and the arrest rate for other sexual offenders remained unchanged for adolescents between the ages of ten and seventeen over the past fifteen years, the rate of placement into residential treatment and correctional settings was moving in the opposite direction. According to data from the U.S. Department of Justice's Office of Juvenile Justice and Delinquency Prevention (Sickmund, Sladley, and Kanf 2005), from 1997 to 2003 the rate of placement of juvenile sex offenders in residential and correctional settings grew a total of 34%. The rate of placement in private treatment settings rose a whopping 62% while the rate within public settings rose just under 20%. The steep increase in the placement of juvenile sex offenders in private treatment settings is a clear indication of the vast expansion of a cottage industry for treating juvenile sex offenders that occurred during a time period when the arrest rate of juveniles for sexual offenses was decreasing for rape and flat for all other sexual offenses. This data is depicted in table 1.1.

The major limitation to official crime statistics relating to sexual assault among adolescents, such as arrest rates, is that they underestimate the incidence of offenses since a large proportion of sexual assaults are not reported and only those incidents of sexual assault that lead to an arrest are counted (Koss 1992). Studies that utilize an anonymous self-report of sexual assault provide a more accurate measure of the rate of incidence since they are not limited to juveniles who were detected and arrested for a sexual offense. The reliability and validity of self-report measures of

FIGURE 1.2
*Trends in the Precentage of Arrests for Young Juveniles
(Under Age 13) in the United States*

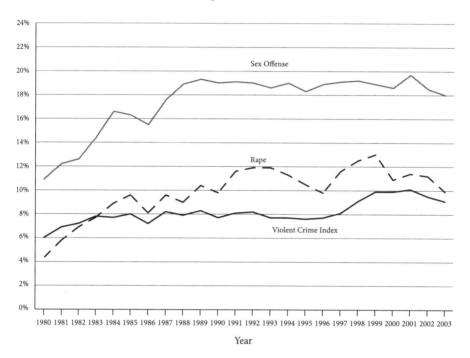

crime and delinquency have generally been found to meet acceptable social science standards (Elliot, Huizinga, and Morse 1987; Hindelang 1979;
Hindelang, Hirschi, and Weis 1981; Huizinga and Elliot 1986). Self-report
measures are not a replacement for but a complement to official criminal statistics. There are obvious limitations to self-report measures as well.
There is the problem of possible underreporting due to concerns about
the potential legal consequences of admitting prior delinquency and the
desire to avoid eliciting negative social appraisals or perceptions from
the interviewer. In studies using retrospective self-report methodologies,
there is also the problem of the accuracy of memory and its general decay
over time. Nonetheless, despite these limitations, self-report measures can
add another dimension to the overall portrait of the prevalence of sexual
assault among adolescents.

TABLE 1.1   *Juvenile Sex Offenders in*
Residential/Correctional Placement, 1997-2003

Year	Total	Public	Private
1997	5,582	3,974	1,608
1999	7,455	5,124	2,324
2001	6,779	4,650	2,128
2003	7,452	4,749	2,608

Source: Sickmund, Sladley, and Kanf 2005.

Self-reports of youth in the community, when compared to official crime reports, provide significantly higher estimates of the prevalence of sexual assault by adolescents. The National Youth Survey was a prospective longitudinal study of delinquent behavior in a community sample of American youth conducted at the University of Colorado at Boulder under the direction of Delbert Elliott and colleagues (Elliott, Huizinga, and Ageton 1985). The project, initiated in 1976, utilized a sample of about seventeen hundred American youth who were between the ages of 11 and 17 at the start of data collection. Elliot and his research team conducted nine waves of data collection. The last one was in 1992, when the group of participants was between the ages of 27 and 33. The overall drop-out rate over the life of the 16-year project was small. The study used personal face-to-face confidential interviews with participants, who were asked about their annual involvement in delinquent behavior. The survey included questions about the occurrence of any incidents of sexual coercion over the course of the prior year. The interviewer specifically asked each research participant whether he had "pressured someone (in the last year) to do more sexually than they wanted to do" (Ageton 1983, 153). The use of such verbally persuasive tactics as "if you love me you will" or "I'll break up with you if you don't" were considered to be instances of verbal coercion. A major limitation of the study is the heterogeneous grouping of sexual offenders—the lumping together of those who used verbal pressure ("you'd do it if you loved me") with those who raped at the point of a weapon.

Over the course of three years of data collection between 1978 and 1980, between 2.2% and 3.8% of the male juveniles between the ages of 13 and 21 reported having committed an act of sexual coercion in the preceding year (Ageton 1983). But about two-thirds of them used verbal coercion. Approximately 1.3% of the sample in 1978, the year with the highest self-report rate, used physical force to commit their sexual offense. There was not much difference with regard to various psychosocial factors between the youth who committed sexual assaults and the youth who committed general delinquency offenses, leading to the conclusion that the explanation for sexual assault is not particularly different than it is for any other form of delinquency.

Victim survey research reveals the highest prevalence rates of juvenile sex offenses compared to official crime statistics and the self-report of perpetrators. The three methods form an "inverted pyramid," with victim surveys providing the highest estimates, followed by self-reports by male perpetrators, and then followed by official arrest or conviction statistics, which yield the lowest rates. The large discrepancy between the rates reported by victims and the other estimates is an indication of the vast amount of official underreporting of sexual assault. The National Youth Survey reported that for the years between 1978 and 1980, the prevalence rates ranged from between 5% and 11% for females reporting sexual assault victimization by male youth (Ageton 1983). However, verbal persuasion was used by between two-thirds and four-fifths of the male offenders, dropping the rate of sexual offenses committed by physical force to as low as 1% or as high as 4%. Most of the sexual assaults were described as unplanned events that occurred in the context of a date, most often at the home of the victim or the perpetrator. For the vast majority of incidents, drugs and alcohol had been used by either the victim or by the perpetrator.

The National Crime Victimization Survey provides data about the rates of sexual victimization through the use of interviews with a random sample of community participants aged 12 years and older. According to the most recent survey results, between 1993 and 2003 the rape and sexual assault victimization rate for youth ages 12 to 17 fell 46% (Snyder and Sickmund 2006). Other researchers estimate that there was a 40% decline in reported cases of childhood sexual abuse between 1990 and 2000 (Finkelhor and Jones 2004) and a decrease of 49% for the substantiation of sexual abuse between 1990 and 2004 (Finkelhor and Jones 2006). This substantial decline in agency statistics matches the declining trend previously reported in the arrest of juveniles for sexual offenses, suggesting that the decrease in reported cases of sexual violence represents a real decline and not an institutional or system change in the way cases were defined or categorized or the way cases were handled.

How is one to make sense of this avalanche of statistics, data, and trends? The rates of reported victimization have gone down significantly, and are probably lower than in any other historical epoch (Bullough 1990). Once again it appears that the ramping up of the legal consequences for juvenile sex offenders occurred during a time when the rate of reported victimization underwent a steep decline. And while it seems possible that the stricter legal responses were in part responsible for the welcomed decline, this hypothesis requires more stringent empirical testing before it can be accepted.

The self-report surveys of victims have been critiqued on a number of grounds, most frequently for their use of verbal coercion as part of the definition of sexual assault. Nonetheless, the rates of sexual violence remain startlingly high. There is a high rate of verbal and physical coercion occurring within the early sexual experiences of adolescents and young adults in America, and this clearly and unambiguously calls for intervention in the form of education and other preventative strategies. The high rates of sexual violence against adolescent girls and young women make it a major public health concern requiring a priority response.

Theoretical models have been developed that explain the problem of the prevalence of sexual assault by reference to sociocultural contexts, focusing on the gendered scripts or roles that legitimate sexual violence and often normalize it (Malamuth, Linz, Heavy et al. 1995; White and Kowalski 1998; White, Kadlec, and Sechrist 2006). These culturally transmitted sexual scripts often support the enactment of power dynamics within intimate relationships whereby males are socialized to be sexually aggressive and females are relegated to the role of "sexual gatekeepers." The high rates of sexually coercive interactions among young males may be a function of the way they have been instructed about what masculinity entails—dominance, sexual prowess, and promiscuity—whereas young females have been instructed that confronting and navigating coercive sexual interactions with boyfriends, dates, and acquaintances are an expectable part of being young and female.

An aspect of this cultural problem not readily revealed in the rates and percentages of the survey research, however, is that sex is a relatively new activity for adolescents. They are learning the rules of sexual engagement as they go along. This fact in no way detracts from the significantly high rates of sexual coercion that occur within youthful sexual relationships. It only argues that these are still immature social actors, and this fact needs to be taken into account when the justice system develops strategies to respond to their actions. It would be incorrect to necessarily conclude that youth who engage in sexual offenses suffer from some deviant sexuality that requires life-long legal and clinical intervention. To consider them as such would illuminate Trilling's notion of a new problem emerging from the well-intentioned attempt to solve some prior problem. The high prevalence rates of juvenile sex offenses point to a broader sociocultural problem about the sexual scripts that are transmitted to boys and girls. Certainly some of the subjects within the research estimates will need strenuous criminal justice intervention. The problem is identifying who they are.

A 16-year-old male adolescent had gathered together in the back of his pickup truck what is often referred to as a "rape kit" by law enforcement professionals, comprised of mace, handcuffs, and duct tape. These were the instruments he used in the brutal rape and attempted murder of an 8-year-old girl he left in a trash dumpster for dead, who miraculously walked away and summoned help. This adolescent's sexual offense bears no similarity to the stories of the juvenile sex offenders previously described in this chapter. They are as far apart on the spectrum of juvenile sex offenders as is probably possible, yet they were treated relatively the same way within the criminal justice system.

It is obvious that these two types of cases call for vastly different legal and clinical responses. However, any book that argues its points from such extreme cases is not doing much work. Cases that exist at the extreme of any continuum are easy to deal with. It is the 90% or so that occupy the various shades of gray in between that are hard. This book will examine the vast landscape of adolescent sexual misbehaviors between the two extremes. What do we know in a scientific way about them? What is to be done legally and clinically about them? These are the uneasy questions the following chapters will examine.

2

The Return of the Blob

The Heterogeneity of Juvenile Sex Offenders

The rumor mill was in full swing at school and Michelle had reached her limit of teasing about her 10-year-old sister, Katie. She had heard enough about how Katie had performed oral sex on Ryan, 14. The incident occurred in a tent in his cousin David's yard during a game of "truth-or-dare." It happened in August but it took until the following spring for the whispered rumors to circulate widely enough for Michelle to finally tell her mother about it. In April 2002 Katie's mother contacted the police and a full investigation into the incident began. Katie's mother knew David, 14. She had baby-sat for him and his siblings when they were younger. David had known Katie for several years from the neighborhood. He had played basketball and other games with her in the past. She had even been over to his house to watch videos. It was commonly known among the neighborhood children that Katie had a "crush" on David's younger brother but that his brother was not interested because, according to David, he "was too young to be into girls."

Katie told the investigating officer she willingly agreed to play the game with David and his cousin, Ryan, but had no idea that the boys intended to lure her into the sexual act. During the game David "dared" her to suck Ryan's penis. When she initially refused she said that David threatened to hurt her. She told police that she was afraid when she complied with David's "dare."

The police next interviewed David and his mother. He immediately confessed. Indeed there had been a game of "truth-or-dare" with Katie in a makeshift tent the boys had set up in David's back yard. According to David, the boys were in the tent drinking beer, given to them by an uncle, and were watching *Sky Kids* on a portable DVD player when Katie came by to watch it with them. He insisted, however, that it was Ryan, not he, who "dared" her to perform oral sex. Later, Ryan told police that it was

David who "dared" Katie to perform oral sex on him. All three parties agreed that Katie had performed oral sex only on Ryan and that it happened only one time, lasting less than a minute. The boys told police that before leaving the tent they made her agree that no mention of what had transpired should ever be uttered outside of the tent. Their story and Katie's are, for the most part, consistent, but they diverge on one important point: she claimed they threatened to hurt her if she did not comply with their demand for oral sex; the boys vehemently denied that any threat was uttered but agreed that they exerted strong verbal coaxing and pressure.

The boys pled delinquent later that July, nearly a year after the incident, and were placed on juvenile probation with the agreement that the rape of child charge would be dismissed and only a nonsexual offense of assault and battery would be entered. They were advised by their respective legal counsels to take the deal because they would not be required to register as sex offenders with the state. They were sentenced to terms of probation and asked to attend regular meetings with their probation officer, to attend school, and to stay away from Katie.

David was the first born of his 17-year-old parents, who had a history of alcohol and marijuana abuse. Though his mother insisted that she did not drink or abuse marijuana while pregnant with David, she resumed her typical pattern of substance abuse shortly after his birth. His father was reportedly physically abusive toward him and his mother. At the age of 2 he was removed from his mother's care and placed within the child welfare system when an aunt reported that his mother was neglecting and physically abusing him and was selling drugs out of the house. He was placed with the aunt for nearly a year before he was returned to his mother's custody.

David's parents divorced when he was 4 years old. He and his younger brother, two years his junior, continued to visit with their father for the next two years, but their father was unreliable about seeing them and often physically abusive. When he was 6 years old his father suddenly left the state and David did not see him again until five years later.

After his parents' divorce, David, his mother, and his brother moved several times. The relocations were prompted by his mother's establishment of new relationships with boyfriends, which were often stormy and brief. Many of the men had substance abuse problems and were physically abusive toward David, his mother, and his brother. His younger sister was born during one of his mother's brief relationships, but her biological father was never a part of the family.

At the age of 11, David had a brief reunification with his father, who had remarried and had other children with his second wife. His father ended their relationship for the second time when his father's wife expressed her disapproval. His father just stopped coming by to see him and then stopped calling altogether.

David was introduced to marijuana by his mother by the age of 13. By the time he was 14 his grades in school had precipitously declined, and it was later discovered that he had begun to regularly abuse alcohol and marijuana. He became angry and more physically aggressive toward his mother and siblings. There was little in the way of any routine at home and minimal supervision. His mother was often out of the house, sometimes for days at a time. The three children had the run of the home, with David cast in the role of caregiver for his younger siblings, often cooking, cleaning, and looking after them. It was during this period that the sexual offense against Katie occurred.

In September 2005 David's probation officer notified the child welfare agency that David and his siblings were being neglected. An investigation revealed that the children were largely unsupervised and poorly cared for and that the house was infested with fleas. David and his siblings were placed in foster care. A short time later David was revoked from his probation, two years after his juvenile court disposition for the sexual offense, when he was arrested for a new crime of breaking and entering and vandalism. He was committed to the state juvenile justice agency and placed in a locked treatment center where he was prescribed sexual offender treatment for the sexual offense against Katie that had happened three years earlier.

Jason was committed to a youth corrections agency until the age of 21 by the juvenile court for three counts of rape of a child when he was 16. The three offenses were against three separate victims, three peer-aged girls with whom he was acquainted, and they all happened in his bedroom when his mother was home. Jason also had a history of nonsexual and nonviolent offenses that included possessing and using drugs, driving a motor vehicle without permission and without a license, and breaking and entering in a public building where he and his peers destroyed property.

All three rapes had a similar modus operandi. Jason would invite the girls over to hang out, watch a movie, or play a video game. On one occasion, when the victim arrived at his house he was watching a pornographic movie that his mother had provided him. On at least two of the occasions, his mother had picked the girls up with Jason and driven them to their house. Often they would drink a few beers or smoke a joint of marijuana, also supplied by his mother. Eventually he would lead them to his bedroom where he would rape them.

The offense would start out as consensual contact between them. He would initiate the interaction by putting his arm around the girl or sometimes making out. When he attempted to go further, such as attempting to fondle her breasts or touch her vagina, she would stop him. He would try to verbally persuade, coax, and pressure her into compliance. When this tactic did not work, he would hold her down and forcibly rape her. Afterwards the girls would get dressed and leave.

Jason was reared in a home with poor sexual boundaries. His mother was described by agency case workers as exhibiting highly sexualized behaviors toward Jason while he was growing up. She reportedly often walked around the house naked in front of him when he was a child and adolescent, used the bathroom without shutting the door, engaged in open sexual relations with men that Jason witnessed, kept pornographic magazines and videos in the house that were readily accessible to Jason, and supplied him with condoms, alcohol, and marijuana, which he interpreted as her being supportive of his becoming sexually active. He reports having been sexually abused as a child by several of his mother's male acquaintances. In treatment it was noted that he appeared to be erotically stimulated by his history of sexual victimization.

Jason developed a number of deviant sexual interests resulting from his exposure to a highly sexualized home environment that modeled poor sexual boundaries. He reports a history of exhibitionism and voyeurism, an interest in cross-dressing, an attempt at sex with a dog, deviant arousal by violent media programming, sexual arousal and fantasies about his mother, and sexual arousal by his own abuse history and even his sexual offense history. His exposure to a sexually deviant home environment where he was overly stimulated by sexuality at an early age and where boundaries and limits around matters of sexuality were loose or nonexistent resulted in a self-concept and an orientation to others that were highly sexualized.

During his offenses he used a variety of cognitive distortions that rationalized his use of force, such as viewing the rapes as consensual, interpreting the victim's refusal and distress as subtle consent and pleasure, and in some cases deliberately ignoring or overriding the victim's resistance because he viewed his needs as more important than his victim's.

Jason spent a total of nearly two years in a locked treatment program where he initially posed complicated behavior-management problems. He engaged in a pattern of self-abuse, such as swallowing staples and inserting them into his penis and anus and voicing suicidal thoughts, requiring that he repeatedly be placed on special observation status and be screened for psychiatric admission. These behaviors were conceptualized by the program staff as rooted in an underlying need for attention and special care. The staff managed them effectively, being sure not to reinforce them, and as a result they decreased and eventually stopped completely.

In treatment Jason revealed the active presence of a number of sexually deviant preoccupations. In sex-offender group therapy he admitted to becoming sexually aroused by some aspects of his sexual offender work, and his disclosures within group therapy about his sexually deviant interests resulted in his being ostracized by the other group members. Toward the later part of his treatment Jason moved beyond these basic behavioral-management problems and entered into a prolonged period of therapeutic engagement on the management and reduction of his risk for sexual assault. In the months prior to his discharge he did not have a single incident of self-harming behavior. In their place, he invested his energy into his treatment and made substantial progress on the control of sexually deviant fantasies, on decreasing his reliance on sex to meet emotional needs, and on expanding his range of possibilities to satisfy self-esteem and interpersonal needs.

Jason was stepped down from secure treatment and placed in a non-secure residential treatment program. He was eventually released back into the community a year later, when he was placed into an independent living program with community supervision and outpatient sex offender treatment. He was eventually discharged from supervision after two years of community monitoring without a known sexual reoffense.

The life histories of David and Jason share some important general features in common. Both are juvenile sex offenders with a significantly troubled past who are in clear need of some sort of intervention. Legal intervention was the first order of business in the case of Jason, but both were in need of psychological intervention to straighten out their disordered pasts. To say they are juveniles with troubled lives is not a particularly differentiating description. This is a broad statement that could be true of a significant number of juvenile delinquents. Both were found delinquent for a sexual offense and each shares in common the legal and clinical category juvenile sex offender, but the differences in their offenses are much greater than the similarities. David committed a single act of child molestation that does not appear rooted in sexual deviance but rather in some other emotional crises operating in his life at that time. He used verbal persuasion, not physical force. He had no reported history of childhood sexual abuse. He would probably emerge as low risk on most sexual recidivism assessment instruments. Jason is an offender of a different sort. He committed multiple acts of violent rape of peer-aged female victims. He seems plagued by possible budding paraphilias to all sorts of sexually deviant practices. The accounts of Jason and his victims depict a pattern of setting up his victims by luring them into his bedroom to gain access to them sexually. Once inside his room he attempted a more subtly seductive approach that quickly escalated to a more physically forceful one when met with victim resistance. He had a significant history of childhood sexual victimization. He would probably emerge as higher risk than David on any instrument assessing sexual offense risk. Despite their differences along all these varied dimensions, they have been joined together and roped off from other juvenile offenders under the banner of "juvenile sex offender."

Adolescents legally identified as sexual offenders have become an expansive category, ranging from adolescents who commit violent rapes to adolescents who engage in sexual behavior that, quite frankly, simply makes some uncomfortable—think back to the case of Glenarlow Wilson. The category juvenile sexual offender is essentially a legal designation but it purports to carry significant clinical meaning. It is a legal designation masquerading as a mental health category. For a category to have any scientific validity and clinical utility, it must be demonstrated that the members of the group share a set of essential or core characteristics; that they have in common a set of preestablished diagnostic criteria; that the between-group variance of the members outside the category is significantly greater than the within-group variance of the members inside the category. It is not sufficient to state that what juvenile sexual offenders share in common is that they have been legally adjudicated for a designated sexual offense. This line of reasoning is tautological. To make juvenile sex offenders a meaningful clinical group, there must be something more than that they share a common legal fate.

The accumulated empirical research on the clinico-legal category of the juvenile sexual offender has failed to sufficiently demonstrate that it is clinically meaningful; the application of the term provides little understanding or insight into who might be its recipient. There are no special markers or clinical signs, apart from the defining sexual offense itself, that distinguish juvenile sex offenders from nonsex offenders, and the amorphous group known as juvenile sexual offenders bears little resemblance to its adult counterpart.

Who gets labeled a juvenile sexual offender? The adolescent boy who videotapes sex with a same-aged peer girl, using a video camera borrowed for a class project, and plays the tape on the LCD monitor of the camera in the high school cafeteria to a clamoring, whooping group of peers; the socially unskilled and cognitively limited adolescent boy in residential treatment, mimicking lines of dialogue recalled from a pornographic movie who overtly stares at his female clinician's body; the 16-year-old adolescent boy without a delinquent past who engages in nonconsensual sex with an intoxicated, semiconscious female acquaintance. All of these examples have been joined together into a single legal category, the juvenile sex offender, along with the adolescent who engages in a violent rape of a peer-aged or adult woman or in repetitive acts of sexual abuse of young children. How useful is a category that can accommodate such a broad swath of individuals?

Obviously, as was the case for David and Jason, meaningful differences among these cases significantly outweigh any similarities. Yet we utilize similar systems of assessment, classification, treatment, and risk management to process them. They are categorized together and regarded as a meaningful clinico-legal group upon which various predictive schemes are based and according to which clinical treatment procedures are applied. These systems of assessment and treatment act to reify juvenile sex offenders, turning a legal construct into a clinical or psychiatric one. Juvenile sex offenders have been stabilized within various classification schemes, typologies, tests, scales, and assessment models, captured and frozen in midair like flies in amber. Closer inspection of the trapped specimen within, however, reveals that they are not as clearly observed as first assumed. The figure of the juvenile sex offender is blurred when observed in juxtaposition to the nonsexual offender. A behavior that seems at first distinct and alarming is absorbed within the matrix of complex developmental variables that yields the juvenile delinquent. Distinct lines of demarcation vanish as he is found to share a similar history with the general delinquent. He is often an aspect of the same generalized phenomenon that produces general delinquency—just a different manifestation.

This chapter will demonstrate that the accumulated empirical evidence does not support conceptualizing the juvenile sex offender as a distinct category of juvenile offenders and that the legal category juvenile sex offender cannot function like a psychiatric category whose members can be reliably distinguished from nonmembers and sorted into well-delineated subcategories or types. More specifically, the following sections will argue that juvenile sex offenders as a group bear little resemblance to adult sex offenders and that the legal schemas and clinical intervention models devised for adults are, therefore, not applicable to them; that juvenile sex offenders are a heterogeneous group who do not appear significantly different from non–sex offending juveniles; and, finally, that there is little empirical support for the conceptualization of juvenile sex offending as a form of psychopathology.

The population of juvenile sex offenders is much more heterogeneous than that of adult sex offenders. These populations—the juvenile sex offender and the adult sex offender—are almost completely separate and distinct. If they are related at all, it is probably best to conceive of the future adult sex offender as occupying a small, static circle within the teeming and fluctuating, amorphous mass known as juvenile sex offenders. While juvenile sex offenders are largely indistinguishable from non–sex offending juveniles, they are quite distinct and separate from the more homogeneous group of adult sex offenders (Caldwell 2002; Letourneau and Miner 2005).

Concern that today's juvenile sexual offender is the budding adult sex offender of tomorrow arose in the 1970s and 1980s when a series of well-known and often-cited research reports discovered that the sexual deviance of adult sex offenders first manifested in middle to late adolescence (Groth 1977; Groth, Longo, and McFaddin 1982; Longo and Groth 1983). These early reports, extrapolating upon the finding that adult sex offenders reported the onset of their sexual deviance in adolescence, put forth the phenomenally unsupportable assertion that the population of adolescents adjudicated for sexual crimes was at risk to progress to more serious forms of offending in adulthood. But it is incorrect to generalize from the rare and narrow range of adult offenders to the large and more heterogeneous population of juvenile offenders. The vast majority of juvenile sex offenders simply do not progress to more serious forms of adult sexual offending. Rather, the opposite is true: most juvenile sex offenders will desist and not go on to commit another sexual offense. The error in reasoning in this early research is obvious. The researchers drew a conclusion about the larger population of juvenile sex offenders on the basis of an exclusive sampling from the high range of the risk continuum—adult sex offenders—and did not calculate into the equation the much larger proportion of juvenile sex offenders who never go on to continue this behavior. The finding that most serious adult sex offenders manifested their deviance in adolescence cannot be used to form the conclusion that, therefore, the vast, heterogeneous array of adolescent sex offenders are adult sex offenders in the making. While it is true that a small high-risk group of juvenile sex offenders will persist into adulthood, it is also true that a much larger share of them will not. The most effective strategy is to develop methodologies to cull the high-risk offenders out from the teeming stream of juvenile sexual offenders, not to subject the entire population to legally and clinically exclusionary forms of restrictive intervention.

Many of the early studies that sounded the alarm about adolescent sexual offenders utilized research methodologies examining the retrospective accounts of adults convicted of serious sexual offenses. One study with the lurid title "The Adolescent Sexual Offender and His Prey" exemplifies the faulty reasoning at the base of this argument (Groth 1977). The study examined the records of twenty-six offenders between the ages of 15 and 17 admitted during the years 1970–1975 to the Massachusetts Treatment Center for Sexually Dangerous Persons. Fourteen of the boys were convicted of rape and twelve were convicted of child molestation. These twenty-six juveniles had been transferred from juvenile court for trial in adult court and were committed to the Treatment Center for possible civil commitment in lieu of a prison sentence. In addition, thirty-seven convicted adult sexual offenders with a history of sexual offending as juveniles were selected and compared to the sample of twenty-six transferred juveniles. The results revealed that a total of 86% of the entire sample had a prior history of a sexual offense. The author argued,

The all too frequent "diagnosis" of "adolescent adjustment reaction," often results in the defects and needs of the offender going unrecognized and in the perpetuation of the jeopardy he constitutes to the community. There is a need for secure treatment facilities for such young offenders if the courts are to make meaningful dispositions for the intervention in such cases. (254)

But the finding of a history of a sexual offense in a high percentage of these cases does not support this conclusion. One cannot examine the individuals at the high end of the risk spectrum and generalize findings to the rest of the individuals across the spectrum. This study examined a very exceptional and rare group: a set of adolescents who had been transferred to adult court for a sexual offense and then sent to a secure correctional program for adult sex offenders for consideration for possible involuntary commitment. This high-risk and rare group bears little resemblance to the larger population of adolescent sex offenders, and what holds true for them is not necessarily true for most others. To discover that this small group of serious offenders shared something essential with adult sexual offenders does not mean that all adolescent sex offenders will as well.

In another study of 231 adult sexual offenders from a maximum security prison, the researchers found that a significant proportion, about a third, exhibited a pattern of escalation of seriousness over time, beginning in adolescence with compulsive masturbation and exhibitionism and escalating to more serious sexual assaults in adulthood (Longo and Groth 1983). They concluded that a number of the subjects in their sample began to exhibit problematic sexual behavior at an early age and because they were unrecognized and untreated were at risk to progress to more serious sexual assaults. But this prediction cannot be argued from the vantage point of this study. One cannot look at the history of adult sex offenders, detect a history of adolescent sexual offending in their background, and then claim that that all juvenile sex offenders are at risk to follow the same downward pathway. What about the vast majority of juvenile sex offenders who did not reoffend in adulthood and did not, therefore, have an opportunity to make it into their sample? A juvenile who commits a sexual offense is in need of legal and clinical intervention, but it is simply not the case that he is necessarily displaying the early markings of a repetitive adult sex offender, and that like an untreated viral infection his condition will rapidly spread into a full-blown case of sexual deviance in adulthood.

This alarmist viewpoint has persisted. An often-cited study to support the early-onset hypothesis was conducted by Abel and Osborn (1992). They report in a confidential self-report study of nonincarcerated men suffering from various paraphilias that a total of 58% of them reported the onset of deviant sexual interests prior to the age of 18. But this means that a high proportion of the sample, 42%, had late onset (Smallbone 2006). Another study has found that late onset is at least as common as, and in some cases more common than, early onset (Smallbone and Wortley 2004). Moreover, many paraphilics— fetishists, for instance—are not typically considered to be sexual offenders (Smallbone 2006). A paraphilia is not necessarily synonymous with a harm-producing sexual offense. Abel and colleagues, echoing the pronouncements of the researchers who preceded them, concluded that "the all-too-frequent diagnosis of adolescent adjustment reaction often results in the adolescent's deviant sexual behavior going unrecognized and thus untreated. The diagnosis is preferred by the legal system so as not to 'inappropriately' stigmatize the adolescent as a sex offender for behaviors that may have been experimental in nature" (Abel, Osborn, and Twigg 1993, 115). Over the course of the last decade their concern has proved to be unfounded as the legal response to adolescent sex offenders has moved to the other extreme, toward the early criminalization of adolescents who have committed sexual offenses. The worry is no longer that they have inappropriately been allowed to escape detection and accountability in an effort to avoid stigmatizing them, but just the opposite. Many have been inappropriately subjected to legal schemes and clinical treatment models better suited to adult sex offenders.

Juvenile sex offenders, as do juvenile delinquents, and even adolescents generally, vary widely on demographic, family, early childhood, social, academic, peer, sexual, and clinical factors. This diversity within the legally designated group of juvenile sex offenders has resulted in their being characterized by many reviewers as vastly heterogeneous (Allan, Allan, Marshall et al. 2002; Butler and Seto 2002; Fagan and Wexler 1988; Letourneau and Miner 2005; Righthand and Welch 2001; Ronis and Borduin 2007; Smallbone 2006; Van Wijk, Vermeirn, Loeber et al. 2006; Weinrott 1996; Zimring 2004). Because of their wide diversity, they have not been found, as a whole, to be significantly different than non–sex offending juveniles. On most demographic, family history, childhood experience, and current clinical functioning factors, they are practically indistinguishable from their non–sex offending delinquent counterparts. The population of juvenile sex offenders is so heterogeneous, so diversified, that it has proven virtually impossible to establish a set of defining characteristics that sets them apart from nonsex offenders.

Comparisons of juvenile sex offenders with juvenile nonsex offenders has generally found that a significant portion of juvenile sex offenders have a history of nonsex offending, suggesting that sexual offenses in juveniles are part of a larger pattern of juvenile offending, rather than a distinct characteristic setting them apart from nonsex offenders (Awad and Saunders 1991; Becker, Kaplan, Cunningham-Rathner et al. 1986; Fagan and Wexler 1988; Fehrenbach, Smith, Monastersky et al. 1986; Ford and Linney 1995; France and Hudson 1993; Graves, Openshaw, Ascione et al. 1996; Jacobs, Kennedy, and Meyer 1997; Ryan, Miyoshi, Metzner et al. 1996). Recall that David and Jason had histories of nonsex offending. The research estimates regarding the presence of general nonsexual delinquency in juvenile sex offenders have varied from lows of about 50% to highs reaching above 90%. These widely disparate results are probably a function of methodological differences among the studies. Studies that differentially sample younger or less serious offenders or draw their samples from juvenile sex offenders within community-based settings as opposed to juveniles incarcerated within secure detention and treatment may yield lower rates of general delinquency. Moreover, samples that include a greater percentage of peer or adult rapists than child molesters (Seto and Lalumière 2006) or that include mixed victim types (Parks and Bard 2006) will yield higher rates of nonsexual offending.

Research studies that utilize convenient samples drawn from a particular treatment setting or program are especially prone to a selection bias that may distort the association of sexual offending and nonsexual offending. Juveniles do not end up in a particular setting through random selection but through a process of successive decisions made by various human decision makers—judges, juvenile justice administrators, case workers, psychologists, and social workers. They are often placed in a particular program for a variety of competing reasons: a good fit between the juvenile's treatment needs and the program's treatment approach; the appearance of an opening at the time a placement decision needs to occur; the low cost of a program; or the overall convenience of the placement for the system. Juveniles within a treatment program are not representative of the larger population of juvenile offenders from which they are drawn. Various sorts of selection biases are in operation, often silently, that tamper with the resulting mix of juveniles who end up being placed in a particular program. The existence of selection biases at every stage of delinquency processing, from arrest to juvenile court adjudication to placement to release, is the bane of the research scientist trying to arrive at stable and generalizable findings about the nature of juvenile delinquency.

Studies that are able to tap into unselected samples, or at least samples that have been less tampered with by the hands of legal decision makers, are more methodologically sound. They are in a better position to sort out true relationships among variables and make more generalizable conclusions. Studies that have used more methodologically sound sampling procedures, controlling for potential selection biases, have uncovered a significantly higher percentage of nonsexual offending among their sample of juvenile sex offenders. The Youth Report Survey, which used an unselected sample of adolescents in the community, found that 93% of the adolescents committing a sexual offense in the preceding year also reported committing a nonsexual offense as well (Weinrott 1996).

A recent study conducted in Missouri used a large of sample of nearly six hundred delinquent youth consecutively admitted, allowing the researchers to obtain a sample of juvenile sex offenders with arrest histories that typically occur within their local jurisdiction (Ronis and Borduin 2007). They reported that 94% of the sex offenders with peer- or adult-aged victims and 89% of the sex offenders with child victims had engaged in one or more nonsexual offenses in the past, a rate similar to the one reported in the Youth Report Survey.

The prevalent finding within the research literature is that juvenile sex offenders are not delinquent specialists, limiting themselves to sexual offenses, but are instead delinquent generalists whose sexual offending is just one facet of a larger pattern of delinquent offending (Lussier 2005). There may be little distinctiveness at all about the offense other than that it is sexual and as such rises to the forefront of attention and concern. While there is a small subgroup of juvenile sexual offenders who exhibit more exclusive and repetitive patterns of sexual offending over the life course, the data shows that this subgroup is clearly the exception rather than the rule.

In a recent report that examined the question of the criminal specialization of juvenile sex offenders, the researchers conducted a meta-analysis that included twenty-four independent studies, published between 1979 and 2003, representing a total of 1,652 juvenile sexual offenders and 8,148 juvenile nonsex offenders (Seto and Lalumière 2006). They found that the age of first contact with the juvenile justice system for both groups was young but not significantly different, averaging about age 12 or 13. Both groups had extensive criminal histories, but the nonsexual offenders had a significantly more extensive criminal history. This result held up even though the nonsex offenders were constrained in their offense histories because they by definition did not have a sexual offense as part of their offense history. Both groups exhibited high rates and diverse manifestations of general conduct problems, but the nonsex offenders had more significant histories of general conduct problems, including school behavior problems, deceitfulness, theft, and serious rule violations. The juvenile sex offenders had a higher rate of involvement in fire-setting and arson. When the variables comprising the conduct problem domain were combined, the results differed significantly according to the source of the data. Juvenile sex offenders self-reported a higher proportion of conduct problems; the nonsex offenders had a significantly higher rate of conduct problems when methods other than self-report, like records, were examined. The study uncovered an interesting finding when the researchers conducted separate analyses for the sex offenders with child victims and sex offenders with peer/adult victims. When juvenile sex offenders who had committed their offense against children were compared to nonsex offenders, they had significantly fewer conduct problems. Juvenile sex offenders who had committed their sexual offense against a peer or an adult had similar patterns of conduct problems to nonsex offenders.

Overall, the results of this meta-analysis provide the best empirical evidence to date against the notion that juvenile sex offenders represent a highly specialized offender group who can be clearly distinguished from nonsex offenders. According to the results in this study, juvenile sexual offenders tend to be deeply involved in prior delinquent acts and manifest diverse conduct problems, often similar to nonsexual offenders. Juvenile sex offenders who commit a sexual offense against a peer-aged or adult victim are especially indistinguishable from nonjuvenile sex offenders. Conversely, juvenile sex offenders who commit sexual offenses against children, though for the most part possessing a delinquent history, tend to be less delinquently involved than sex offenders who commit sexual offenses against peers and adults and nonsexual offenders. This finding, however, was not replicated in the Missouri study, which found equally high rates of nonsexual offending for their samples of child molesters and rapists (Ronis and Borduin 2007).

Another study in support of juvenile sex offenders as nonspecialists followed three cohorts of juvenile delinquents, totaling over six thousand adolescents, from Racine, Wisconsin, in 1942, 1949, and 1955 (Zimring, Piquero, and Jennings 2007). These groups had a total prevalence rate of 37% for police contacts. The researchers discovered that about 1.5% of the sample had some type of sex offense as a juvenile, although nearly three-quarters of these police contacts were for misdemeanor offenses. About three-quarters of the juveniles with a police contact for a sexual incident had only one such incident, and 8.5% had more than two police contacts for a sexual incident. Sex offenses were rare and relatively nonserious for this three-cohort group. Boys with a history of a police contact for a sexual incident had a significantly more active delinquency career than boys without such a police contact. Nearly half of the boy sex offenders had nine or more police contacts while only about 10% of juvenile nonsex offenders had as active an early career.

These community samples of juvenile delinquents were followed longitudinally for as long as fourteen years for the 1942 cohort and as short as four years for the 1955 cohort. A total of 8.5% of the boys with a police contact for a sexual incident went on to have a police contact for a sexual offense as an adult. The most telling finding reported by Zimring and his colleagues was that boys with a prior police contact for a sexual incident were not significantly more likely to have an adult sex offense than juveniles with nonsexual delinquent incidents. Only the group of boys that had no juvenile police contacts had a significantly lower rate of police contacts as adults for a sexual incident. The juvenile sex offenders and nonsexual offenders were relatively equally at risk for an adult police contact for a sexual offense. The frequency of police contacts as a juvenile was a significant predictor of adult sexual offending, while a police contact for a sexual offense as a juvenile was not predictive of adult sexual offending.

Zimring, Piquero, and Jennings (2007) conclude on the basis of these results that juvenile sex offenders do not specialize in sex offending throughout their life course. Rather, it seems to be the case that "sex offenders are frequent (and *generalist*) offenders who roll the dice more often and increase their chances of accumulating a sex offense in their career" (526-27). Additional support for the juvenile-sex-offenders-as-generalist argument was the finding that there were no juvenile sex offenders who had adult-only sex contacts.

The argument against the designation of juvenile sexual offenders as a distinct group of juvenile offenders specializing in sexual offending is further supported by the often replicated finding that juvenile sexual offenders in the aggregate have a low sexual recidivism rate but a much higher recidivism rate for nonsexual offenses, comparable to nonsexual offender's general recidivism rate (Caldwell 2002, 2007; Righthand and Welch 2001; Worling and Curwen 2000; Worling and Långström 2006). A significantly higher rearrest rate for nonsexual offenses among adult sexual offenders has also been reported (Hanson and Bussière 1998; Hanson and

Morton-Bourgenon 2004, 2005). The much higher recidivism rates for general delinquency for juvenile sex offenders provide further evidence that for the most part they are not specialists but are much more like the delinquent generalists who also tend to reoffend at fairly high rates into late adolescence and early adulthood before they trail off and desist in later adulthood (Moffitt 1993, 2003).

The finding that juvenile sex offenders are at higher risk for general recidivism than for sex recidivism has been reported across over sixty years of research beginning with Doshay's (1943) groundbreaking research on recidivism of juvenile sex offenders. Doshay was a psychiatrist working within the juvenile court system in New York City. His samples were composed of 256 male adolescents adjudicated for all sorts of sexual delinquencies in the children's court throughout the various boroughs of New York City beginning in 1928. A total of 60% of his sample had committed other nonsexual delinquent acts. He reported that a total of only 3% of his sample had committed another sexual offense but that 15% had committed another delinquent offense in the followup period.

One method to bring order to the heterogeneity among sexual offenders would be to sort them into separate bins containing more homogeneous members, thereby deriving a typology of juvenile sex offenders. If a reliable and valid system of subtypes of juvenile sex offenders can be established, maybe meaningful differences can be demonstrated between one or more of the subtypes and delinquents who have not committed a sexual offense. Such a system would seek to increase the within-group homogeneity and maximize the between-group differences among the subtypes. The smaller and more homogeneous subtypes might then be meaningfully distinguished not only from each other but also from juvenile nonsexual offenders generally. Researchers advocating this approach argue that the existence of discrete subtypes within the heterogeneous population of juvenile sex offenders may be masking some of the differences between sexual offenders and nonsexual offenders. Separate out the hodge-podge of juvenile sex offenders into more neatly ordered groups and the empirical distinction between them and general delinquents will emerge.

The typology that has demonstrated the most promise is a simple dichotomous system that separates juvenile sexual offenders into child molesters and peer and adult offenders (Hunter, Hazelwood, and Slesinger 2000; Hunter, Figueredo, Malamuth et al. 2003; Seto and Lalumière 2006).

Youth who sexually assault peers or older victims tend to offend against women whereas child molesters target male victims about half of the time. Peer/adult offenders tend to select stranger or acquaintance victims more often than child molesters, who more often select siblings or related victims. Their assaults are also more likely to be group based and to occur in the context of some other criminal enterprise, such as burglary, as opposed to the child molesters, who often act alone and independently of any other criminal activity. Finally, peer/adult offenders more often commit their offenses in a public place, with a third of them occurring outdoors, and with a modus operandi characterized by surprise and violent force that is more often injurious. Child molesters, probably capitalizing on their familiarity with the victim and his or her more vulnerable immaturity, use more opportunistic and subtly coercive techniques, often involving play, to gain victim compliance. These results portray the peer/adult offenders as bearing a closer resemblance to violent delinquents than the child molesters (Hunter, Hazelwood, and Slesinger 2000).

More recent research has attempted to extend the validity of this simple typology, reporting that the groups differ significantly on a number of clinical and psychological dimensions, not just crime variables (Hunter, Figueredo, Malamuth et al. 2003). Child molesters displayed greater deficits in psychosocial functioning, such as social immaturity and emotional regulation problems, were less aggressive in their sexual offense, were less likely to have abused alcohol or drugs at the time of the offense, and were less likely to have used a weapon than peer/adult offenders. Psychosocial deficits were correlated with a juvenile's offender status as a child molester, but their utility as a predictor of group membership—child molester or peer/adult offender—was small. The groups did not differ on personality and attitudinal variables that measure hostile masculinity, negative views toward woman, and acceptance of sexually abusive behavior.

The results support the argument that offenders against children and offenders against peer/adults may have different clinical programming needs (Hunter, Figueredo, Malamuth et al. 2003). This dichotomous grouping of juvenile sex offenders makes rational sense and is consistent with the way adult sex offenders are often described and separated. The typology holds some promise, but it still awaits further validation. Other than the child molesters being more psychosocially immature and more prone to negative emotional states than the peer/adult offenders, the psychological differences between these groups remains uncharted. Recall that the Missouri study found equally high rates of nonsexual offending with its sample of child molesters and rapists. That study also measured these two groups of juvenile sex offenders on a battery of symptom surveys, behavior-rating inventories, and family-functioning scales that were similar to the ones used in the typology studies. The study found no significant differences between the child molesters and the peer-aged/adult rapists (Ronis and Borduin 2007). They differed on none of the psychosocial and emotional adjustment measures, indicating that much more research needs to be done before this simple dichotomous typology can be considered valid and clinically meaningful. Finally, this dichotomous system also does not allow for the classification of the probably sizable number of juveniles who have perpetrated offenses against children and against peers/adults.

Another potential method for developing a useful typology for juvenile sex offenders is to divide then into sex-only and sex-plus categories, a system first suggested by Butler and Seto (2002) and later adopted by Van Wijk, Mali, and Bullens (2007). The sex-only category includes those juvenile sex offenders who have only sex offenses in their official delinquency histories whereas sex-plus offenders have a mix of sexual offenses and nonsexual offenses in their known delinquent backgrounds. Butler and Seto (2002) examined differences between these two types of juvenile sex offenders after they discovered that sex offenders as a whole did not differ significantly from nonsex offenders on early childhood conduct problems, current behavioral adjustment, and procriminal attitudes and beliefs—although they did find that the juvenile sex offenders had a lower expected risk for future delinquency than the nonsexual offenders. When they divided their sample of juvenile sex offenders into sex-only and sex-plus categories, some meaningful differences did emerge between the two groups. The sex-only group had fewer childhood conduct problems, significantly fewer current behavior problems, more prosocial attitudes and beliefs, and a lower expected risk for future delinquency than did the sex-plus offenders, who appeared more antisocial and at a higher acute risk for future general offending.

Van Wijk, Mali, and Bullens (2007), in a replication of the dichotomy suggested by Butler and Seto (2002), found that the sex-plus offenders often begin their criminal careers earlier and persist in offending for a longer period of time. Overall, however, the authors conclude that the results of their study add further support for the commonly reported finding that juvenile sex offenders are a heterogeneous group. For the sex-plus offender, sexually offending comprises only a small portion of their overall delinquency. The sex-only offender, on the other hand, cannot be considered a delinquent specialist who embarks on a future career of sexual offending. In fact, the authors characterize the sex-only offender as most often an "experimenter" and not a sexual deviant.

Another unverified operating belief about juvenile sex offenders, like the notions that they bear some similarity to adult sex offenders and that they can be readily distinguished from juvenile nonsex offenders, is the degree to which their sexual offending is viewed as a manifestation of psychopathology. Sexual offenders are often conceptualized as deeply embedded within a clinical or mental health discourse, as suffering from some form of deviant sexual desire, a paraphilia in psychiatric parlance. They are, therefore, conceived as more complexly intertwined within disordered psychological processes or mental health diagnoses, calling for a greater level of involvement with mental health professionals. The treatment and management of their risk seems more a clinical issue than a purely administrative one, as is the case with other juvenile offender groups.

Mental health clinicians are more often directly involved in decisions regarding their movement and release. Their more complicated clinical treatment, their deeper involvement with clinicians, and the wider reticence of the juvenile justice system and the community at large to place them in the community may translate into juvenile sex offenders spending greater periods of time in secure residential treatment programs where they receive more intensive treatment for what supposedly ails them. Furthermore, community services and outpatient treatment services for juvenile sex offenders are often difficult to locate, requiring a greater level of treatment progress and a more advanced level of risk-management skill to be demonstrated in this offender group than in other offender groups before they are released from residential settings.

One of the often assumed hidden mental health characteristics of juvenile sex offenders is that they have been the victim of sexual abuse and that their sexual offending is in some measure a reaction to or a repetition of this primary trauma. But the research literature about the prevalence of a sexual abuse history in juvenile sex offenders has encountered three problems.

First, most sexual abuse victims do not go on to be sexual offenders. Only a small percentage of sexual abuse victims go on to sexually abuse others later in childhood.

Second, a substantial number of studies have found that the majority of juveniles who commit sexual offenses do not report a history of sexual abuse. The incidence of childhood sexual abuse among samples of juvenile sexual offenders has ranged from a high of 80% in some samples (Becker and Hunter 1997) to a low of 8% in others (Spaccarelli, Bowden, Coatsworth et al. 1997), with other studies reporting everything in between (Barbaree, Marshall, and McCormick 1998; Leguizamo 2002; Longo 1982; Ronis and Borduin 2007; Ryan, Miyoshi, Metzner et al. 1996). There is of course the problem that many juveniles who commit sexual offenses may deny their experience of past sexual abuse because of shame and embarrassment, but this must be counterbalanced by the possibility that the report of a sexual abuse history by juveniles who have committed a sexual offense also provides an easy-to-understand causal explanation for their sexual offense. There exists a motivation to disclose a history of sexual victimization or a pressure to believe that a history of sexual abuse exists when in fact it does not or to create one when one knows it does not exist. At the very least, there will be a greater pressure on the part of the clinician working with the juvenile sex offender to uncover the existence of a history of sexual victimization in the background of the juvenile sex offender and for the juvenile to admit to the existence of such a potentially traumatizing event in his past.

Third, sexual abuse victimization has been found to be prevalent in non–sex offending juveniles as well as juvenile sex offenders. It appears that sexual abuse is a relatively frequent experience of a significant number of juvenile offenders generally. A substantial number of studies have found that a history of sexual abuse victimization did not differentiate juvenile sexual offenders from juvenile nonsexual offenders (Allan, Allan, Marshall et al. 2002; Benoit and Kennedy 1992; Fagan and Wexler 1988; Smith and Monastersky 1986; Spaccarelli, Bowden, Coatsworth et al. 1997).

Estimates of sexual victimization in the histories of juvenile sex offenders vary widely, differing from study to study because of sampling differences. The characteristics of a particular sample of juvenile offenders will vary according to different local practices and characteristics of the juvenile justice system. Different types of samples of sexually aggressive youth may account for the wide diversity of reports about the prevalence of prior sexual abuse (Burton 2008). Samples from residential programs as opposed to community-based programs may contain juveniles with more serious offense histories and more severe victimization histories.

Reports of sexual victimization may vary as a function of when the juvenile is assessed in the adjudication or treatment process. Studies that measure abuse history at pretrial or at intake, just after adjudication, may have lower rates of sexual abuse reporting than if measures are taken further into the process, such as at post-treatment or just prior to discharge (Worling 1995). Such late-stage assessments may capture juveniles at a time frame when they have learned how to define abuse, and they may be more open and trusting in later stages of treatment than in earlier stages. They may also be more motivated to offer justifying causes for their sexual offending or may have come to view favorable release decisions as attached to such disclosures.

In summary, it is difficult to arrive at sturdy figures about the rate of sexual victimization in juvenile sex offenders given the wide variability among the characteristics of the samples. Overall, it seems that sexual victimization is a more prevalent experience among juvenile offenders than children and adolescents outside of the juvenile justice system. While it appears that juvenile sex offenders, particularly child molesters, often have a higher rate of sexual victimization (Awad and Saunders 1991; Ford and Linney 1995; van Wijk, Vermeiren, Loeber et al. 2006), most studies have reported that most juvenile sex offenders do not report a history of sexual victimization. This is consistent with the meta-analytic results of Hanson and Bussière (1998), who found that a history of sexual abuse was not statistically related to sexual recidivism in adults. Though estimates of the rates of sexual victimization vary widely among juvenile sexual offenders, it seems to be overwhelmingly the case that a history of sexual victimization does not condemn one to a future of sexual offending as the vast majority of childhood sexual abuse victims do not go on to sexually abuse others later in life. Sexual abuse does not appear to be a particularly strong marker for sexual offending, and does not figure prominently in the etiology of a significant number of juvenile sex offenders. Most studies report the rate of sexual abuse victimization as below 50% and no study finds a perfect correspondence of 100%, suggesting that sexual victimization is best conceived as "a sufficient but not a necessary condition for future sexual offending" (Barbaree, Marshall, and McCormick 1998, 21).

Deviant sex desire or arousal—defined as sexual attraction to children in the case of pedophiles and sexual arousal to violence or control and power in the case of peer-aged or adult-victim rapists—would appear to be the most likely clinical candidate to distinguish juvenile sex offenders from nonsex offenders. Deviant arousal in adult sexual offenders was the most robust predictor of sexual recidivism in Hanson and Bussière's (1998) meta-analysis. The question remains, however, whether deviant arousal plays a similar role in the sexual offenses of adolescents. Even this seemingly straightforward factor becomes problematic for adolescents.

The most basic problem with the use of deviant arousal as a special clinical marker of the juvenile sex offender is that the vast majority of juvenile sex offenders do not exhibit deviant arousal. Some estimate that approximately 10% of adolescents who engage in sexual offenses exhibit deviant sexual interests (Smallbone 2006; Zimring 2004). A study utilizing a review of archival test results found that 25% of juvenile sex offenders demonstrated deviant interests in prepubescent children (Seto, Lalumière, and Blanchard 2000). Another found that 30% manifested sexual responses to child stimuli (Seto, Murphy, Page et al. 2003). The majority of adolescents, therefore, engage in sexualized misconduct for reasons not rooted in sexual deviance but because of some other set of causes, most likely a developmental life crisis or some other social or emotional stressor operating at the time. The case of David represents a juvenile sex offender whose sexual offense does not appear to be a function of deviant interests as much as opportunity mixed with other emotionally based factors operating in his life at the time. The presence of sexual deviance seems a more critical issue in the case of Jason.

Another problem with the use of sexual deviance in youth is that sexual interest and arousal may be more malleable in adolescents than adults, subject to more developmental change and influence. It is possible that even for the sexually deviant few, for an unknown number of them, their sexual deviance will resolve with maturation. They may manifest sexually deviant interests in a transient and time-limited way. There exists no research on the temporal stability of deviant arousal in children. It is simply not known how many of the adolescents who exhibit deviant arousal to younger children or to violence will mature out of this as they progress into adulthood. They may outgrow their sexual deviancy for no other reason than simple maturation, just as they may outgrow their general delinquency (Moffitt 1993, 2003).

Unresolved questions remain about whether reliable and valid measurement of deviant arousal in adolescent sex offenders is even possible. It is just not clear that deviant arousal can be consistently measured in adolescents, and—putting aside for the moment the problem of reliability of measurement—whether deviant arousal is correlated to the same problems, like sexual recidivism for instance, in adolescent populations as it is in adult populations. This is a validity question. One study found that juvenile sexual recidivists were significantly more likely to have a deviant pattern of sexual arousal; but the presence of sexual deviance was based on clinical judgment through retrospective ratings of therapists—a measure without demonstrated reliability (Schram, Milloy, and Rowe 1991).

The problem of the reliable and valid measurement of deviant arousal is not exclusive to juvenile sex offenders. It is a question that has hounded clinicians and researchers alike who work with and study adult sex offenders. The limitations of self-report of deviant sexual desire are obvious. Offenders may harbor a variety of motivations for being less than forthcoming about their sexual deviancy. Open disclosures can result in negative legal consequences and more restrictive clinical interventions for longer periods of time. Offenders may be ashamed and embarrassed about their deviant sexuality, and may hide it through conscious denial about its lurking presence. Finally, they may suffer from a form of denial at a more primary level, causing them to be confidently insistent about the absence of deviant desire despite its being unambiguously displayed in their overt sexual offenses.

The search for a more objective measure of deviant arousal, free from the untrustworthiness of self-report, has yielded a number of measuring devices. The most established and researched has been the penile plethysmograph (PPG), consisting of an elastic band containing a mercury-filled strain gauge that is wrapped around the male subject's penis about midshaft. The subject then attends to audiotapes, visual slides, or videotapes depicting various appropriate and inappropriate sexual scenarios. The magnitude of the erectile response to the different sorts of sexual stimuli provides a measure of sexual interest. Far from being a lie detector for the penis, the PPG can be readily faked (Kalmus and Beech 2005). The penis is hardly an organ "with a mind of its own" (Friedman 2001), and its responsiveness can be consciously manipulated by the subject. Deniers of sexual deviance can resort to a host of internally distracting strategies to deflect a sexual response, causing the results to "flat-line" or indicate no arousal pattern. Moreover, there is concern about the ethical use of the PPG with adolescents who are exposed to sexually deviant stimuli, typically audiotaped descriptions of deviant scenarios involving rape and child molestation. Potential negative effects emerging from such exposure have called into question the use of the PPG with them (Hunter and Becker 1994).

More recently, various viewing-time measures have emerged as indices of sexual interest. Based on Rosenzweig's (1942) hypothesis that the viewing time for a visual sexual stimulus is related to sexual interest, these instruments measure sustained attention to a particular category of photographs revealing the subject's sexual interests without their awareness of what is being measured. The most well-known of these measures is the Abel Assessment for Interest in Paraphilias (AAIP; Abel 1995), often referred to by the shortened title "the Abel Screen." The test computes the length of time an individual lingers over visual slides depicting males and females of different age categories. Longer viewing times are considered to be an index of sexual interest. The people depicted in the slides are clothed and are not engaged in overtly sexual acts so as not to tip off the subject to the actual intent of the experimenter or examiner. The use of clothed figures not engaged in sexual scenarios also bypasses the ethical concern surrounding the PPG and its use of audiotaped descriptions of sexually deviant scenarios. The AAIP, because it purports to measure sexual interest by means of the amount of time subjects view a category of visual sexual images without their awareness of what is being measured, is considered to be less susceptible to faking. If, however, subjects knows ahead of time what the experimenter or evaluator is up to, they can manipulate their response time.

The widening deployment of the PPG and AAIP in juvenile sexual offender treatment programs has been documented in a number of recent surveys. In 1992, 168 juvenile sexual offender treatment programs reported routine use of phallometric assessment, like the PPG, with adolescent offenders (Knopp, Freeman-Longo, and Stevenson 1992). More recently, 9.9% of a sample of 480 community treatment programs indicated the routine use of the PPG, 25.2% reported using a visual time measure, and a total of 32.2% reported using one or both of these assessment measures (McGrath, Cumming, and Burchard 2003). In 185 residential treatment programs, 9.2% reported using the PPG, 17.7% reported using a visual reaction time measure, and a total of 24.5% indicated they used one or both of these measures.

The overall popularity of these measures of sexual interest has waned from the higher rates of use in the early to mid-1990s, probably in part due to research that has failed to establish their validity for adolescents. Surprisingly, given a recent report by the National Research Council (2002) regarding its questionable merits, polygraph use as a measure of sexual deviancy has increased since 1992, with 42.5%

of community programs and 30.6% of residential programs for adolescent sex offenders reporting routine use (McGrath, Cumming, and Burchard 2003).

Despite the continued use of the PPG and visual time measures like the AAIP, their validity with adolescents has not been firmly established. There have only been a few empirical studies published over the past two decades on the validity of the PPG with adolescent samples. Because of the fluctuating nature of sexual interests in developing adolescents, the results of the PPG for adolescents are more ambiguous and difficult to interpret (Becker and Hunter 1997). The relationship between phallometrically measured deviant arousal and other clinical characteristics in juvenile sexual offenders may be weaker than in adult sex offenders (Hunter, Goodwin, and Becker 1994). The PPG is just less valid for adolescents and, therefore, has limited clinical utility. The greater developmental fluidity of adolescents may mean that the majority of juvenile sex offenders have not developed relatively fixed patterns of sexual arousal and interest. Juveniles are more likely to have victims of both genders as compared to adults, more often engage in multiple paraphilic behaviors, and are likely to cross over from incest into nonincest offending and vice versa. They are simply all over the sexual deviance map, exhibiting a much greater fluidity and instability. PPG results may just be less predictive and informative about adolescents than adults.

There has been only one published study that has attempted to test the PPG's ability to predict recidivism in a sample of juvenile sex offenders (Gretton, McBride, Hare et al. 2001). The study, conducted at the Youth Forensic Psychiatric Service in Vancouver, British Columbia, found that the PPG was not correlated with the Psychopathy Checklist-Revised (PCL-R), the most firmly established measure of the psychopathic personality, and was not correlated either with sexual recidivism or with general and violent recidivism. The interaction of high psychopathy and sexual deviance as measured by the PPG was correlated with general and violent reoffense in the followup but not with sexual reoffense. This was probably due to the low base-rate of sexual reoffense in the sample. The higher rate of nonsexual reoffense within this sample of juvenile sex offenders led the researchers to conclude that their subjects were not so much specialized sexual offenders as they were general, versatile offenders who had happened to commit a sexual offense along the way, echoing a general trend in the scientific data against the notion of the juvenile sex offender as a deviant sexual specialist (Lussier 2005).

In the final analysis, the current state of the science on the use of the PPG for juvenile sex offenders indicates that there is just not enough research to support its employment in the routine assessment and treatment of juvenile sexual offenders

Measures of visual time reaction have not fared much better than the PPG for assessing sexual deviance in adolescents. An initial, independent study of the AAIP, or the Abel Screen, outside of the laboratory of Gene Abel, the instrument's inventor, for a sample of juvenile sexual offenders produced low reliability or consistency over a two-week interval; that is, subjects' scores taken at an initial assessment were poorly correlated with measures taken again after two weeks (Smith and Fischer 1999). If sexual deviancy is considered to be a characteristic with a fair amount of stability over time, a high correlation would be expected over so short a time interval. Either the Abel Screen is not able to measure a relatively stable characteristic like sexual interest, or the Abel Screen is accurate and adolescent deviancy is an unstable and erratic process. Either way, whether the problem lies with the measure or the thing being measured, the study shows that the Abel Screen is not able to measure adolescent deviant sexual interest with sufficient consistency. The researchers go on to challenge the validity of the AAIP because it was not able to discriminate sexual offenders from nonoffenders. Yet, this could be the case because most of the juvenile sex offenders, as the research has mostly indicated thus far, do not have deviant sexual interests and are in fact indistinguishable from the nonsexual offenders on this characteristic.

Abel and colleagues (2004) attempted to redeem the applicability of the AAIP with juvenile sex offenders with a large sample of seventeen hundred juvenile sexual offenders. They report that juveniles who admitted to having molested children lingered longer over pictures of children than juveniles who had engaged in other types of sexual offenses. Moreover, those juveniles who had more child victims and committed more total deviant acts viewed the pictures of children longer. However, the instrument was not able to significantly discriminate between child and non-child offenders, prompting the researchers to caution that further research and refinement of the test was still needed and that it should not be used alone in the absence of other assessment measures. A critical limitation of the study was its use of subjects who admitted to their sexual offenses. Whether the AAIP can identify adolescents who deny their offenses remains untested. Additionally, the study did not address the question of changes in sexual interest due to the effect of treatment or the AAIP's ability to predict sexual recidivism. To date the AAIP has never been tested on its ability to predict who is at greater risk to reoffend sexually. A final cautionary note regarding the AAIP is the lack of a validation study outside of the lab of Abel, the developer of the test. Before the test can be accepted as valid, it is crucial that the research be conducted by researchers independent of the test developer. A test that has only been validated by its inventor and only within his research lab should always be regarded with suspicion.

An alternative viewing time procedure called Affinity was recently reported by Worling (2006). It operates on the same principles as the Abel Screen. Subjects are shown clothed pictures of various age and gender groups and their total viewing time is calculated. The Affinity procedure was able to significantly differentiate those adolescents with a male child victim from those adolescents who never offended sexually against a male child. The Affinity could not successfully differentiate adolescents with female child victims from those who offended sexually against other groups, suggesting that adolescents who offend sexually against girls may not be motivated by deviant arousal. The Affinity could not be used to correctly classify youth into subtypes, such as boy vs. girl molesters, for instance. The study used the self-report of the subject as the criterion to measure the accuracy of the Affinity procedure. Deniers of sexual offending were not in the sample and so the ability of the Affinity procedure to identify deviance in them is unknown, a critical limitation for clinical practice. Finally, the sample did not include nonsexual offenders or community controls and so it is unknown what the base rate of deviant arousal or viewing time is for either of these groups compared to the sample of sexual offenders.

A related problem in the research literature on the sexual deviancy of juvenile sex offenders is the paucity of research assessing deviant sex desire in adolescent nonsex offenders or even for adolescents generally, for that matter. The prevalence rate of deviant sexual fantasies in adolescent boys is unknown. At the present time, there exist no systematic comparisons of the topography of fantasies in different adolescent sex offender groups and a control group comprised of males drawn from the general population.

There has, however, been some research about these matters for adult males, and the results provide a convincing argument for reexamining the role of sexually deviant fantasies in sexual offending in light of the high rates of fantasies about the sexual coercion of women and about sex with children reported by men who deny a history of sexually offending behavior and do not have a history of arrest for such misconduct. Early studies that compared the sexual fantasies of adult sex offenders and nonsex offenders found no significant differences in their deviant fantasy content or frequency of fantasies (Rokach, Nutbrown, and Nexhipi 1988; Langevin, Bain, Ben-Aron et al. 1985). A more recent research report found that most sex offenders reported having nondeviant sexual fantasies involving consenting women, and much fewer reported deviant fantasies involving children or nonconsenting victims (Langevin, Lang, and Curnoe 1998). While a self-reporting bias may be operating here, the researchers assumed that all the sexual offenders had admitted to their offense history and/or deviant sexual desire, making deception less of an issue. Furthermore, the report of fantasies was uncorrelated with a measure that examined response bias. Deviant fantasies were not able to predict group membership as either a sexual offender or a nonoffender. Overall, the nonsexual offenders reported having more sexual fantasies of any kind than did the sexual offenders. Also, about 9% of them report having deviant fantasies but do not appear to act on them. It is difficult to determine the nature of these deviant fantasies, whether they were fleeting and momentary or more elaborate and complex. It would appear that deviant fantasies are not the sole province of sex offenders, as a sizable number of nonoffenders reported having them.

Sexual fantasies about rape scenarios are not as rare as one might assume. A review of the research on sexual fantasies found that on the average, across seven studies, about a third of males in the general population reported fantasies of forced sexual contact (Leitenberg and Henning 1995). In one study 35% of the male undergraduates reported that they would commit rape if they could get away with it (Malamuth 1986). A later study found that many men who do not report a history of sexual aggression exhibit arousal to rape scenarios, particularly when the victim is portrayed as initially resisting and then surrendering (Malamuth and Check 1983).

Sexual fantasies about children are not rare either. A study of male undergraduates found that 21% admit that "little children sometimes attract me sexually" and that 9% report having sexual fantasies regarding children (Briere and Runtz 1989). However, fantasies and even sexual arousal to children do not, taken alone, mean that someone is a pedophile or likely to sexually molest a child. None of the participants in the study anonymously admitted they had molested children. Another study found that 60% of a sample of adult men admitted to having a sexual fantasy of initiating sex with a young girl (Crepault and Coutour 1980). Still another found that 17% of their sample of male undergraduates indicated that they had recently had a fantasy of having sex with a girl under the age of 15, with 5% indicating that the girl was under the age of 12 (Templeman and Stinnett 1991). Finally, in a study of nonoffender controls, nearly 20% demonstrated arousal to prepubescent children on the PPG (Barbaree and Marshall 1989; Fedora, Reddon, Morrison et al. 1992).

There has been a relative absence of research comparing sexual fantasies of juvenile sex offenders and normal controls. One of the few studies to do so was a study that compared the self-reported fantasies of incarcerated youthful sex offenders with those of incarcerated nonsex offenders and a control group drawn from the general population (Daleiden, Kaufman, Hilliker et al. 1998). The samples were drawn from incarcerated youth in Ohio, Oregon, and Texas and college students in an introductory psychology classes. Adolescent sex offenders reported more nonconsenting sexual experiences and more paraphilic interests than the nonsexual offenders. All groups had high rates of interest in voyeurism. The study did not uncover a distinct pattern of fantasy among the sexual offenders. The juvenile sex offenders did not demonstrate elevated levels of deviant fantasy but had fewer fantasies with nondeviant content, leading the researchers to conclude that sexual offending, at least for adolescents, may not be related to elevations in deviant fantasies but to deficits in nondeviant fantasies. It is not the presence of deviant fantasies alone, since many nonsex offenders reported having them, but relative deficits in nondeviant fantasies, or maybe an unfavorable ratio of nondeviant to deviant fantasies, that seemed most distinguishing between the groups.

The results of this study indicate that the presence of deviant fantasies in adolescent sex offenders does not appear to play an important role in the etiology and maintenance of sexual offending. The reported deficits in nondeviant fantasies may contain important considerations for the treatment of adolescent sex offenders. Maybe what is important is the development of nondeviant sexual interests and skills, of normal or nonharmful sexuality, as opposed to the restructuring or extinction of deviant fantasies. It may be more therapeutic, maybe even easier, to add a positive than to delete a negative.

The results from this collection of studies provide a persuasive argument that the role and exclusivity of deviant fantasy or arousal needs to be reassessed in the face of the high percentage of males who do not report a history of sexual offending but admit to having sexual fantasies that incorporate force or have children as their object of desire. Can something be defined as deviant when so many report having it? It may perhaps be deviant in the moral/legal sense but certainly not in the normative sense. Given the taboos against coercive sexual relations and sex with children, the percentages are probably much higher than reported in these research studies (Leitenberg and Henning 1995). It would seem, according to these results, that having deviant fantasies and even experiencing deviant arousal to coercive sex and sex with children is not exclusive to sex offenders, as many nonsex offenders report or manifest them on the PPG.

The category juvenile sex offenders, while a meaningful legal designation, appears to have little validity as a specialized clinical category. In the aggregate they bear little resemblance to adult sex offenders. Most juvenile sex offenders do not in fact go on to continue along sexually deviant pathways into adulthood. Most desist in adolescence and do not carry their youthful sex offending with them across the threshold of maturity, a reality that calls into question the predictive validity of a juvenile sex offense in the history of a juvenile sex offender. The finding of early-onset sexual deviancy in adult sex offenders is no mark on the majority of adolescent sexual offenders, as only a small minority persist in sexually offending across the lifespan.

In contrast to their limited overlap with adult sex offenders, juvenile sexual offenders are not clearly distinguishable from juvenile nonsexual offenders. These two relatively overlapping groups have more in common than distinguishing differences. Juvenile sex offenders often have a history of nonsexual delinquent offending in their backgrounds and are more likely to recidivate with a nonsexual delinquent offense than a sexual offense, just like their non–sex offending delinquent counterparts. The two groups appear to emerge from a similar set of historical forces operating within and on them. Juvenile sexual offending and general delinquency appear to be the products of similar origins. The evidence for the juvenile sex offender existing as a delinquent specialist characterized by sexual perversion and deviancy is weak. Juvenile sex offending, for the most part, does not bear any readily identifiable clinical signs or marks setting the juvenile sex offender apart from the nonsexual juvenile offender. A history of sexual victimization, sexual deviancy, or any other sign or symptom has not emerged as a strong distinguishing feature of the juvenile sex offender. In the final analysis, most juvenile sexual offenders appear to be little more than juvenile delinquents with a sexual offense.

3

Test Authors in Search
of a Clinical Population

*Risk Assessment Instruments
for Juvenile Sex Offenders*

J.P. was sentenced to thirty years with a minimum of fifteen years to serve before parole eligibility for the aggregated sexual assault of two women and the attempted aggravated sexual assault of a third. The offenses occurred in 1982 when J.P. was 14 and 15 years old. The three sexual assaults all involved a similar modus operandi. In each case, J.P. grabbed a stranger adult female victim from behind at knife point, threatened to kill her, forced her to a secluded area, and took her money. In the first offense, he removed the victim's clothes but she managed to escape before he was able to rape her. In the other two cases, he forcibly raped his victims (*In the Matter of the Commitment of J.P.* 2001).

He was transferred to adult court on the basis of the nature of the charges and his extensive juvenile record. He had prior delinquency adjudications beginning in 1980 for shoplifting, receiving stolen property, burglary, theft, robbery, and sexual contact offenses.

J.P. remained in the New Jersey state prison from 1983 until 2000. He was not offered sex offender treatment but did complete a substance abuse program and earned a GED. During his seventeen years of incarceration, he received a total of twelve institutional charges for fighting, possessing drugs, refusing to obey, and lying to staff. The drug infraction occurred in 1991. In 1998 he was evaluated by a psychologist as being "psychologically appropriate" for minimum-security or community placement.

Prior to his parole, however, the state of New Jersey filed a petition in 2000 that J.P., now 32 years old, was a sexually violent predator who suffered from a mental abnormality or personality disorder that placed him at risk for future sexual offending. The state argued that he should not be granted parole, but instead should be civilly committed for treatment until such time as he no longer posed a risk of sexual violence. The state based its petition on the evaluation results of a number of mental health professionals who had assessed him while he was in prison. A psychiatrist diagnosed him as having an Antisocial Personality Disorder, a mental disorder characterized by "a pervasive pattern of disregard for, and violation of, the rights of others that begins in childhood or adolescence and continues into adulthood" (American Psychiatric Association [APA] 1994, 645), and a substance abuse problem. He was rated as high risk on the Minnesota Sexual Offender Screening Tool-Revised (MnSOST-R), an actuarial instrument that purports to measure risk of sexual recidivism. An actuarial assessment instrument is based on static risk factors that are part of a person's demographic profile and life history. The scores are, for the most part, immutable and unchanging and have been statistically correlated with later sexual recidivism. The psychiatrist concluded that J.P. suffered from a mental abnormality or a personality disorder that made him likely to commit sexual acts of violence in the future. A second psychiatrist evaluated him and agreed with the conclusions reached by the first.

Later, another psychiatrist and a psychologist, both employed by the state, evaluated J.P. The psychiatrist concluded that J.P. was a sexually violent predator who needed continued confinement. The appeals court would later comment that this expert did not appear familiar with J.P.'s criminal and institutional history. His testimony that all individuals with Antisocial Personality Disorder should be incarcerated did not bolster his credibility with the appeals court. The psychologist reviewed a number of psychological tests and the results of two actuarial sexual-reoffense risk-assessment instruments: the MnSOST-R and the STATIC-99.

During her testimony in his sexually violent predator commitment hearing, the psychologist stated that she had used her clinical judgment in scoring J.P. as having an unstable employment history even though he was 15 and a full-time high school student at the time of his arrest. Under cross-examination, she also admitted that she had scored the STATIC-99 incorrectly by double counting his first sexual offense but stated that this error did not change his high-risk classification.

A psychologist testified on behalf of J.P., stating that his substance abuse problem was in remission and that J.P. was a different person than he was at age 15. He had better volitional control and insight into his antisocial past. The psychologist further testified that the DSM-IV (APA

1994) required that there be a pervasive pattern of antisocial behavior that persists into adulthood in order for a subject to qualify for the diagnosis of Antisocial Personality Disorder, and that J.P.'s antisocial conduct did not extend into adulthood. His history of prison rule violations was not distinctive enough to support the diagnosis of Antisocial Personality Disorder because, the psychologist testified, 70% of all inmates have histories of institutional infractions. He further testified that the results of the actuarial assessment instruments lacked validity for J.P. since he had made significant developmental changes since the time of his offenses.

The judge in her summation of the expert testimony concluded that indeed J.P. suffered from an Antisocial Personality Disorder and a Substance Abuse Disorder that affected his volitional capacity and predisposed him to commit sexual acts of violence in the future. The judge did not find J.P.'s challenges to the use of the actuarial tools in his case convincing and claimed that she "found these tools . . . assist me in finding that there is a very high risk, a very real and present risk, and the public needs protection" (60). In his appeal of his commitment, J.P. challenged the admissibility of the actuarial assessment instruments, claiming that all of his offenses were committed while he was a young adolescent. The appellate court agreed, stating, "we have some doubt whether actuarial tools can be used to evaluate a sex offender's risk of recidivism under such circumstances" (61). The court observed that the ability of actuarial assessment instruments to predict future dangerousness of sexual offenders whose only offense was committed while they were juveniles was never addressed in the trial. Moreover, even if sex offenses committed while a juvenile can be included in the scoring of the adult actuarial assessment instruments, "when an individual's last sex offense was committed while he was age fifteen, and he has been incarcerated since, the static nature of the instruments effectively freezes that person in his adolescence, making no allowances for the process of maturity" (61).

The court used some of the items on these tests to illustrate the problem of their application to adults who committed their offense as juveniles and have been incarcerated since that time. The MnSOST-R does not provide criteria for how to score the instance of a person who has been incarcerated since age 15 on the employment history item. They noted that the manual for the STATIC-99 does not recommend that the instrument be used for adolescents younger than age 18, but the statement is unclear as to whether it refers to adolescents who are younger than 18 at the time of the assessment or younger than 18 at the time of the sexual offense. They also picked up on the problem of rating an item about the offender having lived with a lover for at least two years in the case of an adolescent. They concluded that "thus the instruments themselves cast doubt on whether they are reliable predictors of future dangerousness when applied to a sex offender incarcerated since early [adolescence]" (62) and found that the judge had erred in admitting testimony based on these instruments. The case was remanded for an evidentiary hearing concerning the admissibility of actuarial assessment instruments in a case of an adult whose only offense occurred as a young adolescent.

The last decade has seen the development of a variety of risk-assessment instruments specifically for juvenile sex offenders. Many of these instruments have been modeled after risk-assessment instruments for adult sexual offenders. Presently there exists little research support for these instruments designed for juvenile sex offenders. There exists research evidence establishing that the factors comprising these instruments can be consistently scored in a similar way, by more than one user for the same juvenile offender (interrater reliability) and that the scores obtained are reasonably consistent over time for a juvenile (test-retest reliability); that the items making up a particular scale within these multiscaled instruments are correlated with each other, indicating that the scale measures some unidimensional construct or factor (internal consistency); and that the scales correlate with some other generally accepted test that has established its validity (concurrent or criterion validity). What has yet to be established is whether these risk assessment instruments can adequately predict recidivism (predictive validity). Predictive validity is the ultimate criterion to determine the clinical utility of a risk-assessment instrument.

The pursuit of predictive validation of juvenile-sex-offender risk-assessment instruments is in its early stages; the returns thus far are not promising. The biggest stumbling block to predictive validation has been the consistently low base rate of reoffense of juvenile sex offenders; too few juvenile sex offenders recidivate. How can a researcher establish predictive validity for a newly fashioned risk-assessment instrument if the juvenile sex offenders that the assessment instrument is designed to categorize do not reoffend at a rate high enough to actually allow the instrument to sufficiently test its own accuracy? A sufficient degree of variability in the criterion behavior, in this case sexual recidivism, is necessary in order for the instrument to do its intended work. The most optimal condition for predictive validation occurs when the target behavior has a close to even chance of reoccurring (Meehl and Rosen 1955). Under this condition, the instrument has the best shot at improving upon chance. If the target event has a 50-50 chance of reoccurring, the instrument only needs to have a small amount of predictive accuracy to improve upon the coin flip that an even chance of reoccurrence presents.

The paradox of low reoffense rates of juvenile sex offenders begs the question of why such instruments are needed in the first place. What is the need of a risk-assessment instrument if the vast majority of juveniles it intends to identify only reoffend at a rate of 15%, 10%, or 5%? A psychological assessment instrument is hard pressed to outperform a "no recidivism" decision that is right 85%, 90%, or 95% of the time.

There is an inherent problem with the prediction of low-base-rate events. The prediction of human behavior is exceedingly difficult to begin with. Add the statistical problem of a low base rate of occurrence to the equation and the problem is that much more compounded. In situations where the base rate is extremely low, as in the case of serious violence, such as homicide or suicide, even the best constructed assessment instrument will seldom, if ever, do better than an automatic "no" decision in every case, regardless of the history and other clinical characteristics that the juvenile presents to the clinician.

The field of violence prediction was initially problematized in the 1970s and 1980s by Steadman and Cocozza (1974) and Monahan (1981). Since their discrediting of the clinical prediction of violent behavior, each has spent the better part of the last three decades attempting to disentangle the field from the problem they first articulated. The field is still coping with the crisis they set off. The irony is that the major figures who first identified this "paradigmatic crisis" (Simon 2005) about the assessment of risk and the prediction of dangerousness would later be at the center of its rescue, trying to set right what they had toppled (Monahan, Steadman, Silver et al. 2001).

It was John Monahan (1981) in an often-cited monograph, *The Clinical Prediction of Violent Behavior*, who lay to rest the assumption that mental health professionals could separate through clinical judgment the dangerous from the nondangerous mentally ill when he uttered his now famous dictum that "psychiatrists and psychologists are accurate in no more than one out of three predictions of violent behavior over a several-year period among institutionalized populations that had both committed violence in the past . . . and who were diagnosed as mentally ill" (Monahan 1981, 47). The errors of prediction were mostly in the direction of the identification of a high number of false positives—that is, a person judged to be danger-ous who proved later not to be—a case of miscategorization with serious negative consequences for the person.

A major innovative idea in Monahan's monograph was a reconceptu-alization of assessment from the dichotomous identification of danger-ousness/no dangerousness to the identification of risk as existing along a continuum. Rather than thinking about dangerousness as an all-or-noth-ing phenomenon, wherein a patient is either dangerous or not dangerous, one should think about the level of risk that a particular patient poses for violence in the future at a particular circumscribed point in time or under a set of identifiable conditions. Dangerousness is more akin to a trait, a static condition, something like an identity. Risk is a more fluid and dy-namic phenomenon that can change as a person's circumstance or clinical functioning changes. Risk better captures the complexity of an individual's violence potential. Risk of violence, he posed, exists along a continuum, extending from low (probably never zero in the case of a person with a violence history) to medium to high. Furthermore, an individual's risk level can change or shift depending on the presence or absence of various conditions or situations such as intoxication, access to weapons, associa-tion with a peer group that supports violence, involvement in a conflicted relationship, or the acuity of violence-prone psychiatric symptoms such as paranoid delusions or command hallucinations. The movement from the concept of dangerousness to the concept of risk also readily lends itself to the strategy of identifying risk factors that contribute to violence and then managing and, even better, modifying these risk factors in order to effec-tively lower an individual's likelihood of violence in the future.

The movement from dangerousness to risk presented a major para-digm shift in the field, linking violence risk prediction with public health models for medical conditions such as heart disease and cancer. Violence could now be framed as a public health problem, an epidemiological phe-nomenon that is determined by the accumulation of empirically supported risk factors governing its occurrence. The shift revolutionized the field of violence prediction through its call to focus on the empirical identifica-tion of factors of risk for violence that are correlated with the incidence of violence rather than focusing on dangerous individuals (Steadman, Mo-nahan, Appelbaum et al. 1994). The assessment of risk would no longer be based on clinical judgment relying on untested theories about the causes of violence or aggression or clinical hunches based on a clinical reading of an individual's violent past. Instead, clinical assessment would consist of identifying factors of violence risk for an individual that have been empirically associated with the incidence of violence, just as a primary care physician or cardiologist bases an estimation of the risk of coronary heart disease and treatment on the presence of certain risk factors exhibited by the patient related to the incidence of a heart attack. The hope was that the risk estimate could even be quantified, calculated, presented as a percentage based on prior research on subjects with similar risk factors who went on to recidivate. Violence prediction would be an actuarial or statistically informed process, not a clinically intuitive one. As long as the individual being evaluated could be reasonably matched to the research sample—that is, be identified as emerging from the same population that comprised the sample upon which the research was based—such a quantification of risk seemed possible.

Debates about the superiority of actuarial versus clinical approaches to assessment of risk have been waged for fifty years, ever since Paul Meehl (1954) first threw the gauntlet down when he declared that actuarial techniques almost always outperform clinical methods in predicting any class of human behavior, including future violence. More recently Meehl reasserted his position in more definitive terms (Dawes, Faust, and Meehl 1989; Grove and Meehl 1996). The ensuing fifty years of research, which has not amounted to more than a few studies pitting clinical judgment against statistically derived decisions, in no way softened his view but instead further solidified it.

Meehl may have been the first to provide a definition of actuarial assessment:

> We may order the individual to a class or set of classes on the basis of objective facts, concerning his life history, his scores on psychometric tests, behavior ratings or check lists, or subjective judgments gained from interviews. The combination of all these data enables us to *classify* the subject; and once having made such a classification, we enter a statistical or actuarial table which gives the statistical frequency or behaviors of various sorts for persons belonging to a class. The mechanical combining of information for classification purposes, and the resultant probability figure which is an empirically determined relative frequency, are the characteristics that define the actuarial or statistical type of prediction. (Meehl 1954, 3)

Meehl also provided a definition for unstructured clinical methods of data combination or decision making.

> On the basis of interview impressions, other data from the history, and possibly also psychometric information . . . we formulate, as in a psychiatric staff conference, some psychological hypothesis regarding the structure and dynamics of this particular individual. . . . This type of procedure has been loosely called the clinical or case-study method of prediction. (Meehl 1954, 3)

Meehl was clear that even the most abstract clinical judgment could serve as an actuarial data point provided that it can be coded or quantified reliably. Actuarial assessment referred to a mode of data combination and decision making, not necessarily to the kind of data employed. Actuarial data was not necessarily limited to static variables that are readily verifiable and unchanging aspects of a person's demographic status or history. Dynamic clinical variables that are subject to change can also be considered actuarial data as long as it can be demonstrated empirically that the variable can be consistently scored by more than one clinician.

Meehl was firm in his view that these two procedures—actuarial prediction and clinical prediction—were mutually exclusive and independent from each other. He left no room for any middle-ground position or an integrated method whereby the two can work harmoniously together. A decision had to follow from one or the other procedure. If mental health experts employing an actuarial classification of risk put their own clinical spin or twist on it, adjusted it down or up on the basis of unvalidated clinical judgment, they were operating within a clinical-prediction mode of assessment. Meehl did not necessarily argue against this practice as long as it was rarely employed and the clinician could point to a valid reason why he or she was abandoning the actuarial rule. In fact, Meehl believed that only a clinician could identify occasions when an actuarial classification, no matter how well validated its results, should be ignored on the basis of some reliable data that the clinician had access to that was not picked up by the actuarial assessment instrument. For instance, the utterance of a direct threat or a stated intention to reoffend sexually does not make its way onto any of the current actuarial assessment instruments for sexual offense risk. Only a clinician would be available to hear and record such a statement and take it into account. An actuarial assessment instrument would probably miss or not be attuned to capture a statement that might invalidate the actuarial rule. Meehl granted the clinician this prerogative but cast some doubt on how often such an event would actually occur in clinical practice.

Meehl (1954, 1986) has been joined by numerous others (Garb 1998; Hanson 1998; Monahan, Steadman, Silver et al. 2001) in the view that actuarial assessment of risk is superior to unstructured clinical assessment. (See Litwack 2001 and Litwack, Zapf, Groscup et al. 2007 for a counterview.) Grove and Meehl (1996) conclude in their review of the literature on the question of actuarial versus clinical prediction that "to use the less efficient of two prediction procedures in dealing with such matters is not only unscientific and irrational, it is unethical" (320). Monahan, Steadman, and Silver et al. (2001) came near to declaring a moratorium on further research on the question about which of the two methods is best and argued that to continue such a research program "seemed to be overkill [as] that horse was already dead" (7).

Beginning in the 1990s, in answer to the call for empirically supported and evidence-based assessments of risk, there was a proliferation of actuarial instruments for assessing sexual offense risk for adults. The Rapid Risk Assessment for Sex Offense Recidivism (RRASOR; Hanson 1997) was one of the earliest developed actuarial assessment instruments for adult sexual offenders. Other actuarial assessment instruments include the Sex Offender Risk Appraisal Guide (SORAG; Quinsey, Harris, Rice et al. 1998), a 14-item actuarial device that includes the results of the Hare Psychopathy Checklist-Revised (PCL-R; Hare 1991) and the penile plethysmograph; the Sexual Violence Risk-20 (SVR-20; Boer, Wilson, Gauthier et al. 1997), which functions more as an assessment guide than as a strict actuarial assessment tool; the Minnesota Sex Offender Screening Tool-Revised (MnSOST-R; Epperson, Kaul, and Hesselton n.d.), another brief actuarial assessment instrument that includes dynamic treatment variables that take into account an offender's progress in treatment; and the STATIC-99 (Hanson and Thornton 1999; Harris, Phenix, Hanson et al. 2003), an expanded version of the RRASOR.

All of these actuarial measures were developed according to similar construction methods. Generally, one begins with a sample of sexual offenders where it is known whether they reoffended or not over a specified period of time. Next, the two groups, the recidivists and the nonrecidivists, are compared on a range of variables that have shown some predictive promise in past research, such as general criminality and deviant sexual interests. The variables are tested to see which of them are significantly associated on a statistical basis with the recidivist group. Particularly strong predictor variables, those with substantially larger statistical relationships with recidivism, are often assigned a greater weight or value. A human judge, in contrast, is very poor at assigning differential weights to multiple predictor variables and will probably weigh them equally (Meehl 1986; Grove and Meehl 1996). If a sufficient number of factors are found to be sufficiently predictive, they can be combined to form an instrument or a test. Cut-off scores for the instrument, the scores that divide the high-, medium-, and low-risk subjects, are determined by figuring the scoring threshold that yields the best classification results—the score that correctly classifies the most subjects as recidivists or nonrecidivists. This instrument is then cross-validated on an independent sample. If a sufficiently large number of subjects are included in the original development sample and subsequent validation samples, estimates of likelihood of reoffense can be provided, expressed in probability estimates (e.g., 20% chance for reoffense for a particular score, 60% chance of reoffense for a higher score).

Overall, independent research has generally indicated that these instruments have moderate predictive validity. There has yet to be declared any clearly superior instrument among them as they all do about equally well in direct comparison with each other (Barbaree, Seto, Langton et al. 2001; Hanson and Morton-Bourgon 2004, 2005; Langton, Barbaree, Seto et al. 2007). Furthermore, the combined use of any of the instruments has not yielded superior results to their use singularly (Seto 2005).

All of these actuarial assessment instruments are variations on a theme with significant correlations among them (Langton, Barbaree, Seto et al. 2007) since they all are developed upon the empirically supported twin pillars of sexual recidivism risk: general criminality or antisocial orientation and deviant sexual interests (Hanson and Bussiere 1998; Hanson and Morton-Bourgon 2004, 2005).

The celebratory hoisting aloft of actuarial risk assessment for sexual offenders is not universal, however. Hart, Laws, and Kropp (2003) cite the lack of independent prospective studies that measure a sample on an actuarial assessment instrument for sexual offenders and then measure recidivism after they have been released to the community; the marginal increment in accuracy (hit-rate) for actuarial assessment over clinical assessment; and the lack of any empirical studies that directly compare the accuracy of an actuarial assessment instrument and a clinical judgment approach. They conclude that "our overall evaluation of the 'state of the field' is less than sanguine" (217) and that "the superiority of actuarial decision making is an article of faith rather than fact" (221).

• • •

By far the most widely used actuarial assessment instrument for adult sexual offenders in the United States is the STATIC-99 (Hanson and Thornton 1999; Harris, Phenix, Hanson et al. 2003). About 48.4% of residential programs that treat adult sexual offenders and 54% of community programs surveyed report using the STATIC-99 (McGrath, Cumming, and Burchard 2003). A recent survey reported that the STATIC-99 is used in sixteen of the seventeen states that had involuntary civil commitment laws for sexual offenders (Seto 2005). The STATIC-99 is the actuarial assessment instrument subjected to most replication studies to date (Langton, Barbaree, Seto et al. 2007).

The STATIC-99 was developed as an extension of its predecessor, the Rapid Risk Assessment for Sex Offense Recidivism (RRASOR; Hanson 1997). The term "static" refers to the instrument's use of static or unchanging historical risk factors (e.g., offense against a male or offense against a stranger child) or demographic factors (e.g., age or history of involvement in a cohabitating sexual relationship) as opposed to clinical or dynamic factors (e.g., treatment progress or sexual deviancy), which are theoretically subject to change over time or by way of clinical intervention. The "99" refers to the year the instrument was first made available.

The STATIC-99 is composed of ten variables that do not require an interview with the individual in order to be scored (figure 3.1). All the information necessary to score the instrument can be obtained from demographic information and the accumulated criminal record of the individual. The cohabitation item is an exception and is often scored according to the self-report of the individual, but confirmation through collateral sources in the record is recommended. The total scores can range from zero to twelve, and individuals are assigned to one of seven risk bins ranging from lowest risk (score = zero) to highest risk (score of six or more). A table of recidivism rates obtained retrospectively from archival records lists the percentages of sexual and violence recidivism for each score or risk category (table 3.1). For instance, a score of three obtained by a 21-year-old male who has never had a cohabitating relationship and has a history of one prior conviction for a sexual offense is associated with a 19% probability of recidivism over a 15-year period of time. A score of six or more, regardless of what items comprise the score, is associated with a 52% probability of recidivism over the same followup period.

The original development sample of approximately thirteen hundred adult sexual offenders included some individuals who had committed a sexual offense as a juvenile (under the age of 18) and were released as

FIGURE 3.1 *Static-99: Items and Scoring*

Item	Score
1. Age	
Aged 25 or older	0
Aged 18–24.99	1
2. Ever lived with lover for at least two years?	
Yes	0
No	1
3. Index nonsexual violence-any convictions	
No	0
Yes	1
4. Prior nonsexual violence-any convictions	
No	0
Yes	1
5. Prior sex offenses	

Charges	Convictions	
None	None	0
1–2	1	1
3–5	2–3	2
6+	4+	3

6. Prior sentencing dates (excluding index)	
3 or less	0
4 or more	1
7. Any convictions for noncontact sex offenses	
No	0
Yes	1
8. Any unrelated victims	
No	0
Yes	1
9. Any stranger victims	
No	0
Yes	1
10. Any male victims	
No	0
Yes	1

Score	Risk Category
0–1	low
2–3	moderate–low
4–5	moderate–high
6+	high

Source: Harris, Phenix, Hanson, and Thornton 2003.

adults. The test developers allow for the use of the STATIC-99 for juveniles but recommend that caution be exercised "as there is a very real theoretical question about whether juvenile sex offending is the same phenomenon as adult sex offending in terms of its underlying dynamics and our ability to effect change in the individual" (5). Nevertheless, "if the juvenile offenses occurred when the offender was 16 or 17 and the offenses appear 'adult' in nature (preferential sexual assault of a child, preferential

TABLE 3.1   *Static-99 Scores and Recidivism Percentages*

Score	Sample Size	Sexual Recidivism			Violent Recidivism		
		5 yrs	10 yrs	15 yrs	5 yrs	10 yrs	15 yrs
0	107 (10%)	.05	.11	.13	.06	.12	.15
1	150 (14%)	.06	.07	.07	.11	.17	.18
2	204 (19%)	.09	.13	.16	.17	.25	.30
3	206 (19%)	.12	.14	.19	.22	.27	.34
4	190 (18%)	.26	.31	.36	.36	.44	.52
5	100 (9%)	.33	.38	.40	.42	.48	.52
6+	129 (12%)	.39	.45	.52	.44	.51	.59

Source: Harris, Phenix, Hanson, et al. 2003.

rape type activities) the STATIC-99 score is most likely of some utility in assessing overall risk" (Harris, Phenix, Hanson et al. 2003, 5). The instrument developers recommend against using the STATIC-99 for adults whose only sexual offense occurred when they were 14 or 15 or for those adults whose juvenile sexual offense looks "juvenile" (e.g., a sexual offense against a peer-age victim that is part of a larger pattern of antisocial conduct). They offer little information about how one is to make a decision about whether a particular offense appears "juvenile" or not.

The development sample did not include any juveniles under the age of 18 at the time of release. Therefore, the validity of the STATIC-99 with juvenile sex offenders is entirely speculative at this point. The test developers cite an unpublished study that utilized a sample of forty-five juvenile offenders released at the age of 19 from the Texas Youth Commission and found a positive correlation between their score on the STATIC-99 and their recidivism rate (Poole, Liedecke, and Marbibi 2000). This single study should be regarded with some caution as it was unpublished and not subjected to the rigors of peer review and utilized a small sample, making it vulnerable to spurious results.

There are scoring problems for the STATIC-99 when it is used with juveniles that are not discussed by its developers but that were identified by the New Jersey Court of Appeals in the case of J.P. First, juveniles will automatically get a discrediting point for being young since a youthful age, defined here as being between 18 and 25, has been statistically correlated with a higher risk of sexual reoffense. Young adults, often younger than 25, are at the highest risk for general criminal recidivism (see Hirschi and Gottfredson 1983) and specifically for sexual recidivism (Hanson 2002). Second, there is a problem with the item "Ever Lived with an Intimate Partner for a Minimum of Two Years." A cohabitating relationship with an intimate partner has been statistically correlated with a low risk of sexual reoffense. The absence of such a relationship in the life of a sex offender earns a discrediting point. The scoring rule explicitly states that if the individual is young and has not had an opportunity to establish an intimate domestic relationship of two years' duration, he should be scored as never having done so. The problem is that an adolescent who has committed a sexual offense while still a legally dependent individual, as is the case for almost all contemporary adolescents and even many young adults, who then serve significant time in a juvenile or adult facility postconviction, as was the case for J.P., cannot help but get a discrediting point for the fact that he has never lived within an intimate domestic relationship. Add to this the discrediting point he receives for being young and his automatic score of two translates into a probability of 16% for sexual recidivism over a 15-year time frame. Add to this a possible point for a prior petition under PINS (Person in Need of Supervision) or a CHINS (Child in Need of Supervision), a petition filed in juvenile court for stubborn or unruly children, for a violent act against a parent resulting in his being removed from home, which the STATIC-99 considers "a Conviction for a Prior Non-sexual Violent Offense," and the individual is up to a STATIC-99 score of three with a 19% probability of sexual recidivism over a 15-year period before any other risk factors are even considered, a probability estimate that exceeds the recidivism rate of 5-15% typically reported for juvenile sex offenders (Righthand and Welch 2001; Weinrott 1996; Worling and Långström 2006; Zimring 2004).

No published research exists regarding the use of the STATIC-99 with juvenile sex offenders. This has not prevented some from advocating that the STATIC-99, and other actuarial instruments designed for adults, be used for juveniles. Doren (2006), for instance, despite his conclusion that "there is reason for some unease in using these instruments to assess juvenile offenders' sexual recidivism risk" (105), does not rule out using such instruments to assess the sexual-offense risk of older juvenile sex offenders. For the STATIC-99, he states that "the extrapolation from findings with adult offenders . . . to older juveniles is reasonable [but] to younger juveniles [it] is not." He advocates using the results of the STATIC-99 for older juveniles "as simply suggestive of high risk, but not as clearly indicative of it" (105) but offers no way to precisely calibrate the doubt that arises when using it with older juveniles.

•   •   •

The first structured assessment instrument specifically designed for juvenile sex offenders was the Juvenile Sex Offender Protocol (J-SOAP; Prentky, Harris, Frizzell et al. 2000). The J-SOAP differs from most of the actuarial risk-assessment instruments for adults, such as the RRASOR or the STATIC-99, which use only static historical variables. The J-SOAP also incorporates clinically derived dynamic variables that purportedly can change over time through maturation or treatment. It combines historical and clinical data and derives a total score that can be subjected to validation testing with objective criteria, such as recidivism data.

The instrument has a short history and few empirical studies to support its utility, but this has not prevented its increased use and prevalence in the field. It is the most widely used risk-assessment instrument for juvenile sex offenders in the United States, with nearly a third of residential and community programs reporting its regular administration (McGrath, Cummings, and Burchard 2003).

The J-SOAP-II, a revision of the original instrument, is comprised of twenty-eight items within four subscales (figure 3.2). Items were selected on the basis of a review of the literature regarding child and adult sexual offenders and general offenders. Two of the scales are intended to measure the two major static historical domains empirically related to sexual recidivism: Scale One—Sexual Drive/Sexual Preoccupation; and Scale Two—Impulsive, Antisocial Behavior. The authors state that the "core" of Scale Two was adopted from the Childhood and Adolescent Psychopathy Taxon Scale (Harris, Rice, and Quinsey 1994), which attempted to identify psychopathy in adults with the use of childhood variables. These two scales make up the Static Summary Scale. The other two scales, Scales Three and Four, capture potentially relevant dynamic factors that purportedly can change over time and are believed to be related to reoffense risk: Scale Three—Clinical/Treatment; and Scale Four—Community Adjustment. They are combined to make up the Dynamic Summary Scale.

The initial validation sample consisted of ninety-six juvenile sex offenders from inner-city Philadelphia ranging in age from 9 to 20, with an average age of 14.2, who were referred for assessment and treatment (Prentky, Harris, Frizzell et al. 2000). Two-thirds of the sample were adjudicated delinquent for a sexual offense and the other third were referred from the child dependency system for sexually problematic behavior. About 70% of the sample was made up of child molesters, defined as having had a victim younger than 11 years old and at least five years younger than the offender. These ninety-six juvenile sex offenders and children with sexual

FIGURE 3.2   *J-SOAP-II: Scales and Items*

1. Sexual Drive/Preoccupation Scale[a]
   1. Prior legally charged sex offenses
   2. Number of sexual abuse victims
   3. Male child victim
   4. Duration of sex offense history
   5. Degree of planning in sexual offense(s)
   6. Sexualized aggression
   7. Sexual drive and preoccupation
   8. Sexual victimization history
2. Impulsive/Antisocial Behavior Scale[a]
   9. Caregiver consistency
   10. Pervasive anger
   11. School behavior problems
   12. History of conduct disorder
   13. Juvenile antisocial behavior
   14. Ever charged or arrested before age 16
   15. Multiple types of offense
   16. History of physical assault and/or exposure to family violence
3. Intervention Scale[b]
   17. Accepting responsibility for offense(s)
   18. Internal motivation for change
   19. Understands risk factors
   20. Empathy
   21. Remorse and guilt
   22. Cognitive distortions
   23. Quality of peer relations
4. Community Stability/Adjustment Scale[b]
   24. Management of sexual urges and desire
   25. Management of anger
   26. Stability of current living situation
   27. Stability of school
   28. Evidence of positive support systems

Source: Prentky and Righthand 2003
Note: All items are scored on a trichotomized scale (0, 1, or 2).
   a. Sexual Drive/Preoccupation Scale and Impulsive/Antisocial Behavior Scale are Static/Historical Scales.
   b. Intervention Scale and Community Stability/Adjustment Scale are Dynamic Scales.

behavior problems had a total of 132 known victims, of which 96% were known to the perpetrator.

The J-SOAP was completed on all ninety-six subjects as part of their intake assessment and then again at discharge, on average about twenty-four months later. The instrument was coded entirely from existing records by two independent clinicians. Subjects were followed for twelve months in the community for reoffense after discharge. They reported good inter-rater reliability (two independent raters scored the same item similarly for the same juvenile) and good internal consistency (test items within a scale are highly correlated and appear to measure the same construct) for three of the scales. The exception was Scale One, Sexual Drive/Sexual Preoccupation. This scale later encountered additional problems on another sample of juvenile sex offenders where the internal consistency of the scale continued to be low to moderate, leaving the researchers to conclude that "Scale One has performed suboptimally" (Righthand, Prentky, Knight et al. 2005, 26). It would appear that reliable clinical judgments about the presence of sexual deviancy in juvenile sex offenders are hard to come by.

Problems emerged in the testing of the predictive validity of the instrument, however. In the 12-month followup only 3.1%, or three juveniles, were identified as having committed another sexual offense while in the community. As discussed, low base-rate sexual recidivism is a problem that has haunted test developers in their search for predictive validity. It is exceedingly difficult, and at the lower extremes nearly impossible, to validate an instrument's ability to predict recidivism if an insufficient percentage of the subjects does not recidivate. If the base rate of sexual recidivism is too low, as was the case here, there is little to predict. This is a theme that repeats itself throughout the various research attempts to validate the predictive ability of actuarial assessment instruments for juvenile sex offenders. It would be exceedingly difficult, if not statistically impossible, for an instrument, regardless of how statistically sound its construction is, to overcome an automatic decision that none of the juvenile sex offenders will recidivate with a new sexual offense in the following year, and, for this sample, that would yield an overall accuracy rate of 97%. The test developers openly acknowledged this limitation, conceding that "given the very small number of detected sexual recidivists, formal testing of group differences was not attempted" (Prentky, Harris, Frizzell et al. 2000, 80-81).

The J-SOAP was revised in response to the weaknesses encountered in the initial development study. The revised instrument, J-SOAP-II, made substantive changes in Scales One and Two. Prentky and Righthand (2003), in the latest issue of the manual, state that at this point in its development, the J-SOAP-II cannot be considered an actuarial instrument but that they hope that research support will eventually allow it to be so. Instead, they characterize the instrument as an empirically informed guide to aid clinicians in the assessment of variables and factors that might be related to high risk for sexual recidivism. They offer no cut-off scores or thresholds or item weightings since there is no empirical data measured against sexual recidivism to establish such figures. They strongly advocate that decisions regarding recidivism risk not be based exclusively on the result of the J-SOAP-II (Righthand, Prentky, Knight et al. 2005).

In another sample of fifty-four juvenile sex offenders whose records were retrospectively analyzed, once again a low base rate of sexual offense, 11%, was found (Prentky and Righthand 2003). This time the followup period spanned ten to twelve years. The J-SOAP was not able to predict reoffense when the total score was considered; however, there was some evidence that Scale One analyzed alone improved prediction above chance, though this evidence was based on a sample of only six sexual recidivists. The authors conceded that "the very low rate of sexual recidivism has been a methodological impediment that has hindered our ability to examine in greater depth the predictive validity of the J-SOAP" (Prentky and Righthand 2003, 4).

Another sample of 153 juvenile sex offenders from the state of Maine provided evidence about the concurrent validity of the J-SOAP-II (Righthand, Prentky, Knight et al. 2005). In a study designed to test concurrent validity, a sample is assessed on a new instrument and on a measure with previously established validity. If the new instrument has a reasonably strong correlation with an instrument with established validity, the new instrument can be considered to be valid. Concurrent validity is not as vital as direct empirical evidence of predictive validity, but it does provide some indirect evidence of an instrument's predictive abilities.

The J-SOAP-II correlated significantly with a measure of general delinquency that had established predictive validity, the Youth Level of Service Inventory/Case Management Inventory (YLS/CMI; Hoge and Andrews 1996). The YLS/CMI is a risk-assessment inventory for general delinquency recidivism, not sexual recidivism, so it has yet to establish itself as able to identify high-risk youthful sexual recidivists. The researchers also found that juvenile sex offenders placed in correctional or residential settings had higher scores on the J-SOAP-II than those in the community, another instance of concurrent but not predictive validity.

The validity of the J-SOAP-II has been tested in a number of independent studies in other states. A study of 261 juvenile sex offenders from two treatment programs in Virginia also reports an exceedingly low recidivism rate for sexual offense, 4.7%, over a followup period of ten years (Waite, Keller, McGarvey et al. 2005). This study used a modified version containing eight of the eleven variables from Scale Two (Impulsive/Antisocial Behavior) of the original J-SOAP. The researchers divided their sample into three groups—low, medium and high—based on their score on Scale Two. They reported no significant differences among the groups on various demographic, historical, and clinical factors. But they did find that juveniles scoring high on impulsive/antisocial behaviors as measured by Scale Two were more likely to be rearrested for any offense, not specifically a sexual offense, than were low scorers. The mean survival time (the time in the community before a new offense was detected) was fifty-seven months for the high Scale Two juveniles versus seventy-two months for the low Scale Two juveniles. The study provides evidence for the predictive validity of Scale Two of the J-SOAP for general reoffense. But the low reoffense rate for sexual offending did not allow testing of the predictive properties of Scale Two for sexual recidivism.

A sample of 156 male juvenile sex offenders from the state of Oklahoma was divided into three groups based on type of victim: child offenders, peer/adult offenders, and a mixed group (Parks and Bard 2006). The J-SOAP-II and the Psychopathy Checklist-Youth Version (Forth, Kosson, and Hare 2003), a measure that identifies adolescents at risk to develop a psychopathic personality in adulthood, were scored from available records. Scale Four, Community Stability, of the J-SOAP-II was not scored since the subjects were all incarcerated when the archival records were constructed. Overall, the mixed group scored significantly higher on the J-SOAP-II and the PCL-YV and had lower rates of treatment completion. Sexual recidivism for the sample was once again low, 6.4%. Only ten of the 156 subjects recorded a sexual reoffense. A total of 30.1% of the sample recorded a nonsexual offense in the community. The results indicated that the total scores of neither the J-SOAP-II nor the PCL-R were significant predictors of sexual recidivism. The Scale Two, Impulsive/Antisocial Behavior, score of the J-SOAP-II was predictive of sexual recidivism, as were the Interpersonal (Factor One) and Antisocial (Factor Four) factors of the PCL-R. The correlation between Scale Two of the J-SOAP-II and Factor Four of the PCL-R was highly significant, suggesting that they were measuring the same construct. The total score of the J-SOAP-II was not predictive of nonsexual recidivism. One interesting finding worth noting is that the child offenders scored significantly higher on Scale One, Sexual Drive/Preoccupation, than either the peer/adult offenders or the mixed group, suggesting that child offending may be associated with a higher level of sexual deviance while peer/adult offending is associated with general antisocial behavior, opportunistic sexual offending, and a high degree of impulsivity and a lack of planning.

A study of sixty juvenile sex offenders between the ages of 12 and 18 in a community-based treatment program in New York examined the ability of the J-SOAP-II to predict general and sexual recidivism (Martinez,

Flores, and Rosenfeld 2007). A unique aspect of this sample is that it was comprised mostly of minority youth, with half of the participants identifying themselves as Latino and nearly 30% as African-American. A total of eight, or 13.3%, of the sample recorded a sexual reoffense, measured by arrest, self-report, or a third party, such as a parent or a probation officer, at followup. The Dynamic Summary Scale (Scales Three and Four) and the total score of the J-SOAP-II was significantly correlated with sexual recidivism and with any recidivism. The Static Summary Scale (Scales One and Two) was not significantly correlated to sexual or general recidivism. No data about the accuracy of prediction is provided, so it is not possible to calculate the rate of false positive (subjects rated as high risk who do not sexually recidivate) or false negatives (subjects rated as low risk who do sexually recidivate).

A methodological limitation in the study, threatening its validity, is that the treating clinicians quite familiar with the youth rated them on the J-SOAP-II after their reoffense had occurred, possibly contaminating the clinical ratings. The use of "blind" raters with no knowledge of the offenders outside of the data in the clinical record who conducted their ratings of subjects before entrance into the program and after completion of treatment would have remedied this validity problem. In its current design it is not a predictive study but is postdictive, looking backwards in time at a sample of subjects who had a sexual offense already in their history. Also, Scale Four (Community Stability) on the Dynamic Summary Scale was not rated reliably by the clinicians but was entered into the validity analyses anyway.

Finally, most recently a study utilizing 169 male adolescents in a residential treatment program for juvenile sex offenders in a midwestern city between 1992 and 2005 was conducted to test the ability of the J-SOAP-II to identify sexual recidivists (Viljoen, Scalora, Cuadra et al. 2008). Trained raters blind to the youth's subsequent charges completed the J-SOAP-II and the J-SORRAT-II, an actuarial instrument for juvenile sex offenders reviewed later, based on the youth's program file. Subjects had spent an average of about a year in treatment prior to discharge, and they were followed for over six years in the community to determine whether they committed a sexual reoffense or general reoffense.

Interrater reliability measures for the J-SOAP-II and the J-SORRAT-II were excellent, and the scores of the two measures were highly correlated with each other. A total of twenty-eight youth, or 16.6%, of the sample were rated as having engaged in sexual aggression while in the treatment program, and fifty-one, or 30.2%, engaged in nonsexual violence during the treatment period. The J-SOAP-II scores at the time of admission did not significantly predict sexual aggression during treatment, but the Sexual Drive/Preoccupation scale did. The total score on the J-SOAP-II was, however, able to predict nonsexual aggression during treatment.

The overall rates of sexual reoffense postdischarge were low, as only fourteen, or 8.3%, of the youth in the sample were charged with a post-discharge sexual offense. A total of 12.7% were charged with a postdischarge nonsexual violent offense, 10.1% for a serious nonsexual violent offense and 42.8% for any offense. Total scores on the J-SOAP-II did not significantly predict reoffending of any type. Furthermore, the false positive rates for the J-SOAP-II were high, but particularly high for a younger group of offenders between the ages of 12 and 15, suggesting that the J-SOAP-II is especially prone to errors in classification for this younger age group.

Thus across a total of six independent samples from six separate states (Maine, Massachusetts, New York, Virginia, Nebraska, and Oklahoma) representing three geographical regions of the United States, the J-SOAP-II has not as yet demonstrated predictive validity for juvenile sex offenders or proved its mettle as an actuarial assessment instrument for juvenile sex offenders. This failure to demonstrate predictive validity is no fault of the test developers. They followed standard procedures in test development and validation. Indeed, their work could serve as an exemplar in test construction and validation. The problem does not lay in shoddy test construction or half-baked validation procedures; the problem lies in the absence of an opportunity for the test developers to demonstrate the effectiveness of their instrument. Their pursuit of predictive validation reads like a story of a skilled craftsperson who forges a carefully honed cutting tool but can find no object on which to test it. It exists in the world, cutting this way and that, without ever having proven whether it cuts with the precision intended. We have no way to know if the line it cuts is straight and true.

The Estimated Risk of Adolescent Sexual Offense Recidivism (ERASOR; Worling and Curwen 2001) is another risk-assessment instrument for juvenile sex offenders developed after the J-SOAP and the J-SOAP-II, and though not as widely used as its predecessor, it is receiving increasing attention. The ERASOR is the second most utilized juvenile-sex-offender risk-assessment instrument within residential and community treatment programs after the J-SOAP-II, with a total of about 20% of programs re-porting its regular use (McGrath, Cumming, and Burchard 2003). The ERASOR bears close resemblance to the J-SOAP-II, though no empirical studies have actually derived a correlation between the measures. Unlike the J-SOAP-II, which can be scored from an archival review of records, the ERASOR is specifically designed to be completed by clinicians fol-lowing a clinical assessment. Most of the items are dynamic clinical fac-tors that are conceptualized as targets of treatment that can be reassessed through the course of treatment (Worling and Curwen 2001; Worling and Långström 2006). A total score is not derived from the summation of the item scores.

The test authors advocate that the ERASOR be used as an empirically guided checklist to aid clinical assessment, like the Sexual Violence Risk-20 (SVR-20; Boer, Wilson, Gauthier et al. 1997), an adult empirically guided assessment instrument upon which the ERASOR was modeled. They rec-ommend that users have a high level of training and experience regard-ing the assessment of adolescents; that evaluators assess multiple domains of the offender's functioning; that multiple methods of data collection be employed to form opinions regarding risk; that multiple sources of infor-mation be used; and that assessments of risk be properly qualified and the limits of the opinions be clearly recognized. It is intended for use for indi-viduals aged 12-18 who have previously committed a sexual assault.

The ERASOR consists of twenty-five risk items divided into five cat-egories: (1) Sexual Interests, Attitudes, and Behaviors; (2) Historical Sexual Assaults; (3) Psychosocial Functioning; (4) Family/Environmen-tal Functioning; and (5) Treatment (figure 3.3). The only historical fac-tors are contained within the nine items comprising the Historical Sexual Assault Scale. The other sixteen items are dynamic factors to be assessed within the time frame of the past six months. The instrument contains a number of items that specifically assess family functioning factors such as level of family stress, degree of parental rejection, level of parental sup-port for sexual offense–specific treatment, and degree of opportunity for future sexual offenses provided by the family environment. These items can be rated on the basis of interview data, including interviews with the parents and data contained in records. The instrument also includes a va-riety of factors about the offender's recent level of general psychological functioning, such as the presence of an antisocial orientation, social isola-tion or lack of peer relationships, aggression, recent escalation in anger or negative emotions, and impulsivity. Many of these items can be scored

FIGURE 3.3 *ERASOR (Version 2.0): Scales and Items*

Sexual Interests, Attitudes, and Behaviors

1. Deviant sexual interests (younger children, violence, both)
2. Obsessive sexual interests/preoccupation with sexual thoughts
3. Attitudes supportive of sexual offending
4. Unwillingness to alter deviant sexual interests/attitudes

Historical Sexual Assaults

5. Ever sexually assaulted 2 or more victims
6. Ever sexually assaulted same victim 2 or more times
7. Prior adult sanctions for sexual assault(s)
8. Threats of, or use of, violence/weapons during sexual offense
9. Ever sexually assaulted a child
10. Ever sexually assaulted a stranger
11. Indiscriminate choice of victims
12. Ever sexually assaulted a male victim (male offenders only)
13. Diverse sexual-assault behaviors

Psychosocial Functioning

14. Antisocial interpersonal orientation
15. Lack of intimate peer relationships/social isolation
16. Negative peer associations and influences
17. Interpersonal aggression
18. Recent escalation in anger and negative affect
19. Poor self-regulation of affect and behavior (impulsivity)

Family/Environmental Functioning

20. High-stress family environment
21. Problematic parent-offender relationship/parental rejection
22. Parent(s) not supporting sexual-offense-specific assessment/treatment
23. Environment supporting opportunities to reoffend sexually

Treatment

24. No development or practice of realistic prevention plans/strategies
25. Incomplete sexual-offense-specific treatment

Other Factor

Source: Worling and Curwen 2001.
Note: All items are scored present, partially/possibly present, not present or unknown. Clinician gives an overall risk rating as low, moderate, or high on the basis of clinical judgment.

on the basis of the results of psychological tests or general assessment instruments. Finally, the instrument includes two items regarding treatment progress: development of realistic relapse prevention plan skills or strategies and incomplete sexual offender treatment. The instrument does not include clinical factors that have highly valued currency within clinical practice as they have not demonstrated empirical relation to risk of sexual reoffense. These include such items as denial of the sexual offense, lack of victim empathy, and a history of sexual abuse. The instrument also does not add discrediting points for a history of general delinquency and the level of seriousness of the sexual offense. Neither of these factors has found support in the research literature as related to sexual risk.

Initial studies regarding the instrument's interrater reliability are good, with a high level of internal consistency (Worling and Curwen 2001; Worling 2004). Risk estimates of low, medium, or high are assigned not by total scores but by means of a clinical judgment of the overall number and particular constellation of risk factors for the individual. At this time there are no formal rules governing the designation of risk level. There are no arithmetical formulas or algorithms. It is left to the discretion of the evaluator to make risk estimates. Thus the ERASOR is an empirical guide to the collection of risk data and is not an actuarial assessment instrument. Clinical judgment still forms the core of the risk estimate.

In an initial validation study, a sample 136 juvenile sex offenders was divided into eighty repeaters and fifty-six nonrepeaters (Worling 2004). Repeaters were defined as adolescents assessed for a sexual assault that occurred after they had already been detected and sanctioned by parents, teachers, police, or child-protection workers for a prior sexual offense. Nonrepeaters were those adolescents who were being assessed absent a history of a prior sanction for a sexual offense. This method of validity testing was utilized as a means to address the probable underestimation of recidivism rates that use arrest and conviction rates (Kenny, Keough, and Seidler 2001; Thornton 2002). Sexual offenses by adolescents are less likely to be reported than sexual offenses by adults, and official crime or conviction reports are an underestimate of recidivism. A possible methodological way to bypass this underestimated rate is to use rates of repeated sexual offending after initial detection or sanction. This method provides a proxy measure of recidivism that allows predictive validation. It can also provide a method of overcoming the universal problem of low base rate of recidivism obtained by rearrest or reconviction data.

A critical limitation of the method was that it was not prospective. Subjects were not assessed at the time of the sanction or intervention and then followed in the community to determine which ones repeated and which did not. Instead, records were reviewed to determine who would qualify as a repeater and who as a nonrepeater and to then test whether the ERASOR could statistically differentiate them from each other.

Worling (2004) reports tentative support for the validity of the ERASOR, as both the overall clinical ratings (low, medium, and high) and the total score significantly differentiated those adolescents known to have reoffended after sanctioning (repeaters) from those who did not have a history of sanctioning (nonrepeaters). Data regarding the accuracy of classification, the rates of false positives or false negatives, was not provided. A potential methodological problem with the classification of repeaters and nonrepeaters is that some of the nonrepeaters may actually be repeaters who have not been detected.

Additional validation is suggested by the finding that subjects in a residential program had higher risk scores than subjects in the community. It is assumed that higher-risk subjects would be removed from the community while lower-risk subjects would not. Finally, lower risk scores were found at the time of discharge than at intake for the entire sample. The problem with these two later findings, however, is that they are subject to rater/clinician bias or contamination, which threatens the validity of the study. Raters/clinicians may score subjects in residential settings as at higher risk on the basis of their assumption that higher-risk subjects would be in such settings and that risk ratings would be assumed to be higher at intake and lower at discharge. The methodology of the study was not able to control for these threats to validity.

As noted by Worling (2004), the major problem of the study was that it was retrospective, based on archival data. The hallmark of any predictive instrument is its ability to parse out future recidivists from nonrecidivists. Differentiating repeaters from nonrepeaters is not the same as predicting recidivism. This would require a prospective study that measures subjects at baseline near the time of the sanction and then follows them out into the community to see if the ERASOR can identify the repeat offenders from those who do not repeat. At this point the ERASOR has not demonstrated an ability to do this.

The most recently developed actuarial assessment instrument for juvenile sex offenders is the Juvenile Sexual Offense Recidivism Risk Assessment Tool-II (JSORRAT-II; Epperson, Ralston, Fowers et al. 2006). The goal of the test developers was to devise an actuarial risk-assessment instrument that would be easy to use, utilizing mostly static and behaviorally anchored factors that could be scored from archival and case record data. The developmental sample consisted of 636 male juvenile sex offenders adjudicated for a sexual offense in the state of Utah between 1990 and 1992. About three-quarters of their sample were white, ranging in age from 11 to 18 with an average age of a little over 15. The base rate of sexual recidivism for the sample prior to the age of 18, defined as any arrest for a new sexual offense, was 13.2% (84 of the 636 subjects). The total or any-time sexual recidivism base rate, defined as any arrest for a sexual offense as a juvenile or an adult, was 19.8% (126 of the 636).

FIGURE 3.4   *JSORRAT-II: Items*

1. Number of adjudications for sex offenses (including current adjudication)
2. Number of different victims in charged sex offenses
3. Length of sexual offending history based on charged sex offenses
4. Under any form of supervision when they committed any sex offense for which they were eventually charged?
5. Was any charged felony-level sex offense committed in a public place?
6. Use of deception or grooming in any charged sex offenses?
7. Prior sex offender treatment status
8. Number of officially documented incidents of hands-on sexual abuse in which the offender was the victim
9. Number of officially documented incidents of physical abuse where the offender was the victim
10. Any placement in special education?
11. Number of education time periods with discipline problems
12. Number of adjudications for nonsexual offenses

Source: Epperson, Ralston, Fowers, DeWitt, and Gore 2006.
Note: Scoring criteria not included in the figure.

The first step in the development of the JSORRAT-II, as was the case in the development of all the other actuarial assessment instruments reviewed thus far, was to derive a set of variables purported to separate juvenile sexual recidivists from the nonrecidivists. The resulting twelve variables that accomplished this distinction are listed in figure 3.4. The next step was to test this set of variables on its ability to distinguish juvenile sexual recidivists from the nonrecidivists, thus determining the predictive accuracy of the newly derived JSORATT-II factors.

The authors admit that this is not a "true" test of predictive accuracy since they used the same sample of subjects in the test as was used in the initial derivation of the factors. The test is essentially circular. The initially derived factors were selected because of their ability to separate the recidivists from the nonrecidivists. To then test those factors on the very same sample of subjects used to derive them is hardly an independent test of their predictive accuracy. It's like a tailor taking precise measurements of a customer, constructing a suit, and then marveling at the fit of the suit. Testing for predictive validity requires an independent validation sample of subjects not involved in the derivation of the factors. The use of the same sample to derive the factors in a test of predictive accuracy will result in an artificially inflated accuracy rate. Testing with an independent sample would probably result in some "shrinkage" of accuracy—just as a tailor-made suit will not fit another man of similar measurements as well as it will fit the man it was specifically made for—but it will be a "truer" test of predictive accuracy.

TABLE 3.2   *Classification Table of Predicted Juvenile Sexual Recidivism Using a Probability Cut Score of .70 as Low Risk and .30 as High Risk*

Predicted Outcome

Observed Outcome	Nonrecidivist (Low risk)	Recidivist (High Risk)	Row Total
Nonrecidivist	430	122	552
Recidivist	12	72	84
Column Totals	442	194	636

Positive Predictive Power = .37
(72/194)
Negative Predictive Power = .97
(430/442)
False Positive Rate = (1-PPN) = .63
(1 - .37)
False Negative Rate = (1-NPP) = .03
(1 - .97)

Sensitivity = .86
(72/84)
Specificity = .78
(430/552)
Overall Accuracy = .79
(430+72/636)

Source: Epperson, Ralston, Fowers et al. 2006

Key:
Positive predictive power—probability of juvenile sexual recidivism occurring when the juvenile sex offender has been designated (predicted) high risk (true positive rate).
False positive rate (1-PPN)—juvenile sex offender is predicted to be high risk but does not sexually recidivate (false alarm rate).
Negative predictive power—probability of juvenile sexual recidivism not occurring when the juvenile sex offender has been designated (predicted) to be low risk (true negative rate).
False negative rate (1-NPP)—juvenile sex offender is predicted to be low risk but does sexually recidivate (miss rate).
Sensitivity—proportion of juvenile sex offenders who sexually recidivate correctly classified as high risk (hit-rate).
Specificity—proportion of juvenile sex offenders who do not recidivate correctly classified as low risk (pass-over rate).
Overall accuracy rate—proportion of juvenile sex offenders correctly classified.

The predictive accuracy of the JSORRAT-II can be examined by way of a classification table of predicted outcomes versus actual outcomes using the approximately 70% of cases scoring in the low and moderately low range, or scores of four or under, as the low-risk or nonrecidivism-predicted outcome group, and the approximately 30% of cases scoring five and above, comprising the moderate, moderately high, and high classifications (table 3.2). This 70-30 split is not arbitrarily chosen. It is the suggested cut-off posed by Epperson, Ralston, and Fowers et al. (2006) for making decisions about who should get minimal intervention and who should get more intensive treatment services, even presumably commitment to either secure or nonsecure residential treatment programs. The authors suggest that only the approximately 30% or so of those scoring at five or above should be recommended for these more intensive services while the approximately 70% scoring four or below should receive a more minimal interventionist approach.

Their division of the developmental sample into these two groups—30% as needing high-intensity services and 70% as needing low-intensity services—highlights an important point often overlooked in the rethinking of risk as dimensional as opposed to binary (dangerous and not dangerous). Even when risk is dispersed along a dimension, set off in multiple categories, be it in three (low, moderate, or high) or five (low, low moderate, moderate, high moderate, and high) categories, legal and clinical decisions are often binary. A juvenile sex offender adjudicated delinquent must be committed to a program or placed on probation in the community; transferred to adult court or retained in the juvenile court; released to the community after a period of involuntary treatment or retained in treatment; discharged at the age of majority or retained beyond the age of majority; made to register or not made to register as a sex offender; civilly committed as a sexually dangerous or violent predator or released at the end of his period of confinement. Risk can be conceptualized as infinitesimal points along a continuum, but at the end of day a decision must be made to deprive the youth of his liberty or not to, to subject him to intensive treatment regimes or not to. Clinicians can describe risk as a gradient, but the legal and clinical decisions are often all or nothing when it comes to the liberty and treatment of the offender.

The JSORRAT-II identified 48.0 % (305 subjects with a score between zero and two) of the developmental sample as being within the low range of risk, with a juvenile sexual recidivism rate of 1%. Another 21.5% scored within the moderately low range, with scores of three or four and a juvenile sexual recidivism rate of 6.6%. A total of nearly 70% of the developmental sample had scores between zero and four, scoring within the low to the moderately low range with a predicted sexual recidivism rate of 2.7%. A moderate-risk group, scoring five to seven on the JSORRAT-II, comprised 16.8% of the sample and had a juvenile sexual recidivism rate of 24.3%. A moderately high-risk group with scores from eight to eleven made up 10.2% of the sample, with a recidivism rate of 43.1%. A high-risk level with a score of twelve or more was found for only 3.5% of the developmental sample, who had a juvenile sexual offense recidivism rate of 81.8%.

When the data from Epperson, Ralston, and Fowers et al. (2006) is entered into a classification matrix, as depicted in table 3.2, with the low-risk category at scores of four or below (70% of sample) and the high-risk category at scores of five and above (30% of sample), as expected, the JSORRAT-II performed admirably. Overall, for this sample of 636 juvenile sex offenders, 13.2% (84/636) recidivated and 86.8% (552/636) did not. For subjects scoring five or higher, about 37% of them later sexually recidivated as a juvenile, while those scoring four or below sexually recidivated at a rate of 2.7%. The JSORRAT-II correctly identified seventy-two of the eighty-four juvenile sexual recidivists as high risk, for a hit-rate (sensitivity) of 86%. Conversely, it missed 14% (12/84) of the sexual recidivists, whom it incorrectly identified as low risk. It correctly identified 430 of the 552 nonrecidivists as low risk for a rate of 78% (specificity) but mistakenly identified 22% (122/552) of the nonrecidivists as high risk.

A major concern emerges in the rate of cases mistakenly predicted to be high risk that did not recidivate. These were false positives. A total of 63% (122/194) of those subjects identified as high risk did not go on to be juvenile sexual recidivists. A total of 2.7% (12/442) of those subjects identified as low risk went on to be sexual recidivists. These were false negatives. Overall, the JSORATT-II was correct 79% of the time.

As a demonstration of the problem of a high false positive rate, let's say that one thousand juvenile sex offenders are scored on the JSORATT-II. If their base-rate estimate of juvenile sexual recidivism is taken as 13.2%, it could be extrapolated that about 132 of a thousand juvenile sex offenders would be expected to be sexual recidivists. The instrument would identify about 86%, or about 114 of them. It would do about as good a job at identifying the nonrecidivists, picking up 78% of them. The major problem lies here: about 63% of the cases identified as high risk would not go on to recidivate. The hit-rate of 86% is at the expense of mistakenly mislabeling a large number of nonrecidivists as high risk. The hit-rate, or the proportion of sexual recidivists correctly captured as high risk, is impressive at 86% but at the expense of a false positive rate of 63%, meaning that nearly two-thirds of the three hundred juvenile sex offenders who scored five or above would have been designated high risk but would not go on to recidivate and would probably have been deprived of their liberty for some period of time and exposed to high-intensity treatment within a potentially criminogenic environment unnecessarily. For one thousand juveniles administered the JSORRAT-II, that would extrapolate into mistakenly netting about 186 juvenile sex offenders along with the correctly netted 114 sexual recidivists.

The setting of the gauge of the net is a bit like picking your poison: too wide and one lets a higher proportion of sexual recidivists slip through; too fine and one ensnares a large share of nonrecidivists. This is the case largely because even though a base rate of 13.2% is on the higher end of the recidivism rate reported in the literature, it is still a low base-rate event in the absolute sense. This is not necessarily a shortcoming of the JSOR-RAT-II, and has more to do with the perils of prediction of low base-rate events. The overall accuracy of decisions using four as the cut-off score is 79%. This is below what could be achieved by simply concluding "low risk" for everyone. Of the sample, 86.8% did not sexually recidivate as juveniles. Saying "no risk" or "low risk" for every case guarantees an overall accuracy rate of 86.8%.

The final analysis by Epperson, Ralston, and Fowers et al. (2006) was the predictive accuracy of the instrument for adult sexual recidivism. Generally, they found that while the scores on JSORAAT-II predicted adult sexual recidivism better than chance, the rate was somewhat lower than it was for juvenile sexual recidivism, leading them to suggest that the factors that predict sexual recidivism in adulthood may be somewhat different than they are in adolescence. Adult recidivism may not be predictive from adolescent data because of the complexity of the maturation issues that occur during adolescence. The results stand as a challenge to the notion that long-term prediction of sexual recidivism is possible for juvenile sex offenders. Epperson, Ralston, and Fowers et al. (2006), on the basis of this finding, conclude that risk assessments for adolescent sex offenders should have an "expiration date" that should end at age 18, calling into question the practice of civilly committing young adults whose only sexual offense occurred during adolescence, as was the case for J.P. in New Jersey. There is no strong empirical data to support the notion that we can identify life-time persistent sexual offenders when they are juveniles.

Epperson, Ralston, and Fowers et al. (2006) describe these preliminary results of the predictive accuracy of the J-SORRAT-II as "promising." But as they state throughout, it is really unknown whether the JSORRAT-II can accurately predict risk of sexual recidivism for juveniles beyond the 636 predominantly white juvenile sex offenders from Utah. There is no way to know at this point whether these results would hold up in other samples, or in other geographical regions, where different juvenile justice selection procedures are used to process juvenile sexual offenders. Juvenile justice systems vary widely across the states. It is unclear whether the JSORRAT-II factors will translate across state lines. Many of the factors selected by the JSORRAT-II, such as history of sexual offenses, number of victims, and length of time engaged in sexual offending, have been found to be predictive of recidivism in the empirical research and are included in other actuarial risk assessment instruments. But others, such as a history of childhood sexual abuse as a victim, have not been found to be predictive of recidivism, raising the potential problem that this factor, and possibly others, may be specific to this sample and will not hold up as predictive in cross-validation research. Until this cross-validation occurs, the authors refer to their instrument as experimental and recommend that it be used to guide clinical decision making and not be used as an actuarial assessment instrument.

In the only published cross-validation of the JSORRAT-II, Viljeon, Scalora, and Cuadra et al. (2008) report that it was not able to predict sexual aggression or nonsexual aggression in the behavior of youth in a residential treatment program. Moreover, it did not predict sexual reoffense in the community, or any kind of offending, for that matter, postdischarge.

Recidivism rates for juvenile sexual offenders vary from study to study, ranging from 0% to nearly 40%, with most estimates landing somewhere between 5 and 15%. A recent report published by the Office of Juvenile Justice and Delinquency Prevention (Righthand and Welch 2001) declared, contrary to what is probably the current assumption among the public and even various professional groups, that "the results of research investigating recidivism . . . typically reveal relatively low rates of sexual recidivism" (xvii). Zimring (2004) concluded from his analysis of recidivism studies that "the existing data on the general run of juvenile sex offenders provide solid evidence that young offenders are much less likely than adult offenders to commit further sex offenses and that known rates of sex reoffending for juveniles are also *very low* in absolute terms" (62, italics added).

There have been a number of published reviews of recidivism studies of juvenile sexual offenders over the past decade. Each echoes these conclusions. Weinrott (1996) examined twenty-three studies that reported recidivism rates for juvenile sex offenders and concluded that, overall, "most boys who sexually abuse younger children do not reoffend, at least not sexually, during the 5-10 years following apprehension" (84). Caldwell (2002) reviewed twenty-five studies that followed a sample of juvenile sexual offenders into the community and measured recidivism by new charges and reconvictions. He reports a consistent trend for lower rates of sexual recidivism than is generally reported for adult sex offenders. Caldwell's review revealed that the juvenile sexual offenders were, on average, six times more likely to be arrested with a nonsexual offense than with a sexual offense. A more recent study by Caldwell (2007) reported that in a sample of 249 juvenile sex offenders and 1,780 nonsexual offenders, the prevalence rate for sexual offenders for a new sex-offense charge was 6.8% compared to 5.7% for the nonsexual offenders, a nonsignificant difference. At the same time, juvenile sex offenders were nearly ten times more likely to have been charged with a new nonsexual offense than to have been charged with a sexual offense.

Worling and Långström (2006) examined twenty-two published followup studies of juveniles who had committed a sexual offense. Many of the same studies were utilized in the Caldwell (2002) review. The average recidivism rate measured by a new charge for a sexual offense was 15% across the studies. A more conservative measure, conviction for a new sexual offense, did not significantly decrease the rate of reoffense; it was 14%. When the rate of being charged with a new criminal offense, including a sexual offense, was examined, the recidivism rate skyrocketed to 54% and 42% for an arrest and a conviction for any new offense, respectively. This substantially higher rate of recidivism for nonsexual offending among juvenile sexual offenders has been a consistent finding in the research literature.

The trend for low recidivism rates for juvenile sexual offenders appears to be a stable finding over time. The first reported study by Doshay (1943) included 256 sexual delinquents in New York City whom he followed into the community for four years. He found that none of the juveniles who had committed only a sexual offense reoffended sexually, while 3.1% of the general delinquents with a reported sexual offense reoffended sexually. The recidivism rate for nonsexual offending was 16.8%. Atcheson and Williams (1954) utilized a juvenile court clinic sample in Toronto between 1939 and 1948. An interesting historical aspect of this study was that there was a tenfold higher rate of sex delinquency for girls than boys, as it was customary at the time to adjudicate girls as "sex delinquents" if they engaged in any form of sexual behavior (Alexander 1995). They provided recidivism data for only the boys, however. They reported that only 2.6% of the sample of 116 juvenile sex offenders was rearrested in a 10-year followup period.

A few studies of the sexual recidivism rates of juvenile sexual offenders have yielded relatively higher rates. Rubenstein, Yeager, and Goodstein et al. (1993) examined the adult outcomes of a small sample of nineteen violent, sexually assaultive adolescent males committed to a correctional school in Connecticut in the 1970s. They followed the group into the community for eight years postrelease and found that 37% of them had committed a sexual assault as an adult. Borduin, Henggeler, and Blaske et al. (1990) examined the treatment outcome of sixteen juvenile sex offenders. The sixteen subjects were randomly assigned either to treatment with Multisystemic Treatment (MST)—an intensive form of outpatient treatment that focuses its interventions on the various systems a juvenile is embedded within, such as the family, school, and community—or to individual psychotherapy (control group) in an outpatient setting. The researchers then followed the subjects for three years after the completion of treatment to determine which group had a higher rate of recidivism. Sexual recidivism as measured by arrest for the group treated with MST was 12.5%, or one subject out of eight, and the rate was 75%, or six subjects out of eight, for the comparison treatment or control group. The higher rates of reoffense in these studies may be a function of the instability of the small sample sizes.

Weinrott (1996) discusses a study that extracted data from the National Youth Survey and found a reoffense rate of 22% after a period of fifteen years in a sample of sixty-six adolescents who self-reported a sexual offense but who had not been arrested by the police or placed in sex-offender treatment. The unique aspect of this study is that it looked at recidivism in a sample of undetected "offenders" in the community who were never arrested or processed through the juvenile or criminal court for a sexual offense. Their self-reported sexual recidivism occurred free from the potentially restraining influence of detection and official sanctioning or treatment.

There are a number of factors that might explain the generally low sexual recidivism rates for juvenile sex offenders over the past half-century. First, the lower recidivism rate may in part be a function of their heterogeneous makeup, the group's mix of deviant and nondeviant members, low- and high-risk offenders, anomalous and repetitive offenders, all roped off under the same clinico-legal categorical banner of the juvenile sex offender. The heterogeneity of juvenile sex offenders will reduce the overall sexual recidivism rate. Many of the studies that report high recidivism rates of over 20% utilize high-risk groups of offenders (Parks and Bard 2006). A study that uses an outpatient sample will probably draw a very different group of subjects, particularly as it regards their risk of reoffense, than a study that uses a sample drawn from residential treatment or a correctional setting.

Second, the length of time postrelease also differs widely among studies and will have a major effect on the reported rate of recidivism. Studies with longer postrelease time frames will yield a higher rate of reoffense, although most studies indicate that the bulk of reoffense will occur within the first year, often within the first six months, and then taper off. Caldwell (2002) reported a strong correlation between reconviction rate and length of follow time in his reanalysis of twenty-five studies that report sexual recidivism rates for a sample of juvenile sexual offenders.

Third, the method used to measure recidivism, the dependent variable, will also affect the rate of recidivism. Whether a study uses arrest, conviction, self-report, or the report of some other third-party informer, will affect the obtained rate of recidivism. Criminal arrests and reconvictions underestimate recidivism rates by failing to identify recidivists who move under the radar of official detection because their offenses may not be reported by victims. In her sample of juvenile sex offenders, Bremer (1992) found that the self-reported rate of sexual offending was higher than the conviction rate. Reconviction is a particularly problematic index of sexual recidivism as the vagaries of plea bargaining and the reduction of charges can all work to reduce sexual recidivism rates.

The use of retrospective reports of current adult offenders about the onset of their pattern of childhood and adolescent sexual offending has been a method used in some research as a way to provide some general or global estimate of sexual recidivism of juveniles (Abel, Mittleman, and Becker 1985). This method, as previously discussed in chapter 2, has a number of critical flaws beyond the obvious one regarding the reliability and accuracy of retrospective reporting. Deriving empirical evidence about juvenile sex offenders by working backwards from adult sexual offenders, many of whom may be sexually dangerous persons, will lead to distorted results. It is uniformly the case that research into the history of sexually dangerous persons has consistently found that they often manifest sexual deviance in adolescence. Adult sexually dangerous persons do not just spring out as fully formed sexual deviants in adulthood. They often, maybe almost always, have origins, early deviant rumblings, that extend back until at least adolescence. While this may be true, it is an instance of faulty reasoning to then presume either of the following: (1) juveniles who get into trouble for their sexual behavior will go on to do so as adults; and (2) since early sexual deviance in adult sexual offenders was covert and undetected, adolescent sexual deviance is rampant and out of control.

The following statement from Prentky, Harris, and Frizzel et al. (2000) demonstrates the fault line within these assumptions: "*given . . . the general acceptance that these offenders progress from less to more serious offenses and constitute a 'high-risk group'* one would expect that this group of young offenders would have been the focus of rigorous empirical efforts to enhance the accuracy of predictive decisions" (72, italics added). The fault line of the argument is obvious from the previous review of research: according to the recidivism research with juvenile sex offenders, they do not generally progress from less to more serious offenses, thereby coming to constitute a high-risk group. In fact, just the opposite appears to be the case: the vast majority of juvenile sex offenders desist from sexual reoffending though they may go on to wreak havoc in other sorts of nonsexual ways during adolescence before desisting from this as well in adulthood. The "stability" and "continuity" of such behavior appears to be the exception rather than the rule. Using retrospective reports of adult offenders as a method to estimate adolescent recidivism distorts the picture of juvenile sex offending by exclusively focusing on a small, high-risk sector of the population and ignoring the larger low-risk sectors. Missing from the analysis is the vast majority of juvenile sex offenders who did not go on to continue sexual offending in adulthood. This method derives estimates about the whole from a rare and exceptional subgroup.

The self-report of sexual recidivism as a method to overcome the underestimation of recidivism as measured by rearrest and reconviction has rarely been used as a method to validate actuarial assessment instruments for juvenile sexual offenders. The limitation of this method is obvious: subjects may be less than forthcoming about their undetected sexual offending. At the same time, the self-report and the report of collateral agents proved a fruitful strategy in the MacArthur Violence Risk Study (Monahan, Steadman, Silver et al. 2001), enabling the researchers to boost their sample's base rate of violence, which was undoubtedly beneficial to their eventual ability to develop an actuarial assessment instrument. However, violence is a much more public phenomenon than is sexual offending, which is more secretive and cloaked and much more socially stigmatizing. Subjects may be much more willing to admit to a violent incident than to a sexual offense. Self-report and collateral reporting methods may pose some added complications not present in violence research. Despite the evidence that the self-report of sexual offending within the general population of adolescents is higher than the rates contained within official statistics, the development of an actuarial assessment instrument based on the self-report of juvenile sexual recidivism in the community is unlikely to yield any more promising results than have been found using other research strategies.

In the final analysis, there is currently no empirically validated actuarial assessment instrument of sexual-offense risk for juveniles ready for use in the clinical and legal arena. The three most widely cited instruments that have received the most attention and focus—J-SOAP-II, ERASOR, and the JSORRAT-II—are all examples of well-developed instruments that have used a combination of rational and empirical methods of item selection and construction. There is some overlap of the items that comprise these instruments. All three have items for the number of prior sexual offenses, the number of victims, a history of nonsexual juvenile offending, and a measure of progress in sex-offender treatment. Nonetheless, there is a fair degree of divergence of items as well, which is to be expected as some, such as the JSORRAT-II, focus mostly on static variables and others, such as J-SOAP-II and the ERASOR, include a wide range of dynamic variables. All three instruments have meticulously followed standardized psychometric procedures for the establishment of reliability (consistency) and validity (accuracy) for their respective instruments. The one aspect of test validation, arguably the most important, that has consistently eluded all of these tests is predictive validity. The detected sexual recidivism rates in the developmental and cross-validation samples have been too low to allow for robust testing of predictive validity. None of these instruments has sufficiently demonstrated its ability to designate high-risk offenders or predict sexual recidivism beyond what can be achieved by an automatic decision of low-risk or no sexual recidivism because of the consistently low base rate of reoffense for the population of juvenile sex offenders.

The low base rate of recidivism for juvenile sexual offenders functions like a predictive barrier that may be impossible to overcome. Wollert (2006), in his analysis of actuarial assessment instruments for adult sex offenders, demonstrated that they were inaccurate for identifying recidivists, particularly older adult offenders, and misclassified many nonrecidivists as recidivists (a false positive problem). He argued that actuarial assessment instruments have limited predictive accuracy for populations with base rates lower than .25, and it would seem to be the case that juvenile sex offenders generally recidivate at too low a rate for any instrument to capture them without netting a significant number of nonrecidivists alongside them.

4

The Adolescent as Sexual Deviant
The Treatment of Juvenile Sex Offenders

A 17-year-old adolescent male adjudicated delinquent for fondling a semiconscious girl intoxicated at a party describes to his therapy group at his residential treatment program a deviant sexual fantasy he recently had while out on a community pass. He was in line at a Burger King at the local mall when he noticed that the girl at the counter was sexually attractive. What is deviant about this? He explained that he learned in treatment that it is inappropriate for him to have sexual fantasies or feelings about a girl with whom he is not involved in a relationship. Furthermore, having a sexual fantasy about a girl without her permission is an instance of "sexually objectifying" her and in a way is like a sexual offense.

A 15-year-old adolescent male who digitally penetrated his 8-year-old step-sister, whom he was baby sitting, describes himself as "disgusting . . . a real monster . . . a horrible person." He has been told by his therapist that he can never be in the presence of a younger child without supervision again and should never have children of his own when he becomes an adult because he is at risk to sexually abuse them

A 16-year-old adolescent male who fondled the genitals of his younger male cousin in the community pool describes an appropriate sexual fantasy that he has been working on in treatment. In the fantasy he has had a hard day at work and on the ride home looks forward to taking his girlfriend out for dinner and having sex with her afterwards. But in the fantasy he comes to the realization that his plan to have sex with her is an instance of his putting his needs ahead of hers. He decides instead to take her out for ice cream and just hold hands with her at home.

A 16-year-old adolescent male reports that he recently recovered memories of childhood sexual abuse after a year in individual psychotherapy with a therapist who firmly believed he was the victim of childhood sexual abuse. He claims that he has a vague and indistinct memory of his mother fondling his genitals as she bathed and diapered him when he was about eighteen months old. He claims to have made the connection in his therapy between his victimization and his sexual abuse of a younger child in the neighborhood.

Juvenile-sex-offender treatment is often a dogmatic exercise, practiced by well-intentioned clinicians, often working from a manual, who apply the same approach in a rote manner without much attention to the individual needs of the adolescent. The list of unsupported beliefs promulgated within these programs is mind-boggling (Chaffin and Bonner 1998): all adolescents who have committed an inappropriate sex act must receive this particular form of treatment; all juvenile sex offenders have a history of sexual victimization, and if you look deep enough, you will find it; adolescents must admit that their sexual abuse was traumatic and damaging; their denial must be broken down with persistent in-your-face confrontation; they must admit to deviant fantasies or hidden perversions and are provided fantasy logs in which to record them; treatment must be long-term, restrictive, and located in quasi correctional settings that often replicate the abuse of power in their early lives; they must make their offense fit a stock, prefabricated dynamic involving the need for power and control or the presence of perversion or deviancy; they must face the fact that they have an incurable condition, like a chronic disease, that is lifelong and that they can never be around children unsupervised again and should certainly never have their own children; and they are dangerous predators who must notify their community and neighbors about their presence and keep the police and other agents of community safety aware of their activities and whereabouts.

There is little evidence that any of these tenets are true, and by continuing to promulgate them, clinicians may in fact be doing considerable harm. Treatment forges identity; it alters the self. The persistent use of these unfounded treatment tenets may aid in the creation of the very objects of our concern—adolescents who come to incorporate the sexual-deviant label tagged on them. In the process, the juvenile justice system fails to devote limited resources to the very small high-risk spectrum of juvenile sex offenders who actually need intervention.

Juvenile sex offenders are subjected to the same treatment technologies developed for adult sex offenders without much thought as to whether these treatment processes are necessary, effective, or even harmful. Most contemporary treatment approaches for sex offenders are based on a modified addiction model that teaches the offender that his sexual deviance is like alcoholism, a life-long condition that needs to be managed and controlled—that a wary eye must be cast upon the self for the omnipresent rumblings of deviancy that are churning just below the surface. One is never cured of one's sexual deviancy, and the offender must be on perpetual guard against its inevitable return. While there is some empirical support for the effectiveness of these approaches with adult sex offenders, there is little to no empirical support for the application of this model of treatment to juvenile sex offenders.

The treatment of juvenile sex offenders has become something of a "cottage industry" in the United States (Zimring 2004). In 1982 there were twenty treatment programs in the United States for juvenile sex offenders; by 1993 there were over eight hundred, an increase of about 4,000% (National Adolescent Perpetrator Network 1993). By 2002 there were 937 treatment programs dedicated to juvenile sex offenders and 410 servicing children with sexual behavior problems, typically focused on children younger than twelve (McGrath, Cumming, and Burchard 2003). In 2002, programs treated an estimated total of 21,587 adolescents and 4,498 children—a combined total of over twenty-six thousand youth. A total of nearly three-quarters of the residential programs for juvenile sex offenders and 90% of the community programs were operated by private agencies. Approximately 90% of the programs that clinically service children with sexually abusive behavior problems were private. These statistics may underestimate the growing privatization of juvenile-sex-offender treatment since many public institutions, like juvenile prisons and training schools, are often operated by private agencies. Nearly 12% of the residential programs for adolescent boys were situated within prison settings in 2002.

The dominance of the mostly private-based service industry for juvenile sex offender is made all the more a cause for concern in comparison to the world of adult sexual offenders, where the opposite situation prevails. About 70% of adult sexual offenders are treated in public institutions, most often prisons. The large-scale privatization of juvenile-sex-offender treatment and its transformation into a "sexually-at-risk youth" industry raises the specter that profits and bottom lines may be driving many of the services, which tend to be increasingly long-term residential placements. This trend toward increased numbers of treatment programs and longer-term residential treatment has occurred despite the generally accepted empirical research finding that community-based treatment is more effective than residential treatment. Treatment on average is much longer for juvenile sex offenders than for general delinquents (Letourneau and Miner 2005). The average length of residential treatment for adolescent sex offenders in 2002 was eighteen months and for children about sixteen months (McGrath, Cumming, and Burchard 2003). In a more recent survey of forty-nine juvenile-sex-offender treatment programs, a similar average length of treatment of about 16.9 months was reported (Walker and McCormick 2004). A possible reason why longer-term residential treatment of juvenile sex offenders has persisted, in contradiction to the available research on effectiveness is that bureaucratic inertia and convenience has combined with economic incentives to perpetuate this situation.

The National Center for Juvenile Justice reported a 22% increase in the institutional population of juvenile sex offenders in the United States from 1997 to 2001 (Zimring 2004). What makes this rise in the confinement of juvenile sex offenders so perplexing is that it occurred during a time when the overall arrest rate and the total number of juvenile court cases for juvenile sex offenders was essentially flat. Moreover, the tremendous expansion of juvenile-sex-offender programs across the country over the past twenty years has occurred in the absence of empirical evidence that supports their effectiveness.

The early proponents of juvenile-sex-offender treatment criticized what they described as the overly permissive view that sexual offending was the result of sexual experimentation, a benign manifestation of an errant developmental process that would correct itself over time, a normal part of the sexual development of boys (Barbaree and Cortoni 1993; Ryan 1997). They advanced instead the view that adolescent sexual offending was part of a much more serious and insidious process that, if left unchecked, would expand and spread to more frequent and serious forms of sexual offending. According to this gateway theory, early indications of sexual boundary violations and inappropriate sexual precocity were considered as precursors to more serious problems, such as rape and pedophilia, just as marijuana is thought to lead to heroin.

The National Adolescent Perpetrators Network's Task Force Report on Juvenile Sexual Offending (NAPN 1993) supported mandatory treatment for nonadjudicated as well as adjudicated juvenile sex offenders—that is, those who were found delinquent by a juvenile court as well as those who were found not delinquent but who had a complaint for a sexual offense filed against them. The Network criticized the diversion and decriminalization of juvenile sex offenders, believing that their rerouting out of the criminal justice system to the mental health or child dependency system would encourage denial and minimization and incite more offending. The Network discouraged plea bargaining, suspended sentencing, and outright dismissals. Adolescent sexual offending, in the Network's view, was not properly confined to a mental health problem, or even a problem requiring more normalizing interventions like instruction and education, but was a matter for the police, the local prosecutor, and the juvenile court judge. The only effective intervention was the criminal justice system. The Network asserted that treatment by necessity must be long-term, typically twelve to twenty-four months, and that the release of an untreated or incompletely treated youth always posed a danger to the community. The Network assumed that sexual victimization was often a primary cause of sexual offending and that youth would often deny their victimization because of embarrassment or shame, or might not recall it because it had been repressed or cut off from awareness by the process of dissociation. They provided some clinical signs that should make the clinician concerned about the hidden presence of previous sexual abuse, including drug abuse, sudden loss of interest in school, sports, church, and extracurricular activities, precocious sexuality, and extensive knowledge of sex.

The field is not short on guidelines for treatment, but these are based on expert opinion and consensus about accepted clinical practice and are not evidence based (Burton, Smith-Darden, and Frankel 2006). Treatment guidelines promulgating best practices have been issued by a number of professional organizations, such as the National Adolescent Perpetrator Network (1993), the American Academy of Child and Adolescent Psychiatry (1999), the National Offense-Specific Residential Standards Task Force (Bengis, Brown, Freeman-Longo et al. 1999), the Association for the Treatment of Sexual Abusers (2000), and the International Association for the Treatment of Sexual Offenders (Miner, Borduin, Prescott et al. 2006), to name just a few. The agreement among these various organizations is high, but again, these standards are based not on empirical research about what works but on general consensus on what the membership *believes* works. At this point in time, evidence-based practices for juvenile sex offenders do not exist (Chaffin 2006).

Weinrott's (1996) conclusion about the state of the treatment-outcome literature for juvenile sex offenders, written over a decade ago, has not lost any of its relevance: "The prevailing view is that early intervention is needed to break the cycle of sexual deviance, and that intervention should take the form of lengthy, offense-specific, peer-group therapy. There is not a shred of scientific evidence to support this stance" (85). A less prophetic statement by Weinrott was that "the groundswell of support that launched so many juvenile sex offender treatment programs will eventually die out for want of data on effectiveness" (88). He couldn't have been more wrong; just the opposite has occurred. Juvenile sex offender programs have flourished despite the absence of evidence to support their effectiveness.

All the news is not negative, fortunately. The field has progressed beyond the nihilistic proclamations of the 1970s and 1980s that "nothing works" (Furby, Weinrott, and Blackshaw 1989). At least three meta-analyses have provided limited empirical support for the effectiveness of juvenile-sex-offender treatment, though not necessarily for restrictive residential treatment programs per se. Alexander (1999) claimed a moderate "treatment effect" for 1,025 juvenile sex offenders who completed treatment, with an overall sexual recidivism rate of 7.1%. The analysis did not include a comparison with an untreated control group. It is not therefore possible to determine whether treatment was the cause of this low rate of recidivism or whether this would have occurred even without the benefit of treatment.

Walker, McGovern, and Poey et al. (2004), in a meta-analysis that included a total of ten studies of treatment outcomes for 644 juvenile sex offenders, reported an overall moderate treatment effect averaged across three outcome variables: sexual recidivism, self-report of reoffense and deviant arousal. As was the case in the first meta-analysis, a limitation of the study was that eight of the research reports used in the meta-analysis did not include a control group, so it is not possible to determine whether the claimed "treatment effects" were larger than a no-treatment control or some other generic form of treatment.

More recently, Reitzel and Carbonell (2006) included a total of nine studies, four published and five unpublished, with a total of 2,986 adolescent sexual offenders, in their meta-analysis. The average followup period was about five years. The average recidivism rate for sexual offenses was 12.5%; for nonsexual violent offenses it was 24.7%; and for nonsexual nonviolent offenses it was 28.5%. When separate sexual recidivism rates were calculated for the treatment versus the no-treatment controls, the treatment groups (7.37%) had a significantly lower sexual recidivism rate than did the control groups (18.93%). There was no difference in the recidivism rate for juveniles receiving primary sex-offender treatment versus a comparison group receiving a non–sex-offender-specific form of treatment, however. Reitzel and Carbonell (2006) found a significant effect of treatment on sexual recidivism with Multisystemic Treatment (MST), a community-based intervention for general delinquents that is not specific for sex offenders and does not include any of the typical features of sex-offender treatment. MST, which targets interventions at the various nested systems—the family, the school, the community—that a juvenile offender exists within, had the significantly highest treatment effect among all the treatment models tested in their analysis.

The treatment of juvenile sex offenders has been dominated by a set of well-worn mantras, repeated as self-evident truths without any empirical support to bolster them. The first general step of treatment, a principle imported from the quasi religious model of Alcoholics Anonymous, is taking responsibility for one's sexually abusive behavior, like the sinner taking responsibility for his or her moral transgressions. The idea operating behind this universally accepted principle is that accepting responsibility, reducing denial and minimization, and owning the truth about one's abusive behavior will open up therapeutic avenues such as the production of empathy and the acceleration of motivation. Many programs will not accept individuals into group therapy unless they have relented and given up their defensive denial. But empirical evidence for the necessity of taking responsibility does not exist.

Group therapy with co-led teams is usually advanced as the treatment of choice. But there is no existing study that demonstrates that such a mode of treatment is more effective than individual treatment or family therapy. Moreover, there is no empirical research data to support the assumption that the treatment of juvenile sex offenders must be sex-offender–specific and must target the sexual deviance that is hypothesized to reside within the offender. And there is no evidence that treatment must be provided by practitioners specially trained in the psychology of juvenile sex offenders. Treatment is presumed to have to be long-term, often lasting several years, in restrictive, structured and controlled, sexually antiseptic environments that pathologize all forms of sexual expression. Again, there is no empirical evidence to support this view. It is based entirely on presumption.

Relapse-prevention training was initially developed as a treatment for substance abusers (Marlatt and Gordon 1985). The approach is premised on the theory that drinking or drug taking is cued by various stimuli in the environment—walking past a favorite bar, social contact with a set of drinking or drug-using friends—and that certain mental or mood states act as conditioned stimuli for substance use—feeling depressed or angry, becoming bored or lonely, experiencing a diminution in self-esteem. The goal of treatment is to identify the high-risk situations that elicit the impulse or desire to abuse substances and teach the patient how to avoid them or, if the patient is unable to completely stay clear of them, to manage the patient's response to them. Patients are taught to recognize patterns of self-defeating thinking that place them at risk for substance use and to correct these patterns. For instance, the patient is counseled to expect, and even predict, momentary lapses of self-control and will power; backslides are bound to occur. Such discrete episodes are labeled lapses. Patients are fortified with cognitive self-help skills so that they can quickly intervene and correct these lapses and get back on the right track; they are taught not to view lapses as catastrophic, as such a view can lead to full-blown relapses into substance abuse. Instead, the patient learns to accept that lapses are a necessary part of recovery and that they need to use various effective coping strategies to deal with high-risk situations and lapses.

Substance abuse is conceptualized not as a spontaneous act that arises without warning but instead as a behavior that is prompted by antecedent conditions and situations that are identifiable. Relapse is understood as a process that unfolds in a predictable manner, beginning with the patient's encounter with high-risk situations, environmental triggers, or confrontations with negative mental or mood states. The operation of these antecedent factors sets off a pattern of negative cognitions that rationalize, justify, or explain away the significance of the return of the desire to drink: "I'll just have one drink and stop"; "I've been good and have worked hard and deserve a reward"; or "I don't want to hurt my friend's feelings by refusing his offer of a drink. That's rude." These patterns of thought help clear the way for the patient to drink by minimizing the significance of the lapse, and if these thoughts are left unchecked or allowed full reign, they will eventuate in a full relapse. The patient, through his or her understanding of this cycle of relapse, is instructed to intervene early in the cycle to circumvent a lapse or relapse before reaching "the point of no return," when sheer will power alone is unlikely to offset the strong mounting desire to drink. The earlier in the cycle a patient can intervene, before momentum builds up, the more likely the patient is to resist the return to old patterns of substance abuse.

The relapse-prevention model was later adapted for sex offenders, with clinicians importing the ideas of high-risk situations, the cycle for relapse, lapses, cognitive restructuring, and cognitive distortions and applying them to sex-offending treatment, which had prior to this been dominated by psychoanalytic models of treatment that had proven to be ineffective (see Pithers, Marques, Gibat et al. 1983). The arrival of the relapse-prevention model of treatment for sexual offenders was initially heralded with great enthusiasm. Relapse prevention already had established research support from the addictions field. Its more structured and manualized approach lent itself to easier training of paraprofessionals and to outcome studies. It was easier to implement than psychoanalytically based approaches, which required a high level of theoretical know-how and the clinical training of advanced clinicians and was a nightmare to test given the great variability in the way practictioners conducted their treatment sessions.

The implementation of relapse prevention with sex offenders preceded any research on its effectiveness, but this did not worry its early practitioners, who were eager to apply a new treatment approach. Barbaree and Cortoni (1993) express the enthusiasm that surrounded the arrival of relapse-prevention training some fifteen years ago when the movement was still in its early stages: "As yet, no studies of outcome have been reported for relapse prevention, but most clinicians are optimistic that relapse prevention will eventually be shown to be an effective component of therapy" (257). In the 15-plus years since this statement was made, the enthusiasm for relapse prevention has not waned, but the hoped-for effectiveness studies have still not arrived for juvenile sex offenders.

The relapse prevention model was easily adapted to fit the population of sex offenders. Within its theoretical canopy, sexual offending was recast within a sexual assault cycle that was constructed from the original addiction cycle. Sex offenses are not impulsive acts, but the culmination of a process that builds over time and is governed by antecedent triggers and distorted thinking that can be conceptualized within the components of the sexual assault cycle. Lapses are understood to be reoccurrences of thoughts, feelings, fantasies, or behaviors that are precursors to sex offenses. A reoffense is too serious an event to be referred to as a lapse and is instead considered a full-blown relapse. High-risk situations in this context are exposures to any environmental triggers that increase the risk of relapse. For a pedophile, a high-risk situation might be living, working, or taking daily walks near an elementary school. For a rapist, a high-risk situation might be viewing particular types of pornography or indulging in violent sexual fantasies. Relapse prevention instructs patients on how to avoid and cope with high-risk situations and identify and correct cognitive distortions that might facilitate further sexual offending: "Sex with a child is not abusive if the child consents," "I knew the victim wanted to have sex with me because she dressed in such a provocative fashion," etc. The goal of relapse prevention for sexual offenders is to enhance the offender's self-management skills; treatment is viewed as an active problem solving process.

Sexual offending in this approach is treated as if it is like an addiction for which there is no cure. The most the offender can hope for is to develop an ability to control and manage what is considered to be a life-long condition. This is the Alcoholics Anonymous model grafted onto sexual offending. Gray and Pithers (1993) state,

> we directly tell clients that they have engaged in a criminal behavior for which no cure exists, but that they can learn to control their decision making and behavior. Clients are told that treatment may decrease their attraction to abusive sexual behaviors, but that abusive fantasies may recur at least momentarily in the future. Clients are informed that the return of an abusive fantasy does not necessarily signify that they are going to reoffend. They learn that a crucial part of their treatment involves learning what to do when they feel drawn to abusive sexual behaviors again. (300)

Relapse-prevention training is more akin to the promotion of a lifestyle choice than a discrete form of psychotherapy. Relapse prevention, as it is practiced in many programs, is a way a life, a manner of comporting the self in the world. The task of treatment is no longer to cure or provide relief from suffering but to reduce and manage the risk the patient poses to others. The client has become the community and the patient someone the therapist must be on guard *against* so that he does not wreak harm on the general population. The opening credo of the National Adolescent Perpetrator Network's (1993) report on juvenile sexual offender, its first assumption within its body of 387 assumptions, is that the community is the client. The "community first" position has also been endorsed by the Association for the Treatment of Sexual Abusers (2000). This shift from cure to management has brought about the replacement of the language of diagnosis and treatment with the language of risk and its attendant factors. It is the factors of risk that are treated, not the patient. What the client suffers from is a severe impairment in self-control, where deficits in coping that impair his ability to manage stressors, anger, impulses, and behavior is the affliction. He is taught skills of living, self-control, and appropriate behavioral comportment. The goal is not self-fulfillment or self-actualization, the traditional aims of psychotherapy, but restraint and good citizenry. Therapy is replaced by the administration of moral conduct and behavior.

Relapse-prevention training has reconfigured the basic patient-therapist relationship, inserting a new figure between them, the community. Through their work with clients, therapists labor on behalf of the community, thereby generating a new identity for the therapist: that of the adversarial therapist who often regards his or her forensic client as the enemy who must be controlled and managed. The therapeutic alliance has shifted from the therapist and his or her client to the therapist and the community. Within this new configuration, the interests of the offender and the community are often rationalized as unified and shared. In a practical sense, however, this is often not the case. When the offender's liberty is at stake, his interests are often diametrically opposed to those of the community. But it is not clear that "the community" can be construed as a client. A therapeutic alliance with the community opens up new potential problems within the enterprise of psychological treatment, raising the real possibility that community-as-client can lead to abuse of power by the therapist, who prowls the gates of treatment on alert for any sign of risk that his or her patient-offender might pose to his or her community-client, ensuring that the offender does not walk through the door and into the open world until every hidden potential form of risk has been addressed.

This new therapeutic alliance is often realized through the therapist's communicative linkage with the criminal justice system. The therapist is often in direct contact with the offender's probation or parole officer. Often treatment is a central part of the community supervision plan of the offender. The probation or parole officer is privy to the treatment. He or she is informed about whether the treatment actually occurred and, often, what the content of treatment was and whether there was sufficient progress. The offenders' liberty is often contingent on their being in treatment and making progress. The National Adolescent Perpetrator Network

(1993) asserts that treatment for juvenile sex offenders should only proceed when mandated by the criminal justice system. Involuntary treatment is the only condition that will provide the necessary leverage and force to ensure compliance and cooperation. Otherwise treatment is doomed to fail because the defensive posture of the client will pose an insurmountable obstacle. The Network asserts that few, if any, offenders, especially sex offenders, will freely and of their own accord take full responsibility for their sexual offending and admit to the full range and depth of their deviance without the fist of the criminal justice system to persuade them to open up.

McGrath, Cumming, and Burchard (2003) report that about two-thirds of juvenile-sex-offender community-based programs and about 40% of residential programs across the country require that their clients sign a waiver of confidentiality allowing them to talk openly about treatment with agents of the criminal justice system. A total of 40% of programs that treat children with sexually abusive behavior problems in the community and residential settings have their parents sign such a waiver. Nearly every respondent to the survey reported that he or she works collaboratively with probation and parole officers. The NAPN (1993) states, "Confidentiality cannot apply in the treatment of this population because it promotes the secrecy that supports offending" (37).

Within the treatment discourse about juvenile sex offenders, there is a strain of thinking that tends to demonize them, as though they are alien creatures that are by nature devious, deceptive, and untrustworthy, such that the therapist must either be continually on guard or risk falling prey to their devious and deceptive ways. They are seen as somehow different from other youth, even different from other delinquent youth, despite the contemporary research that, as we have seen, now casts doubt on this difference. Consider this statement from a book about the treatment of juvenile sex offenders: "The sexually abusive youth thinks differently from other youth" (Ryan and Lane 1997, 305). Or consider this statement from another book about treatment: "The adolescent sex offender's motivation is to mislead the clinician so that the offender can appear to cooperate with treatment while not being forced to confront difficult topics such as his offense pattern" (Perry and Orchard 1992, 63). Further along this volume states,

> The adolescent sex offender tends to be unlike other delinquent groups. He may present as cooperative, compliant, and agreeable: "a nice boy."

Too often the therapist is convinced by the youth that his sexual offense was a momentary aberration which will not recur. This represents one of the most dangerous mythical beliefs about adolescent sex offenders. That pleasant, seemingly remorseful young man is at risk of committing another sexual offense. (63-64)

Juvenile sex offending has often been viewed as a misdirected attempt to compensate for early histories of victimization, a strategy to regain lost power and esteem. Becker (1990) states, "Victims, without therapeutic intervention, are often *destined* to a future of repeated victimization of themselves, the inability to protect others, or the development of similar abusive behaviors toward others" (111, italics added). She further theorizes that "by overpowering, exploiting, manipulating, or controlling others, he may be attempting to undo or protect himself against the impact or implications of his own victimization, or be over-identifying with the aggressor. In his role as perpetrator, he now perceives himself as powerful and able to protect himself" (111). Over time, without corrective intervention, sexual deviance becomes repetitive and ingrained. Often the reinforcement is further propelled by the "thrill of secrecy" of sexual offending. The build-up of deviant fantasies and the planning and stalking act as addictive tonics to the juvenile, necessitating that he seek more and better "highs." Every instance of offending and getting away with it acts as an instance of reinforcement.

Treatment in the hands of practitioners who follow this model takes on the cast of a police interrogation process. In treatment offenders must be confronted and made to admit their crimes. The confession to fantasies is as important as is the admission to acts, because for all sexual offenders, the fantasies are seen as preludes, rehearsals to offenses. The deviance is believed to be reinforced by the offender's continual masturbation to them. "Breaking through his original denial often takes levels of confrontation beyond anything mental health practitioners are accustomed to using. . . . He [the juvenile] needs to reach a level of discomfort sufficient to motivate disclosure and facilitate change" (Ryan, Lane, Davis et al. 1987, 388). Understanding and controlling the sexual assault cycle is believed to take months or years; it will take that long to break through the youth's manipulations, secrecy, and covert assertions of power. Kahn and Lafond (1988) give clinical advice that provides a chilling reminder of the moral hysteria that gripped the country in the 1980s regarding nursing and child-care centers: "Since it is known that sexual offenders frequently lie, distort, or minimize, it makes sense that the treatment process should proceed on the assumption that police reports and victim statements are accurate" (141). They go so far as to provide the following simple advice: "Instead of asking closed-ended questions such as 'did you hurt your victim?', it is generally more productive to ask questions that do not give offenders opportunities to deny. For example, "when your victim started crying, what did you do?'" (141).

Treatment becomes a form of exorcism whereby the demonic forces that resist treatment and cling to the underlying deviancy must be confronted and attacked in order to free the adolescent residing within. To counteract these forces, clinicians must have the strength and authority of the criminal justice system behind them when they enter battle. They are ill-equipped to fight against these forces alone. They must be prepared to take charge and confront denial and deviancy in all its manifestations. They should not be afraid to sanction the offender with threats of termination, which bring the risk of probation or parole revocation. The therapist must demand that the offender take responsibility at all times and must not tolerate any excusing or justifying of beliefs. And this must all be done within a relational framework that is sensitive, empathetic, and supportive. Gray and Pithers (1993) described this odd conglomeration of attributes as "compassionate accountability."

Chaffin and Bonner (1998), in a brief introductory paper, aimed one of the first major critiques at the state of clinical practice in the treatment of juvenile sex offenders: "There are still no true experimental studies comparing outcomes of treated adolescents versus untreated adolescents and no prospective data on either risk factors or the natural course of the behavior. . . . Largely, the field is still using treatment models and assumptions borrowed and adapted from programs for incarcerated adult pedophiles. These things have not changed" (314).

More recently, Chaffin (2006), echoing the commentary he made nearly a decade earlier, concluded that the treatment of juvenile sexual offenders still lacks any firmly established, evidence-based practices. The field is still predominated by interventions that are based on clinical lore as opposed to scientific outcome research. The efficacy of cognitive-behavior treatment and relapse-prevention training has not been sufficiently demonstrated empirically for juvenile sex offenders. More recently this approach has drawn increasingly more criticism as a "one-size-fits-all" approach that is often applied dogmatically and inflexibly (Bumby 2006).

The treatment tends to be workbook oriented, measuring change according to how accurately a client's homework assignments adhere to a standard. Progress is often measured by how well a client is able to regurgitate and parrot his therapist's remarks. Clients who are able to adopt the lexicon of treatment, present well-formulated offense cycles that they have constructed in groups, and display comprehensive relapse-prevention plans are usually deemed ready to step back into the community without much of a sense of whether their ability to produce such therapeutic texts translates into internal change and lower risk, or even whether their risk was high enough to warrant such treatment to begin with.

Treatment devices, like offense cycles, are prefabricated models, and it is unclear whether an offender's work with sexual-assault cycles decreases recidivism. There is no evidence for this. Yet it remains uncritically accepted by the field, and has become an institutionalized staple in sex-offender-treatment programs. Many programs use bibliotherapy methods—journaling and autobiographies—and fantasy work in the absence of any research on these specific techniques (Burton, Smith-Darden, and Frankel 2006).

Despite the absence of empirical data regarding its efficacy, cognitive-behavior therapy continues to be the leading mode of treatment for juvenile sex offenders across the county. Cognitive-behavior theory or its close variants, relapse prevention and psycho-education, are the most frequently identified program theories, with nearly 90% of survey respondents endorsing one of these as their primary program theory or philosophy (McGrath, Cumming, and Burchard 2003). About 90% of the programs endorsed the use of relapse prevention, cognitive restructuring, victim-empathy training, and offender responsibility taking as a therapeutic technique in the program. Another, more recent survey (Walker and McCormick 2004) reports the overwhelming predominance of a cognitive-behavior treatment model focusing on techniques for relapse-prevention training, development of empathy skills, and cognitive restructuring.

Pharmacological treatment was used in over a third of the residential programs and almost half of the community-based programs. Medication included the use of anti-androgen agents, like Depo-Povera, to reduce sexual drive, and the SSRIs, like Prozac and Zoloft, to address what is described as the compulsive-like sexual behavior of some juvenile sex offenders and also to lower sexual drive. The practice of treating juvenile sex offenders with medication is proceeding without any controlled studies about its effectiveness.

Recently the relapse prevention model for treatment of juvenile sex offenders has come under increasing criticism as a method too restrictive to address behavior as complex and multidetermined as sexual offending (Bumby 2006; Laws 2001; Ward 2002). The major limitation identified has been relapse prevention's singular focus on managing and regulating risk—its instruction on what one should not do—which neglects helping the offender learn what he should do instead. The "don't do it" message of relapse prevention has become hollow and insufficient. According to the criticism, the juvenile sex offender needs more; he needs to know what to do instead. The exclusive focus on risk factors has come to be viewed as necessary but not sufficient. The relapse-prevention model is too narrow in the ways in which it accounts for sexual offending, forcing the juvenile to fit his offense into the rigid structure of the sexual-assault cycle, leaving little room for individual differences on the chain of events that are purported to lead to a sexual offense, and making every offender shoe-horn his offense into the common pathway of the cycle. The model is intellectualized, filled with abstract concepts and complex language that makes treatment often experience-distant and artificial.

In contrast, Ward and colleagues (Ward 2002; Thakker, Ward, and Tidmarsh 2006) promote a strengths-based approach to the treatment of sexual offenders, which they term "the Good-Lives Model." This model focuses on making treatment a more positive experience, returning to the idea that it is important to build a sound therapeutic alliance with the client. It remains focused primarily in the here and now but is also interested in the client's past, his subjective experience, and his insight into the motivations for his sexual offending. The treatment model shifts the focus back on understanding the primary needs that underlie sexual offending, and then working toward developing strategies to aid the client in obtaining gratification of those needs in a more acceptable and healthy manner.

Robert Longo (2004), who in the 1980s published a few research reports, reviewed in chapter 2, advocating that juvenile sex offenders need immediate intervention before they progress into more serious forms of sexual offending (Groth, Longo, and McFaddin 1982; Longo and Groth 1983), has recently criticized the current excessive focus on relapse prevention, which he views as the result of a "trickle-down effect" from adult treatment programs. He advocates the incorporation of a developmental focus into the treatment of juvenile sex offenders. His Holistic or Well-Being approach, in a manner similar to Ward's Good-Lives Model, returns to the power of the therapeutic relationship, advocating a more flexible approach that is dictated by the particular learning style of the offender. Relapse prevention is based on the premise that sexual offending is habitual and persistent, but Longo, in a reversal of his previous stance, now challenges the universal applicability of these assumptions. He also raises a concern about the wisdom of promoting the idea to juvenile sex offenders and their families and, for that matter, the public at large, that sexual offending is chronic and that at best one can only hope to manage, not cure, the problem. This view can contribute to a "self-fulfilling prophesy" by exposing the juvenile to excessively restrictive criminal justice and mental health interventions, excluding him from normalizing socialization experiences. The Holistic or Well-Being model focuses instead on positive coping and places less attention on the control of risk factors and sexually deviant impulses.

There exist to date very few controlled outcome research studies for juvenile-sex-offender treatment despite the numerous descriptions of treatment approaches in the literature (Chaffin 2006). Evidence-based practices have become a widely recognized standard in the behavioral health care field. In an era of dwindling government budgets for human services, and when insurance companies and other third-party reimbursements are more closely scrutinized, the demand for evidence-based practices has increased. Evidence-based practice seeks to go beyond simple correlational evidence or clinically proven effectiveness, which often is nothing more than the report that a patient or client group indicated improvement on a variable of interest when a particular treatment was introduced. Instead, evidence-based practices often use randomized controlled trials to establish the efficacy of a particular treatment and effectiveness studies that test in the field outside the laboratory.

The only treatment approach that has been researched with randomized controlled outcome studies is Multisystemic Treatment (MST; Henggeler, Schoenwald, Borduin et al. 1998), described earlier. There have been two randomized controlled studies regarding the effectiveness of MST for juvenile sex offenders (Borduin, Henggeler, Blaske et al. 1990; Borduin and Schaeffer 2001). According to Chaffin (2006), "MST is the leading candidate model for any program wanting to adopt an evidence-based practice orientation to treating adolescent sexual offenders" (670).

MST appears to be a promising treatment approach not only for juvenile sex offenders but for violent delinquents generally. The cruel irony here is that while it is the treatment approach with the strongest research support, it may be the one that is applied the least frequently with juvenile sex offenders. Multisystemic Treatment is used by only 6.5% of the programs for adolescent sex offenders (McGrath, Cumming, and Burchard 2003). Instead, state juvenile justice agencies tend to endorse the treatment approach with the weakest research support, namely, residential sexual offender treatment—an approach for which there is simply no outcome research.

MST is based on Bronfenbrenner's (1979) social ecological theory of human development. Within this model, viewing an individual separately and apart from his multiple social contexts is an artificial, atomized perspective promoted by individualistic psychological theory. No individual exists detached from a larger social context and set of interacting social relationships. All individuals are embedded within what Brofenbrenner termed "nested contexts." This is especially the case for children and youth, who exist not in isolation but within various nested systems—family, peers, school, neighborhoods, communities, and a larger culture. The systems that are in closer proximity to the child exert greater influence on the child's self and behavior. For young children, the family is often the most influential and powerful context; for adolescents, the peer group grows in proximity and influence. The goal of MST is to apply interventions to the multiple systems within which the child exists. To solely target interventions at the child, ignoring the interacting systems within which he or she exists, as do relapse-prevention training and cognitive-behavioral interventions generally, risks having those interventions be neutralized later and wiped away when the child returns to the various nested systems that define him. Therapists' interventions are no match for the powerful systems that exist around the child. They are simply outnumbered, and their limited exposure time to their clients is no match for the extra-therapy time that the child will spend with family, friends, school, neighborhood, and community. But targeting interventions at these systems can lead the systems to do the transformative work.

MST has been identified by the surgeon general (U.S. Department of Health and Human Services 2001) as an empirically supported treatment for serious juvenile offenders and has been endorsed by the National Institute on Drug Abuse (1999). It has successfully established itself as an effective intervention strategy for violent and substance-abusing youth. More recently, it has come to be viewed as an effective intervention strategy for juvenile sex offenders (Saldana, Swenson, and Letourneau 2006).

MST is a team approach with three or four therapists assigned to a juvenile offender along with a supervisor and a consultant, often the model developers themselves serving in this role. The sessions occur not in the stale and artificial setting of a detention center or residential program or therapist's office but in natural settings: the juvenile's home, school, and other significant contexts within which the juvenile operates. There is no preestablished time length to sessions or number of sessions. Treatment occurs around the clock, and meetings occur at times and places convenient to the family. The treatment developers insist on a strict adherence to the model. The treatment is based on a set of manualized protocols designed to prevent therapists from drifting away from the tenets of the model and to ensure treatment fidelity. Strict adherence to the model and treatment fidelity are predictive of success.

There have been two randomized controlled trials that found MST to be more efficacious than "usual services," as measured by sexual recidivism and general criminal recidivism rates. In the first study sixteen juvenile sex offenders were randomly assigned to either MST or individual therapy (Borduin, Henggeler, Blaske et al. 1990). The individual-treatment control group was exposed to an eclectic approach that blended psychodynamic, humanistic, and behavioral models. Both treatments were delivered on an outpatient basis. Active treatment lasted from one to seven months for MST and three to nine months for individual therapy. Followup varied from twenty-one months to four years. The research team reported that only 12.5% of the MST group, or one of eight participants, was charged with a new sexual offense, while 75% of the control group, or six out of eight, was arrested for a new sexual offense. This treatment effect was extremely robust, but its meaningfulness is limited by the small sample size and the absence of any measurement of post-treatment differences. The 75% sexual recidivism rate of the control group is probably a function of the low sample size. Small samples are prone to outlying results. The nonsexual recidivism rate was 25% for the MST group and 50% for the controls, another robust finding, suggesting that the treatment intervention has positive effects beyond sexual offending for this sample of youth.

These findings were replicated in a larger study with a longer followup period of eight years (Borduin and Schaeffer 2001). The longer followup allowed the researchers to test whether the therapeutic effects are durable and sustainable. Twenty-four peer/adult juvenile rapists and twenty-four child molesters were randomly assigned to either MST or usual services.

At followup, the researchers found that the youth assigned to MST had fewer reported behavior problems, decreased psychiatric symptomatology, less self-reported delinquent offending, more positive family relations, improved peer relations, and better grades in school than the control group. They also spent fewer days in out-of-home placements and one-third fewer days in adult jail. Most importantly, the sexual recidivism (12.5% vs. 41.7%) and nonsexual recidivism (29.2% vs. 62.5%) rates were three times less for the MST group than the control group. The type of offender, rapist or child molester, did not moderate treatment effectiveness. The researchers report that MST was also more cost effective. Usual services were estimated to be four times more expensive.

A limitation of this study was, again, the small sample size. Also, like its predecessor, it is an example of an efficacy study that demonstrates a treatment effect in a well-controlled research sample of subjects that have been selected for participation. The treatment model awaits validation in an effectiveness study that examines treatment effects on a large, unselected sample, outside the confines of a tightly controlled laboratory-like setting, in a more naturalistic real-world application.

Explanations for the efficacy of MST with juvenile sex offenders has zeroed in on the model's focus on the social ecologies of the juvenile rather than the individual characteristics of the juvenile, such as deviant arousal, thinking errors, and cognitive distortion, the stock targets of traditional sex-offender treatment (Swenson, Schoenwald, and Randall et al. 1998). Individual-oriented therapies do not address the environmental contexts that support violent offending, drug abuse, and school failure—important considerations in the overall treatment approach for juvenile sex offenders, since sexual offenses are complex events that are multidetermined and require interventions aimed at various systems.

As we have seen, sex-offender treatment for juvenile sex offenders has traditionally been based on the assumption that they are somehow different from general offenders and therefore need a specialized treatment approach that addresses their unique treatment needs and risk factors, such as sexual deviance or cognitive distortions. But as we have learned in the previous chapters, it does not seem to be the case that juvenile sex offenders differ that much, if at all, from general delinquents. Juvenile sex offenders have problems very similar to juvenile nonsexual offenders, such as lower social bonding with family and high involvement with deviant peers. Yet they are usually treated as a specialized population by the systems that manage and treat them even though juvenile sex offending may be part of a broader pattern of general delinquency and not indicative of sexual deviance in need of specialized treatment. This may explain why specialized treatment models have not been proven effective and why interventions that address the social ecology of the juvenile, like MST, have demonstrated efficacy (Ronis and Borduin 2007). As we have seen, the finding that general delinquency is common among juvenile sex offenders has led some to question whether sexual-offender-specific treatment is even indicated in most cases (Berliner 1998; Milloy 1998).

The recent success of a model of treatment like MST, a treatment that occurs in the community, outside of the restrictive and artificial secure treatment or detention setting, begs the question about the possible negative effects of residential treatment and traditional sexual-offender treatment. The types of potential harm resulting from the unnecessary placement of children, often in secure residential treatment programs for months and sometimes years, are manifold. First, simply being deprived of one's liberty by being unnecessarily and involuntarily interned in a program is prima facie evidence of harm.

Second is the unavoidable harm that befalls an adolescent taken out of the developmental flow of his life—the life loss that occurs when he is unable to keep pace with his peers educationally, occupationally, and socially because he has been sidelined by placement in a residential program and made to work on sex-offender issues. There is added harm done to the juvenile when he is taken out of society and incarcerated. He falls behind his peers economically and socially by virtue of his having been prevented from participating in the normal channels or pathways of achievement, making it more difficult for him to adjust post-release and move onto a nondeviant life path. Adolescents who are committed to the juvenile justice system are behind their peers to begin with; long-term incarceration trails them behind that much more, making it difficult, if not impossible, for them to make up that lost time and making it more likely that they will continue along a delinquent career path because so many other pathways have been closed off to them.

Third, treatment programs are learning environments. They are training grounds where identities are forged and relationships are formed. Ideas about the self are passed on to the adolescent through the covert and overt operations of a program. Programs hope that the ideas they knowingly instill will make future offending less likely, but that is not always the case, particularly with adolescents. Juvenile correctional programs are often facilitating environments for "deviancy training" (Dishion, McCord, and Poulin 1999), the learning that takes place outside of group when the juvenile is not in treatment. Deviancy training is the learning fostered not by one's clinician but by one's peers, who teach lessons, often modeled, of deeper deviancy, so that what an adolescent ultimately learns is how to be a more effective deviant—if he was even deviant to begin with. In juvenile-sex-offender treatment programs it may be the most deviant few who instruct the least deviant majority.

Within the sterile confines of these programs, there is a very limited opportunity to explore and build a healthy sexual identity—a central task of adolescence, clumsily stumbled through by most adolescents. For youth confined within a juvenile-sex-offender program, there are countless opportunities to internalize the identity of a sexual deviant. One is excluded from other sexual "normals" and grouped with other "deviants," reminded repeatedly, day after day, week after week, month after month, that one's deviancy lives within, hidden away, tightly coiled, ready to spring one into the deviant cycle without one's awareness, leading to the commission of further acts of sexual abuse. The effects on the self can be far reaching and inestimable. Such an experience can significantly impact one's sense of self, as well as one's life chances, closing off many social and occupational doors to the adolescent labeled as a sex offender.

There are unintended insidious negative effects attached to our benevolently rendered interventions. Often interventions can stabilize or amplify deviance rather than correct it. When we persistently label people as deviant, they can begin to internalize the type we cast upon them, doing untold damage to their identities and sense of self. Ian Hacking (2002, 2006) refers to this process as an instance of "making up people," a situation whereby "people spontaneously come to fit their categories" (2002, 100). Hacking makes a distinction between natural kinds and human kinds. Natural kinds are things discovered, like a new species of fish in the Artic Sea. Human kinds are completely different from natural kinds. Human kinds are the categories developed by social scientists to describe people. But people are highly reactive to the categories in which we inscribe them. Hacking refers to this as a "looping effect" that occurs between the category and the person within it. Social science categories are brought into being by human actions. They are not out there to be discovered, as is the case for most objects in the physical or biological sciences. Human categories are fashioned, and then peopled; distinctions are made and then new realities appear. An instance of "making up people," creating a new human or social category, brings about a new social space, a new possibility that did not exist before. "Numerous kinds of human beings and human acts come into being hand and hand with our invention of the ways to name them . . . our spheres of possibility, and hence our selves, are to some extent made up by our naming and what that entails" (Hacking 2002, 113). Mary Douglas, the British anthropologist, had another way of expressing this phenomenon: "Stigma is interesting as a self-fulfilling prophesy. Prejudicial and exclusionary behavior validates itself" (1992, 36). Our methods can often bring about the thing that concerns us most.

5

Creating the
Objects of Our Concern
*Normal Childhood Sexuality and
the Invention of Childhood
Sexual Behavior Problems*

Can a 6-year-old boy form the intent to commit an act of sexual aggression against a female classmate? This question was at the center
of the media maelstrom that swept across the country when the Brockton
Public School District, in a city about twenty-five miles south of Boston,
Massachusetts, issued a three-day suspension on January 6, 2006, to a
6-year-old boy who had touched a same-aged first grade female classmate
inside her waistband (Jan and Burge 2006; Papadopoulos 2006a and b).
The act was labeled sexual harassment because it fit the school district's
definition banning such conduct. The accused child was immediately removed from the classroom and an internal investigation into the incident
was prompted. The result of that investigation led the school district to
refer the incident to the county prosecutor's office, which declined to file
a delinquency complaint since juvenile court jurisdiction does not begin
until the age of 7, the age of reason according to English common law,
when an individual is capable of contemplating criminal intentions and is
legally and morally responsible for wrongful acts.

The mother of the offending child was described in newspaper accounts as outraged by the way the matter was handled by the school district, stating that her son was too young to understand anything about
sexual harassment. "He doesn't even know what that word 'sexual' is," she
was quoted as saying. "I don't see how I'm going to explain it to him. I
can't. He's just too young for that" (Ranalli and Mishra 2006).

During the height of the media tumult that raged in the days following the initial report of the event, the family was surrounded by various

human rights agencies that joined forces to establish a special committee to support the family in its countercampaign against the school district. The mother of the suspended child demanded that her son be transferred to another school. The school district apologized to her, granted her request, and promised to revisit the sexual harassment policy.

The problem with any moral panic—like the one about children and adolescents as budding sexual predators—is that they are poor discriminators of events. Everything gets bulldozed in their path. New school policies and new curricula designed to prevent sexual harassment are rational responses to a real problem. Schools are right to take the problem of sexual harassment seriously. But the incident in Brockton is symptomatic of the problem that emerges when concern about something reaches such critical proportions that people become blinded, seeing any and all possible instances that may even remotely signal the presence of the problem as a call for immediate and decisive intervention. That is the hazard of zero-tolerance policies. They sweep up everything into the advancing threshing combine and package it as though it was all the same thing, even the case of a 6-year-old boy who touches a female classmate on her waistband.

This case begs endless questions. It opens up so many fronts of critical interrogation—not of the offending child but of the system that responded as it did in such a knee-jerk, automatic fashion. It observed an act, interpreted it as a dangerous sign, and set into motion a system of responses that only in the aftermath came under the light of examination. In the end it was the reaction of the school, not the offending child, which became the point of criticism in the media coverage. In a different historical moment this act would have probably been viewed as normal childhood behavior, an instance of playfulness or sexual curiosity or, at worst, an aggressive act that called for adult correction and instruction, not a matter for the police and the district attorney.

The single aspect of this case that makes it such a telling example is that it remains unclear where the "sexual" aspect ascribed to it first emerged. Is it in the act of the offending child or the mind of the observing adults? Is there any way one can determine from the abbreviated description of the act itself whether it was a sexual act in the manner in which "sexual" is typically construed by an adult? Even if the offending child carried within him the idea that his act was "sexual," is his idea of "sexual" the same as has been ascribed to him by the adults bearing witness to his act? Does a 6-year-old boy conceive of sex along the same lines as an adult? Or is this an instance of the "adultification" of a 6-year-old boy? Even assuming for the moment that his act was "sexual" in the way that the adults involved in this drama understood the word "sexual," how does one arrive at the conclusion that the act carried within it an intent to harass or do harm? Furthermore, how does one arrive at the conclusion that the act is injurious—so injurious that it prompted school administrators in Brockton, Massachusetts, to suspend the offending student and refer his case to the district attorney for possible juvenile justice processing? How did we get to point where childhood sexuality is perceived as so potentially dangerous?

It is at once odd and perfectly sensible that G. Stanley Hall, the preeminent child psychologist of his time, would be the one to invite Freud to America for his only visit to the New World to deliver a set of lectures commemorating the twentieth anniversary of the establishment of Clark University in September 1909. Hall is a figure riddled with ambiguity, with a foot firmly set in both the 19th and 20th centuries. He is American psychology's reactionary and visionary. Hall was a consummate organizer and promoter of academic and professional psychology. He established the American Psychological Association and was its first president; he founded the discipline's first major research journals, including the *American Journal of Psychology,* still in publication, and the *Pedagogical Seminary*; and he was the founder and first president of Clark University (Ross 1972). He was among the first in the newly emerging discipline of psychology to see a role and place for psychology beyond the academy and the laboratory, envisioning its application in the school, in child-rearing practices, and in public policy. This is the visionary side of Hall, the modernist Hall, the side that most likely had the stronger affinity for Freud and his still-controversial, if not heretical, ideas about childhood sexuality.

But Hall possessed an intellect and moral sensibility firmly rooted in the 19th century. An ardent advocate of recapitulation theory, Hall believed that the development of each individual replays the evolutionary advancement of the species (Cravens 2006; Ross 1972). Within the psychological unfolding of each person is the sum total of human evolution; the large of the species is writ small within the growth of the individual. "Ontogeny (individual development) recapitulates phylogeny (evolution of a species)." The theory, still widespread in academic psychology at the turn of the 20th century, formed the intellectual underpinning for various racist ideologies such as the idea that the races could be scientifically ranked according to their supposed progress along some evolutionary continuum, with the white race occupying the supreme position atop the ladder while the other, lower, degenerate races—the Africans, Asians, and Eastern and Southern Europeans—occupied some lower rung on the evolutionary scale. These inferior human kinds were viewed as less developed from an evolutionary perspective.

Hall and the recapitulationists viewed children as akin to savages. "Normal children often pass through stages of passionate cruelty, laziness, lying, and thievery. . . . We are told that to magnify the soul of a child before its more animal instincts are reduced to due proportion and control by conscience and reason, would give us the most truculent and menacing forms of criminality" (Hall 1904, 334-35). He even went so far as to equate vicious criminals with children, seeing them as nothing more than overgrown children, childish minds in violent adult bodies. For Hall the true menace facing childhood was precocious exposure to sexual activity and the chief scourge was masturbation, which he held responsible for multiple problems ranging from faulty vision to stunted growth, as well as depression, anxiety, and cognitive and mental deficiencies. He advocated his own version of an abstinence-only curriculum, calling for the suppression and diversion of all sexual activity in childhood. He preached—his works often sound more like sermons than scientific discourse—a prevention strategy that centered on hard work, loose-fitting trousers, and plenty of cold baths. He advised parents to be wary of boys with their hands in their pockets, recommending that tree climbing and other activities leading to incidental genital stimulation be assiduously avoided (Arnett 2006).

For Freud the trip to America was a momentous occasion, an opportunity to present his new ideas to the New World. In Europe his radical psychoanalysis was regarded with great skepticism and often hostile rejection. Psychoanalysis had barely permeated beyond the insular coterie of devotees he assembled around him. Freud was acutely aware of the significance of his visit and his lectures. At the time none of his writings had yet been published in English in America. He was anxious about how his views would be received in America. In a letter to Carl Jung on January 17, 1909, Freud wrote, "I think that once they discover the sexual core of our psychological theories they will drop us. Their prudery and their material dependence on the public are too great" (Freud and Jung 1974, 192).

Freud was scheduled to give five lectures on successive days that he would deliver in his native German. He arrived in Worcester without having prepared his lectures ahead of time, choosing instead to work them out freshly and spontaneously during brisk early-morning walks before his scheduled lectures (Rosenzweig 1992). The fourth lecture, delivered on Friday, September 10, 1909, was on childhood sexuality and would be his most controversial (Freud 1910). In this lecture he acknowledged at the outset his audience's probably incredulous reaction to his ideas about the presence of an erotic impulse implanted at birth. He further anticipated that they might claim that he exaggerated the importance of sexuality with his idea that all psychic symptoms are rooted in the erotic impulse. He assured his audience that the evidence of a sexual basis for all psychological symptoms was incontrovertible if one allowed oneself to sift through the memories and free associations of the psychoanalytic patient. In every case the etiological trail leads back to early childhood, when some sexual conflict was first repressed only to later reappear in disguise as a neurotic symptom. It is repressed sexual wishes, he told the gathered audience of assembled American scholars, that cause psychological disturbance.

Freud assured his audience that his goal was not to provoke them to astonishment, and he invited them to set aside their doubts as he took them through the inner logic of his developing psychoanalytic theory. The child has a sex drive from the outset that begins as an autoerotic impulse. The infant has no developed sense of self or other, only raw drives that seek gratification. Later, as the self emerges, sexual object-choice becomes possible, bringing with it a capacity for sexuality to express itself along relational lines. In the early stages of development the child's first sexual attachments are to its parents. It is within the intimate confines of the nuclear family where sexual conflicts first play themselves out; it is from these sexually charged relationships that the template for all future sexual conflict is cast. But it is not the child alone who is implicated in this sexual drama. Sexual attachments are incited by the parents, whose solicitous and tender care contains traces of an erotic wish, though the aim may be greatly inhibited.

Freud ended his lecture on childhood sexuality by informing the group that later in childhood, sexual impulses eventually fall under the control and dominion of the conscious self, the ego, as the child begins to incorporate the mores of the society. Repression takes over, banishing sexuality to an underlife where it will continue to exert its coded influence on a vast array of behaviors. It is the engaged and theoretically informed psychoanalyst who holds the key with which to decode its riddled language.

The lectures were a crowning success for Freud. They were received openly by the audience and were covered favorably and extensively by the local press (Cromer and Anderson 1970). Childhood sexuality had arrived in America and seemed to have hit fertile soil in the New World. Later Freud would reflect that the lectures and his trip to America signaled a turning point for him, the moment when his ideas seemed to take on a new reality (Evans and Koelsch 1985; Rosenzweig 1992). His ideas had spread beyond his insular group of acolytes to a world beyond his own. As for Hall, he will always bear the historical credit for bringing Freud to America even though he never fully embraced Freud's ideas. Freud wished to free us from the chains of a repressive sexuality; Hall wished to strengthen those manacles. Freud had arrived in America, bringing with him new ideas about the sexual nature of children, but America's conflict, its deep ambivalence about childhood sexuality, did not dissipate with Freud's implantation of childhood sexuality and his return to Vienna. The American prudery that he alerted Jung to would ensure that its deep conflict with childhood sexuality would not only continue but expand during the course of the century.

Despite Freud's efforts to establish the idea of childhood sexuality, nearly a century after his visit to America there remains a paucity of scientific information about the normal sexuality of children and adolescents. The ethical barriers erected against the study of childhood sexuality are immense and difficult to transverse. The concern centers on an irrational fear that the mere act of inquiring about children's sexual behavior would be an incitement—a fear that asking them questions about sex might disrupt their innocent naiveté about such matters and send them rushing headlong into a sexual frenzy. It is difficult enough to secure public funding to support research about adult sexuality; soliciting grant money to study childhood and adolescent sexuality is a downright perilous affair. Alfred Kinsey had his funding for his famous sex surveys in the 1940s and 1950s terminated by the Rockefeller Foundation because of pressure brought to bear by a U.S. congressional subcommittee that threatened to revoke the foundation's tax-exempt status (Hunt 1999).

Some forty years later, in the late 1980s, a team of researchers from the University of North Carolina at Chapel Hill had their grant for a national comprehensive survey of the sexual attitudes and behavior of adolescents pulled by the Department of Health and Human Services after a battle cry was issued by a number of conservative groups that objected to questioning adolescents about their sexual behavior, even though the research protocol called for parental consent. The cancellation of a funded research project, which had already passed muster through the rigors of peer review, was declared unprecedented by the American Psychological Association and the American Sociological Association. They publicly condemned the government's action, characterizing it as a serious threat to the freedom and independence of scientific thought and inquiry (Hunt 1999).

But the Congress meant business and passed a bill sponsored by Senator Jesse Helms, ironically also of North Carolina, banning federal funding of national sex surveys. Congress seemed to be saying that some things, like sex, were meant to remain a mystery, cloaked in secrecy, and that it would not allow federal money to be spent on their illumination. Adolescent sexuality was to remain in the shadows, where it belonged, even if the knowledge gained could potentially aid in efforts to reduce unsafe teenage sexual practices, thereby limiting the rates of STDs and unwanted pregnancy among teenagers. The study of adolescent sexuality originally proposed by the University of North Carolina researchers was eventually conducted as a part of a larger federally funded study of adolescent health but in a much more curtailed and limited fashion (Hunt 1999).

Even in the absence of political barriers, the scientific study of sex, particularly the sexual lives of children and adolescents, is an elusive matter. Most of the research about child and adolescent sexual experiences is derived from retrospective accounts of adults—a notoriously unreliable form of data, prone to all sorts of distortions and inaccuracies due to the vagaries of memory and the tendency for subjects to shape self-reports to comport with perceived social expectations. Surveys of parents about the sexual behavior of their children are also methodologically complicated. Children and adolescents have efficiently learned that sex is something one should conceal from others in order to conform to social rules and norms (Friedrich, Grambsch, Broughton et al. 1991; Money and Ehrhardt 1972). Children are socialized at a young age to view sex as an unspoken and unseen matter, and this makes child sexuality a very difficult phenomenon to study. Having learned quickly that sex is taboo, children have already begun to conceal what the social scientist wants to discover. Much of the research regarding the reports of adults and adolescents about their childhood sexual experiences reveals that these reports are fraught with inconsistency (Fortenberry and Aalsma 2003; Graham 2003). According to one study, only about a quarter of sexually experienced youth reported the same date of their first sexual experience when asked about this on more than one occasion (Upchurch, Lillard, Aneschenel et al. 2002). Boys tend to exaggerate their rate of sexual encounters while girls underreport it (Savin-Williams and Diamond 2004).

The contextual nature of childhood sexuality also makes it a very ephemeral thing to study. A child's sexual behavior will reflect the sexual values of the culture in which he or she is reared. There is no childhood sexuality in a culture-free sense; there is no natural childhood sexuality that transcends culture or history since they define what is to be perceived as sexual and what will be the permissible expressions of sexuality. After Freud, entire panoplies of childhood behaviors were suddenly viewed as sexual. Prior to that, they were not. Childhood sexuality is not something that unfolds outside of a cultural or a historical context. In Norway researchers conducted interviews with preschool teachers about their observations of the sexual behavior of their students. Many of the teachers reported observing their students exploring their own bodies sexually, manipulating their genitals and the genitals of their peers in a process they labeled as "coitus training." A similar description of behaviors in a study conducted in the United States resulted in a recommendation for a preventative education program (Barbaree and Marshall 2006). One culture's healthy sexual development is another's pathology.

Another barrier to knowledge about normal sexuality is that there has been far more research about deviant forms of childhood sexuality—childhood sexual abuse and juvenile sex offending—than there has been about normal childhood sexuality. There is a fundamental validity problem when the bulk of knowledge about childhood sexuality is based on cases referred to clinical and legal agencies for evaluation, treatment, or prosecution. The way to acquire knowledge about normal sexuality is not through study of deviant or abnormal sexuality. Such an approach will inevitably lead to an extremely skewed picture. When not focused on sexual abuse or sexual offending, the research has mostly been centered on other perils and harms associated with childhood and adolescent sexuality, like sexually transmitted diseases, AIDS, and unwanted pregnancies. "The negative cast of research on adolescent sexuality can be interpreted as exemplifying the general tendency to portray sexuality as a source of problems rather than an integral aspect of human development. . . . Although the denigration of adolescent sexuality has been predicated on protecting health and well-being, it might actually do more harm than good" (Savin-Williams and Diamond 2004, 192-93). The aim of much of this research has been to develop strategies to eliminate or at least restrict or limit the sexual behavior of adolescents.

The underlying message of all these research agendas is the same: sex is harmful and needs to be strictly monitored and managed. Joycelyn Elders, the former U.S. surgeon general, warned that "treating sex as dangerous is dangerous in itself. We need to be matter-of-fact about what is, after all, a fact of life" (Levine 2002, x). Unfortunately, she lost her job for doing just that when in the early 1990s she advocated teaching children about masturbation. The result of these limitations has been extensive gaps in knowledge about adolescent sexuality. Consider the conclusion of the following review of the state of the science on adolescent sexuality made over ten years ago: "We have little understanding of what constitutes sexual health, what motivates sexual behavior, how sexual norms are developed and sustained, and how these evolve over time" (Di Mauro 1997, 4). Or consider this more recent conclusion: "Even after decades of research on adolescent sexuality, many fundamental gaps about normative sexual development from prepubescence to young adulthood remain unanswered" (Savin-Williams and Diamond 2004, 189-90).

There is very little interdisciplinary contact between, on the one hand, clinical researchers who study childhood sexual abuse and deviant sexuality, like sexual offending, and, on the other, sexologists who study normal sexuality and researchers who study child development and adolescent health issues. Reference lists in studies about childhood sexual abuse or juvenile sexual offending rarely cite studies from these other research areas, and vice versa. There is virtually no cross-referencing of information and knowledge across this divide. The two groups work in near complete isolation from each other, with little awareness and acknowledgment of the other's work. They do not build on one another's findings or conclusions, instead erecting their own separate theories, knowledge systems, and problems to be solved. One group works to define the limits of sexual normality, the other the limits of abnormality, without the slightest awareness that each group's work crosses into the terrain and territory of the other.

A notable exception to this knowledge divide was the research of the late William Friedrich (see Friedrich 2003; Friedrich, Grambsch, Broughton et al. 1991). Friedrich eventually migrated to the study of normative sexual behavior in children, but he did not begin there. He began by studying the effects of sexual abuse on children. Friedrich's point of departure was a simple enough assumption, still widely held by mental health clinicians and researchers: the presence of sexual behavior in children between the ages of 2 and 12 is indicative of prior sexual abuse. Non–sexually abused children do not exhibit sexual behavior because they presumably do not know about such things. Sexuality is taboo in children, and if they are displaying it, it must mean that they have been prematurely exposed to this knowledge via sexual abuse. Friedrich was merely responding to a common tendency to see such an expression of sexuality as a marker of childhood sexual abuse. What Friedrich came to discover, however, in complete violation of his initial assumption, was that sexual behavior was ubiquitous in children, the sexually abused and the non–sexually abused alike. He started out thinking he was studying the abnormal, but it turned out he was actually studying the normal. He had to realign his prior assumptions when confronted with the finding that sexual behavior is very common in children and that it was even more common in European samples and in children whose parents had higher educational backgrounds and more liberal attitudes regarding sex—another instance of sexuality being contingent on the context of the child's family and culture.

The need to see the prepubescent child as asexual has interfered with the ability to perceive the sexuality of children accurately. The sexually sanitized view of children has resulted in vast cultural denial, even among researchers and mental health professionals, that children are sexual beings, exhibiting a range of sexual behaviors in the absence of sexual abuse. Sexual behavior in children is not pathological. It follows a rather varied developmental course that is normal and healthy. There has been limited interest in mapping the wondrous diversity of childhood sexuality and how a child's unique expression of sexuality informs one about the unique idiom of that person. "Research addressing how adolescent sexuality can be positive and growth promoting is nearly absent from the empirical literature" (Savin-Williams and Diamond 2004, 221). Instead, research into childhood sexuality has been confined to identifying the signs of sexual abuse or other problems attendant to sexual behavior and determining how they can be eliminated.

Alfred Kinsey and his famous sex surveys, which were begun in the 1940s at the University of Indiana, initiated the scientific study of childhood sexuality. Though he and his research team's primary goal was the mapping of adult sexual practices in the United States, his survey data did cover, in a limited way, the sexual experiences of children. Kinsey and his research team made a number of controversial assertions regarding child sexuality in their two-volume study of sexuality, *The Sexual Response of the Human Male* (Kinsey, Pomeroy, and Martin 1948) and *The Sexual Response of the*

Human Female (Kinsey, Pomeroy, Martin et al. 1953). Within the pages of their comprehensive reports, they document the sexual response of infants soon after birth and the existence of the preadolescent orgasm. As for the prevalence rate of childhood sexual activities, they provide data indicating that about half of their sample reported preadolescent heterosexual and homosexual sexual play, but they believed that the rates were probably much higher. They attribute the suppression in the numbers to the reluctance on the part of research participants to disclose early-onset sexual experiences because of concern about the social reaction to such behavior.

Kinsey described the first sexual experiences as emerging from incidental interactions that flow from normal play activities or from innocently initiated imitations of sexual behavior. Generally, he viewed the behavior as normal and healthy, a product of curiosity about sex and sexual anatomy. He did not see the behavior as deviant or as a risk marker for later sexual aggression. He found little evidence that a child's sexual experiences resulted in any lasting damage to his or her psyche or later sexual life. Any residual guilt reaction was induced by the parents and was viewed as more harmful than the sexual experience itself. On the issue of the effects of sexual abuse of children, he had the following to say:

> If a child were not culturally conditioned, it is doubtful if it would be disturbed by sexual approaches of the sort which had usually been involved in their histories. It is difficult to understand why a child, except for its cultural conditioning, should be disturbed at having its genitalia touched, or disturbed at seeing the genitalia of other persons, or disturbed at even more specific sexual contacts. When children are constantly warned by parents and teachers against contacts with adults, and when they receive no explanation of the exact nature of the forbidden contacts, they are ready to become hysterical as soon as any older person approaches, or stops and speaks to them in the street, or fondles them, or proposes to do something for them, even though the adult may have had no sexual objective in mind. Some of the more experienced students of juvenile problems have come to believe that the emotional reactions of the parents, police officers, and other adults who discover that the child has had such a contact, may disturb the child more seriously than the sexual contacts themselves. The current hysteria over sex offenders may very well have serious effects on the ability of many of these children to work out sexual adjustments some years later in their marriages. (Kinsey, Pomeroy, Martin et al. 1953, 120-21)

Kinsey found within his own data an increase in sexual activity for those born after 1920 compared to those born before 1920, indicating a steady but slow rise over the course of the early 20th century in the rate of adolescents participating in sex. Recent data indicates that a greater proportion of adolescents are having sexual intercourse before age 15, with nearly a quarter reporting having engaged in this behavior, and about two-thirds by age 18, suggesting that sexual intercourse during high school is a normative experience for the contemporary adolescent (Sonenstein, Ku, and Pleck 1997). Even more recent data indicates that some of these trends may be reversing, or at least flattening out (Bancroft 2006; Santelli, Lindberg, Abma et al. 2000). Fewer adolescents are having sexual intercourse, but those who do are having it earlier. The decrease in sexual intercourse appears to be offset by more diverse sexual activity, such as oral sex, than in the past (Savin-Williams and Diamond 2004). Overall, there exists a much more sexually active adolescent today than at the time of Kinsey, but the general cultural concern about sexually rampaging teenagers may be much exaggerated.

There have been a number of recent research reports updating the Kinsey data for children and adolescents. Some fifty years after Kinsey and his team, the Kinsey Institute at Indiana University collected more recent research data to identify general changes in the sexual activities and behaviors of adults and children over time. One recent study compared the childhood sexual experiences of a sample of university students with the original Kinsey data (Reynolds, Herbenick, and Bancroft 2003). The researchers asked the sample of participants to recall prior childhood sexual experiences and found an overall increase in such experiences with peers compared to the rates reported by Kinsey and his research team. The rate change was most pronounced for female subjects, who had doubled their rate of involvement in childhood sexual experiences, from 42% to 84%. The male participants reported a more modest increase, from 68% to 87%. The most prevalent reason they gave for their sexual behavior sounded very adolescent—simple curiosity and the thrill of doing something illicit.

They reported differences for the sexes for the first appearance of sexual attraction, with boys estimating their first awareness of a sexual attraction at age 11 and girls being conscious of it at age 13. These estimates must be regarded with some caution since they are based on retrospective recall, a notoriously fallible measuring method. They also found that males reported an earlier onset of sexual fantasies than females, with 55% of boys beginning prior to puberty compared to only 38% of girls. However, these rates may also be distorted by a reporting bias whereby women participants presumed it was socially unacceptable to have sexual fantasies as a child.

There have been other researchers who have followed in Kinsey's footsteps, attempting to define the parameters of childhood sexual experiences. In a study of about one thousand male and female undergraduates who responded to an anonymous questionnaire containing questions about childhood sexual encounters with other children and adults, 42% of the participants reported having experienced a sexual encounter prior to the age of 13 with another child more three years older than they (Haugaard and Tilly 1988). Another way of describing this result is that nearly half of the sample could be defined as having been victims of a juvenile sex offender when they were children, although from their subjective accounts and descriptions of the experience, it is not at all clear that they would characterize the experience this way. The majority reported a single encounter with an opposite-sex friend, and the experiences were mostly limited to sexual hugging and kissing and genital exposure. When direct sexual contact occurred, it was typically limited to genital fondling. Sexual intercourse was rare. When the encounter occurred with a friend, it was typically rated as positive. The type or extent of the sexual contact was not related to the child's rate of enjoying it. Encounters that occurred with strangers or same-sex partners or that were coerced were more likely to be rated as negative. It was the nature of the relation—friend versus stranger or same-sex versus opposite-sex, and the absence of coercion— that determined their level of enjoying the encounter, not the type of sexual act itself.

In another study of 128 college women in the early 1990s, 85% reported having engaged in sexual games or play as children (Lamb and Coakley 1993). The mean age for the initiation of the sexual play was about 7.5 years. About a quarter of the sample played their sexual games with an older peer and about a fifth with a younger one; nearly half reported having engaged in sexual activities with a different-aged peer. The majority of the sample perceived the experience as normal, with 84% of the narratives about the experience being rated as noncoercive. A third of the sample reported genital fondling, and only a few reported oral-genital contact and simulated intercourse. Most indicated that they found the experience arousing and exciting.

The largest scientific survey of the sexual behavior of Americans since Kinsey's report was the National Health and Social Life Survey (NHSLS;

Laumann, Gagnon, Michael et al. 1994; Michael, Gagnon, Laumann et al. 1994). In this national sample, thirty-five hundred adults between the ages of 18 and 59 were surveyed regarding their childhood sexual experiences, subsequent sexual history, and current sexual practices. Because it surveyed such a wide age span of participants, the NHSLS study could identify trends and changes in the sexual behavior of adolescents in America over many decades. The one area where the research team found a high degree of uniformity across age groups was the participants' attitudes about teen sex. A total of 80% of the participants believed that teen sex is always wrong or almost always wrong. This attitude was endorsed even when the person reported an early age of onset for intercourse in his or her own history. There seems to be a long-standing and fairly rigid divide between the attitudes of adults about teen sex and the sexual behavior of teens—even that of the adult survey subjects, given that they described their own teenage sex lives as fairly active.

Over the course of several decades, the survey found a slight trend for earlier experiences of first intercourse but nothing that would indicate a sexual revolution among America's teenagers. Men and women born in the decade 1933-1942 on average had sexual intercourse at age 18. Twenty and thirty years later, those born between 1962 and 1967 had sexual intercourse about a half-year earlier—a rate of change that averaged about two months a decade. Generally, male youth had intercourse earlier than female youth, and black youth, particularly black males, had intercourse at an earlier age than white youth. Survey subjects from intact families and higher educational backgrounds tended to have sexual intercourse later.

An unexpected finding of the survey was the strong regulatory effect marriage had on sexual behavior. First, it is a social institution that a vast majority of Americans participate in, and no matter what their sexual behavior was like prior to their becoming wed, whether they initiated sexual intercourse early or not, or had many premarital sexual relations or not, married people have remarkably similar sexual lives. There was no strong evidence for high rates of extramarital affairs. The single most profound demographic shift having the largest effect on the sexual lives of young people, including adolescents, is the trend for marriage to occur later in life, often into the late twenties. When marriage occurred earlier in life, as early as 17 or 18, it regulated the age at which premarital sexual intercourse was initiated, limited the number of sexual partners, and limited the problem of unwanted teen pregnancy. As marriage was delayed and premarital sex became more common and acceptable, this opened the door for people to have more sexual partners simply because they remained unmarried for a longer period of time and had time to accumulate more partners. It also decreased the age of premarital sex among teenagers. Teenage sex would obviously not be viewed as a social problem within a legally sanctioned marriage, even if the married partners were as young as 17.

Overall, the results of national surveys have generally agreed that there has been a gradual rise in the proportion of adolescents who have experienced sexual intercourse, with a reduction for the age of first intercourse but a significant decrease in the pregnancy rate (Guttmacher Institute 2006). Nearly half of all 15-19-year-olds in the United States have had sexual intercourse at least once. But sex remains relatively rare among very young teens. Only 13% of teens have had sexual intercourse by age 15. By age 19, about 70% of them have engaged in sexual intercourse. The mean age has remained about 17 years old for the onset of sexual intercourse, a full decade before the average marriage age. There is evidence that more recently teens are waiting longer, reversing the slow decrease in mean age that has accumulated over the past five or six decades. Nearly two-thirds of teen girls report that their first sexual partner was between a year and three years older, and more than three-quarters of them report that their first partner was a steady boyfriend, a fiancé, a husband, or a cohabiting partner (Guttmacher Institute 2006).

Another significant change in the sexual lives of adolescents in America since Kinsey's data was collected is that oral sex is a much more prevalent sexual experience among adolescents. In the original Kinsey data oral sex was typically a much more advanced sexual experience, more often occurring after the initiation of sexual intercourse. Since the Kinsey data, oral sex has been placed earlier in the chain of progression of sexual behaviors, more often preceding sexual intercourse. Recent survey data indicates that oral sex is as common as vaginal intercourse among teenage girls (Guttmacher Institute 2006). About half of adolescent boys and girls between the ages of 15 and 19 reported that they had had oral sex, slightly more than the proportion that had had vaginal intercourse. As is the case for sexual intercourse, oral sex is more common among older teens, and teens who report having had sexual intercourse are also more likely to have had oral sex. Nevertheless, nearly a quarter of teenagers who have never had vaginal intercourse have had oral sex. White adolescents and those from higher socioeconomic classes are the subgroup most likely to have had oral sex. The major reasons why teenagers report engaging in oral sex instead of vaginal intercourse are that they want to avoid pregnancy; they perceive oral sex as less in conflict with their moral and religious beliefs; and they want to avoid the risk of STDs. While the survey research indicates that oral sex is more common among adolescents than it was in the past, the data has not supported the recent media scare about an oral sex craze among adolescent girls (Guttmacher Institute 2006; McKay 2004; Remez 2000). Instead, it may be the case that teens view oral sex as less risky and as a less intimate or relationally meaningful sexual expression than vaginal intercourse, a view that may not be shared by adults. There has been some recent research evidence that the "virginity pledges" favored by abstinence-only programs may be unintentionally causing teens to engage in oral sex as a means to technically preserve their virginity (Bruckner and Bearman 2005).

The pursuit of scientific knowledge that flies in the face of prevailing political views is a dangerous affair. On July 12, 1999, in a stunning 355 to 0 vote, the United States House of Representatives forged its own version of government censure of science when it condemned the publication of a scientific paper that challenged the orthodox view on the ravages of childhood sexual abuse (H. Con. Res. 107). The action by Congress, a vote to condemn a scientific paper, is unprecedented in U.S. history. The offending research psychologists were Bruce Rind, a professor of psychology at Temple University, and his colleagues, Phillip Tromovitch of the University of Pennsylvania and Robert Bauserman of the University of Michigan, whose meta-analytic review of the effects of childhood sexual abuse among samples of college students called into question, not by way of opinion but by means of a scientifically quantifiable method of data analysis, the entrenched view that child sexual abuse condemns one to a life of maladjustment and dysfunction (Rind, Tromovitch, and Bauserman 1998).

One would hope that the findings would have unleashed a collective sigh of relief about the resilience and durability of the human spirit to overcome potential adversity. Instead, it brought condemnation to the researchers responsible for the finding and accusations that they were mere apologists for pedophiles and supporters of legally unencumbered access of adults to children for sex. Nothing could be further from the truth.

In the summer of 1998, Rind, Tromovitch, and Bauserman published their research findings in *Psychological Bulletin*, a highly regarded journal published by the American Psychological Association (APA) with a rejection rate of about 90%. The journal focuses on comprehensive reviews of scientific research of important topics in psychology. The journal was established in 1908 and is ranked as one of the most prestigious journals published by APA. The article in question by Rind and colleagues, entitled "A Meta-Analytic Examination of Assumed Properties of Child Sexual Abuse Using College Samples," was subjected to the typical peer review vetting that all manuscripts submitted for publication to *Psychological Bulletin* undergo, and it was published after the recommended revisions by the blind reviewers were made by the authors (Rind, Tromovitch, and Bauserman 2000; Rind, Bauserman, and Tromovitch 2000).

The article proposed to examine the widely held and, as these unwitting researchers would later realize, unshakable assumption that all forms of child sexual abuse are harmful, even devastatingly so. They asserted in the introduction to their article that the association of childhood sexual abuse with long-term harm and maladjustment may be inflated because of the historic reliance on clinical samples in prior research. The exclusive reliance on clinical samples is problematic from a scientific point of view for a variety of reasons. First, clinical samples are not representative of the entire population of people exposed to childhood sexual abuse. They represent only a segment, presumably an extreme segment, as these patients have developed some form of emotional disturbance or maladjustment that may be attributable, though not necessarily so, to their prior sexual abuse. The predominant use of clinical samples excludes from the field of examination those persons who have experienced childhood sexual abuse but do not manifest maladjustment and problems. Thus, leaving them out of the analysis can potentially lead to a spurious association between childhood sexual abuse and the later development of adjustment problems. Second, there are potential built-in methodological problems that occur when clinical samples are used in a retrospective examination of the connection between childhood sexual abuse and later maladjustment. Rind and colleagues warned that "information bias" can arise because patients in search of explanations for their problems are more likely to recall childhood sexual experiences and to perceive them as the underlying cause of their difficulties. Likewise, researchers convinced that childhood sexual abuse is a primary cause of adult maladjustment may set out on a confirmatory search for these factors in the inquiry of their research subjects. A confirmatory bias may also operate at the level of peer review of research wherein reviewers predisposed to connect childhood sexual abuse and adult adjustment problems may favor research articles that confirm their initial beliefs and assumptions.

Rind and colleagues conducted a meta-analysis of fifty-nine research studies that when combined included thirty-five thousand research participants. The participants in the studies were drawn from nonclinical populations. They were all college students who had participated in various retrospective surveys regarding their experience of child sexual abuse and their reactions to this experience. Despite the methodological limitations of retrospective data, the innovative aspect of the Rind, Tromovitch, and Bauserman study was the use of nonclinical participants, which provided a more robust testing of the link between childhood sexual abuse and adult adjustment problems since they had not been selected because they had previously self-identified as clinically in need of mental health services or because they had been identified by the criminal justice system as having committed some illegal act, another form of adult maladjustment that could potentially be explained by their having been the victims of childhood sexual abuse.

Meta-analysis is a well-regarded scientific method that combines research subjects from various research studies into one large research study. The derivation of a large pool of subjects from various studies allows for a more statistically robust testing of hypotheses because of the often enormous sample sizes that are assembled. Meta-analysis is generally considered to be a superior method of data combination to a more subjective review of various studies based on what amounts to a box-score approach, wherein the researchers count the number of studies that support a particular hypothesis and the number of studies that do not support the hypothesis and then decide on the supportability of the hypothesis according to whether there are more studies supporting it than disconfirming it. Meta-analysis bypasses the subjective weighing of a collection of studies by combining the subjects and variables within them into a single large sample and then subjecting them to a quantitative analysis as if they were all part of the same study.

This is essentially what Rind and his colleagues did. They assembled fifty-nine studies that examined the relationship between childhood sexual abuse and later adjustment problems among college students to test whether the deeply entrenched orthodox view about the devastating effects of child sexual abuse would hold up for a sample of nonclinical subjects. If it didn't hold up, a revision of the orthodox view would become necessary.

Rind, Tromovitch, and Bauserman (1998) found that a substantial proportion of the combined subjects reported having been sexually abused as children, with women reporting nearly double the rate of sexual abuse compared to men, 27% vs. 14%. These prevalence rates were generally consistent with what had been previously reported in the research literature. They next examined the association of childhood sexual abuse with poor adjustment and found poor support for the link between the two, with childhood sexual abuse accounting for about 1% of poor adult adjustment; that is, nearly 99% of adult maladjustment seemed to be associated with factors other than childhood sexual abuse. Childhood sexual abuse was associated with poor adjustment, but the association was weak and other factors seemed to account for it better. When the researchers examined the differential effect of family environment on adjustment, they found it to be a much stronger predictor of poor adjustment than childhood sexual abuse.

Childhood sexual abuse is probably confounded by family environment. The two are undoubtedly strongly correlated with each other, maybe even causally connected though the direction of causality may be ambiguous. Another way of saying this is that it is very likely the case that children reared in dysfunctional family systems, ravaged by poverty, conflict, substance abuse, mental illness, or other disfiguring influences, are also more at risk to be sexually abused. Furthermore, it may also be the case that the occurrence of sexual abuse acts as a force producing family dysfunction. The causal arrow between family dysfunction and sexual abuse may be bidirectional; sexual abuse is both a by-product and a cause of a poor family environment. At a basic level it is very artificial to attempt to deal with these two issues as though they were separate variables when they are inexorably intertwined with each other. Nevertheless, when these researchers statistically separated out family-environment factors from child sexual abuse, as artificial as such a separation may be, they found that the association between child sexual abuse and poor adjustment was eliminated, suggesting that the prime cause of poor adult adjustment was family environment and not sexual abuse.

The researchers were meticulous in their explanation that the results uncovered by their analysis applied to the aggregate and that sexual abuse could still be a devastating experience for particular individuals. They never at any time ruled out the possibility that child sexual abuse may be catastrophic for some. But they did introduce doubt that this is necessarily the case for the many.

Rind, Tromovitch, and Bausermann entered treacherous waters when they next examined the effect that level of sexual contact and level of consent had on adult adjustment. It would seem self-evident that the intensity or intimacy of the sexual abuse would be related to adjustment, with more pervasive forms of sexual abuse, like rape, having a more negative effect than noncontact offending, such as exhibitionism. It would also seem likely that the negative effects of child sexual abuse would occur regardless of whether the child consented to the sexual contact or not. Consent in this context—the researchers took great pains to emphasize—did not pertain to legally informed consent, which a child by definition cannot give, but merely to simple consent. Simple consent connotes that the sexual contact was not experienced as forced, coerced, or unwanted. What they found when they isolated these moderating variables was that level of sexual contact was not related to adult adjustment but that level of simple consent was associated with a negative adult adjustment. This differential effect for the level of consent led the researchers to conclude that sexual contact that was simply consented to was not as harmful. It was this finding that resulted in the coming storm that would besiege the researchers despite their attempt to emphasize that their finding about adult-child sexual contact and simple consent does not mean that such contact is permissible or should be decriminalized. The fact that it is established as not empirically harmful (in most instances) does not make it legally or morally permissible in any instance. Rind and his colleagues maintained that adult-child sex is criminal and wrong but properly insist, given their findings, that it is wrong on moral grounds, not empirical ones because they were not able to establish that it necessarily produces harm. This moral-empirical or ought-is distinction is an important one that later got lost in the political fall-out over the study.

Based on their findings, Rind, Bauserman, and Tromovitch (1998, 2000) argue that the current definition of child sexual abuse, which contains all and any form of adult-child sexual contact, works fine as a moral category with proper moral prohibitions but fails miserably as a scientific one. It fails as a scientific category because it is overly expansive and broad, capturing a heterogeneous mix of wanted and unwanted contacts, and as a result it failed to produce predictive validity. The lumping together of all cases of adult-child sexuality as instances of sexual abuse fails to predict harm and maladjustment. Without predictive ability, a construct has little scientific value and meaning. Because of this, in what would later prove to be a misstep, they advocated using a more scientifically neutral term, such as "adolescent-adult sex," for sexual contact where simple consent exists, and reserving the more loaded term "childhood sexual abuse" for instances where such simple consent is absent. They argued that narrowly defining child sexual abuse along these lines will bolster the predictive validity of the term, placing it on better scientific footing. While making the argument of good scientists practicing their craft, they at no time, at any place in the article, suggested that adolescent-adult sex is morally permissible. Being the scientists they are, they simply wanted to be clear that when such a moral position is staked out, it is not based on empirically established grounds of harm.

The firestorm that swirled around the Rind, Bauserman, and Tromovitch (1998) article did not immediately follow its publication. It took about six months for the findings and their implications to settle out and be picked up by the media. But once the controversy hit, it didn't take long for it to wend its way to the floor of the U.S. House of Representatives. The Rind controversy was carried to Resolution 107 on the momentum of a number of socially conservative organizations and media figures (Lillienfeld 2002; Rind, Bauserman, and Tromovitch 2000; Rind, Tromovitch, and Bauserman 2000). The National Association for Research and Therapy of Homosexuality (NARTH; http://www.narth.com), described on its website as "a non-profit organization dedicated to affirming a complementary, male-female model of gender and sexuality," with the core mission of preventing and curing homosexuality, provided the first criticism of the study in December 1998. In March 1999 Laura Schlessinger, host of the *Dr. Laura* syndicated radio program, began an attack on the Rind, Bauserman, and Tromovitch article that lasted several months, referring to it as an instance of "junk science." The Family Research Council (FRC), a socially conservative lobbying group in Washington, D.C., joined the fray, and at a press conference in May 1999 demanded that the American Psychological Association reject the study and its conclusion that children can consent to having sex with adults. Among the participants at the press conference was Dr. Laura, via satellite, a representative from NARTH, and three conservative Republican congressmen: Representatives Delay of Texas, Salmon of Arizona, and Weldon of Florida.

Two days after the press conference, Raymond Fowler, CEO of the APA, appeared on MSNBC defending the peer review process that the study had undergone and the scientific integrity of the study. But a month later, buckling under the mounting criticism and pressure that continued to grow about the study, Fowler wrote a letter to Delay commending him for his stance against sexual abuse and separating the APA from the Rind, Bauserman, and Tromovitch article by declaring that the opinions expressed in the study were not the position of the APA. He reaffirmed the view of the APA that sexual abuse should never be considered harmless or acceptable and that children can never consent to sexual activities with adults. In the letter Fowler, no doubt in an effort to appease the incensed congressman, declared that the APA would seek independent review of the scientific integrity of the article and would take direct steps to advise journal editors to carefully consider the "social policy implications" of controversial topics before deciding to publish them.

Never in its 100-year history had the APA ever moved to have a previously peer-reviewed article reviewed a second time by an independent body, nor had it ever administratively attempted to influence the editors of one of its journals about taking heed before publishing scientific papers that might prove to be controversial or upsetting. The APA asked the American Association for the Advancement of Science (AAAS) to act as an independent reviewer of the Rind, Bauserman, and Tromovitch article. But in the fall of 1999, the AAAS refused to provide an independent review of the article, upholding the integrity of the original peer review process that the editor of the *Psychological Bulletin* had already conducted on the article.

In July 1999, a year after the publication of the controversial article, the U.S. House of Representatives unanimously passed Resolution 107 "rejecting the conclusions of a recent article published in the *Psychological Bulletin*, a journal of the American Psychological Association, that suggests that sexual relationships between adults and children might be positive for them" (H. Con. Res. 107)— although the article never described child-adult sex as potentially positive, only as not necessarily harmful. Resolution 107 furthermore "congratulated" the APA for "clarifying its opposition to any adult-child sexual relations," which, the resolution asserts, will help prevent any pedophile from attempting to cite the article in a legal defense, as well as for taking steps to ensure that the social, legal, and political ramifications of its scientific articles are evaluated prior to publication.

The lessons from the Rind controversy are multiple. Perhaps the most general and overriding cautionary lesson of the story is that it is inherently dangerous when political agendas are allowed to so directly control scientific inquiry and investigation. At some level all scientific activities involve some political agendas, even at the most basic level of what types of scientific studies receive government funding. It is simply naïve to view science as a depoliticized activity. Political and social agendas influence what studies get funded, which studies are to be most widely disseminated, and, at a more fundamental level, even what scientific questions are allowed to be formulated for testing. But there is something utterly sinister when government has such direct overt control on the conduct of science.

The other important lesson raised by the Rind controversy, however, may be more closely associated with the moral panic about childhood sexuality. An important problem to examine from the Rind controversy is why it seems to be the case that the U.S. Congress, the APA, the conservative media, and the various antihomosexual groups got the study all wrong. None of them, it would seem, got the article right. The article in no way ever advocates for making adult-child sex permissible or ever suggests that such sexual relations should be decriminalized because evidence of harm is deficient when the adolescent or child involved is a willing participant on some level. Rind and colleagues were meticulous about maintaining a bright-line separation between the scientific questions and the moral ones at hand. Scientific questions are essentially "is" questions. They purport to depict the state of existence of something. Is it or is it not the case that something is the case? They endeavor to inquire about the state of the world, and in the case of social scientists, the state of the social world as they find it. They do not provide answers to "ought" questions. Whether one ought to do one thing or another is essentially a moral question, and science has very little to say about "ought" issues. Rind and colleagues were careful not to let their "is" conclusions about childhood sexual abuse and adult adjustment get confounded with "ought" questions. The same cannot be said of their critics. They perceived "ought" when Rind and colleagues were talking about "is." Rind and colleagues never in any way conclude that the absence of evidence of harm for *some* forms of childhood sexual abuse should be translated into the conclusion that such sexual relations "ought" to be permissible. Their suggestion to rename willing or simply consensual sex with adults as something more neutral sounding was not an attempt to destigmatize the behavior for the adult—although they might argue that the destigmatization of the "victims" of childhood sexual abuse under these conditions would be a positive development—thereby clearing the way for adults to have unimpeded sex with children. They advocate the name change solely for the purpose of bringing some order to the field of research about child sexual abuse. The cleaning up of the category of child sexual abuse to exclude children who do not manifest harm is a suggestion made to improve the predictive validity of a construct that had come to be too broad to be meaningful. Some housekeeping of the construct would improve the science around it.

Rind, Tromovitch, and Bauserman (1998) advocated a refinement of the concept of childhood sexual abuse. They did not seek to jettison it. This false charge was pinned on them by others reacting in a near-hysterical fashion to any hint that childhood sexual abuse is anything but a disfiguring and permanently scarring event that warps the psyche and spirit of the child victim for life. The question remains as to why all those involved in this sexual drama got it so wrong. How did they miss this point so completely? Why were Rind, Tromovitch, and Bausermann demonized for their research about childhood sexual abuse? Were their critics blinded by the suggestion that childhood sexual abuse may be other than devastating and harmful? What touched off this firestorm reaction that seemed so far off the mark?

James Kincaid, in his 1998 book *Erotic Innocence: The Culture of Child Molesting*, set out to understand the contemporary obsession with child sexual abuse and child molesting. He refers to the endless stories about child molestation that haunt the imagination as Gothic narratives, lurid tales without solutions. They function like horror movies for a culture under stress. Like any good horror movie, these stories create a villain— enter the sexual predator, the pedophile—transformed from a run-of-the-mill criminal offender to some incarnation of pure evil, beyond redemption or salvation. Kincaid translates the cycle-of-abuse notion into a Gothic narrative, where the sexually abused are condemned to sexually abuse others, and so on, with the sexually abused geometrically increasing, like werewolves or zombies. The allure of this narrative is similar to the impulse that gathers strangers together in a darkened movie theater to have the wits scared out of them: the need for a focus, a target, where one can input all of one's fears and play out one's fantasies of mastery and control. The sexual predator appears to explain so much. If only he were contained and mastered, the world could be safe again. He, like the monster on the screen, draws the attention of the audience away from the seemingly insurmountable structural social problems that plague the world, focusing attention instead on him. Regardless of how the statistics are tallied, or how the definition is crafted, childhood sexual abuse has

come nowhere near to the accumulated harm done by the more perni-
cious social problems of poverty, poor education, childhood neglect and
physical abuse, lack of health care, and inadequate housing. Pedophiles
are the target because they are easier to focus on than the other problems
that would require a greater collective commitment.

Concerns about child sexual abuse move along historical cycles, like
a swinging pendulum. Jenkins (1998) suggests that the current wave of
concern may be the third cycle. The first wave occurred between 1890 and
1920 and the second between 1940 and 1950. Each of the cycles is sprung
from a particular historical concern. At the turning of the 19th century
it was immigration; in the 1940s and 1950s it was World War II and the
dawning of the baby boom. Currently it may be a backlash to the wom-
en's movement and women's increasing economic autonomy and entrance
into the work force. While mother was at work, day care centers in the
1980s and 1990s purportedly became overrun by pedophile rings seizing
an opportunity.

Jenkins fears that the current cycle of fear about childhood sexual abuse
may have broken free from its axle, becoming part of the permanent cultural landscape, an inexhaustible metanarrative that explains all social ills
and problems. A peculiar development from the current cycle of moral
panic about sexual abuse has been the expansion of deviant medicalized
labels applied to adolescent sexual behavior that would have previously
been perceived as harmless sex play.

The problem with the romantic idea of the child as sexually pure and innocent is that it wraps the sexuality of children within a frame of fear. The
expression of sex in children evokes anxiety and dread about the worst—
a reaction that is undoubtedly communicated to children. As a result
children are often educated only about the worst aspects of sex. Suzanne
Frayser (2003), a cultural anthropologist specializing in cross-cultural research on human sexuality, argues that the collective denial of childhood
sexuality may carry within it a set of unintended negative consequences.
In the rush to deny childhood sexuality, the opportunity to address sex
in a more rational and accepting manner is foreclosed. The denial of its
existence drives sexuality underground, erecting a wall of silence, pro-
hibiting discussion about sex between adults and adolescents. Frayser
refers to the persistent portrayal of children and adolescents as sexually
innocent, the denial of knowledge about their sexuality, as an instance of
"asexual abuse." The insistence that children are devoid of sexuality does

them more harm than good. Keeping them in the dark will not make their sexuality disappear. Sex will go underground and adolescents will be left to construct their sexual identities from distorted media sources like movies, MTV, and popular music. More harm can result from a lack of knowledge. Knowledge can empower and bring rational choices and sound decision making about sexuality. There may be other potential harm resulting from the ideologically restrictive view of sexuality in children. John Money (1986), the noted sexologist, has warned that many of the paraphilias, including pedophilia, may develop from a lack of knowledge about sexuality or from a rejecting or punishing response to its expression. Juvenile sexual offending, following his line of reasoning, may be due not to oversexualization or sexual abuse but to the denial of sex and the repression of its healthy expression.

The discomfort, the unsettledness, about children and sex, the concern that the premature exposure of children to sexuality will irrevocably harm them, should not be misconstrued as meaning there has been a vast cultural silence about children and sexuality. The denial of childhood sexuality, the persistent portrayal of children as sexually pure and innocent, has been subjected to nonstop discourse. Michel Foucault (1978) was the first to identify the endless discourses that have been promulgated since the 18th and 19th centuries in the emerging medical sciences of the time about the perils of precocious sex, even masturbation, which was thought to result in sterility, feeble-mindedness, and even insanity. The present age is still resonating from this historical moment. Prior to the appearance of these incessant discourses, there was a long-standing freedom of language between children and adults that disappeared when childhood sexuality was banished to obscurity. While strict, impenetrable walls of silence were erected around children regarding matters of sex, the same was not true of childhood sexuality. Instead, new regimes of concern about childhood sexuality were installed, what Foucault called "a deployment of sexuality," wherein childhood sexuality became a constant preoccupation and source of danger. There has been a cultural denial about the existence of sexuality in children but not a denial of constant discourse about that absence. The absence, the lack of sex in children, has been the subject of constant chatter. And from this obsessive chatter has emerged a constant alert with manifold plans for surveillance. "Around the school boy and his sex there proliferated a whole literature of precepts, opinions, observations, medical advice, clinical cases, outlines for reform and plans for ideal institutions" (Foucault 1978, 28).

The constant concern about childhood sexuality has resulted in a massive historical effort to regulate it and place it under pedagogical control. It came under closer scrutiny—indeed, micro-analytical examination—and was continuously sifted and pored over in an effort to uncover every aspect of it, no matter how well hidden in the deepest residues of consciousness and experience. It was diagnosed, treated, subjected to preventive strategies, sanitized, anticipated, and circumvented. Constant attention and focus were required to control and manage it, although there was no hope of ever being able to completely eliminate it. In Foucault's analysis, the goal was never complete annihilation, just sufficient control, a reduction of childhood sexuality to its asymptotic limit.

The sex of children was problematized as a contaminating toxin that zaps intellectual, moral, and spiritual development. The child as sexually innocent and pure was historically implanted, and any violation of this view was greeted as a cataclysmic event. Sex was seen as posing grievous physical harm, moral corruption, and spiritual death. Parents were placed on alert status, and forces of medical and pedagogical experts arose to ally with parents against the sexual scourge. Psychiatry and childhood pedagogy emerged as technologies, imbued not with science but with moral force, with the power to counteract the disfiguring instinct of sex. It was morality, not empirical science, that crept into the ideas about children and sex. The concern about sexual precocity in children and adolescents is as strong today as it was a century ago, and the evidence to support the concern has still not arrived.

"Children who molest children," "children with sexual behavior problems," "abuse-reactive children," "sexualized children"—all are examples of new clinical terminology covering younger and younger children. They express new moral scourges requiring new strategies of eradication, exemplifying a "definitional creep" (Kincaid 1998) of juvenile-sex-offender categories drifting over younger adolescents and even prepubescent children. It is another instance of what Ian Hacking (2002, 2006) referred to as the creation of new human kinds. Sexual behavior in children that in the past or within another cultural context would have barely registered a reaction is now pathologized as a new kind of disorder that carries hidden within it a germ that grows into a sexually deviant adult life form. These newly erected categories are not static and inert, hollowed out boxes that have been waiting to be discovered. They are buzzing, interactive, and productive. The activity of diagnosing new human kinds is not like the biologist walking through the forest labeling the various forms of fauna and flora encountered along the journey. Newly discovered species of plants and animals do not react to the labels placed on them, but children do. The invention of the category "children with sexual behavior problems" has brought forth new regimes of assessment and treatment developed to counteract this new form of pathology. The new categories of sexual pathologies in children are built on the fault line of the assumption that sexual behavior in children is the result of trauma. It is the precocious exposure to sex that prompts the child to sexual expression. Mary Douglas (1966) emphasized the importance of context to a culture's notion of contamination and purity. Dirt found in the garden is considered perfectly natural and organic. Dirt in a garden is not dirty. It is soil, an earthy loam rich in nutrients, something one wants to dig one's hands into. But that very same soil on the bedroom floor is dirt, filth, a contaminant brushed up with broom and dustpan and quickly removed and disposed of. Dirt in the house is "matter out of place." Childhood sexuality works along similar lines: it is behavior out of place and as such it is perceived as representing pathology, abnormality, risk, and harm. The sexual behavior of children, like dirt on the floor as opposed to the garden, is matter out of place and is treated like a polluting substance that needs to be removed and eradicated.

William Friedrich, discussed earlier, began his research career with sexually abused children with the confident belief that sexual behavior in children was a reliable indicator of sexual abuse. He quickly became dissuaded of this notion when it became unavoidably clear to him that a sizable number of the most carefully screened samples of nonabused children displayed sexual behavior, even some of the more advanced forms of sexual behavior, such as "putting mouth on genitals of other children" and "insertion of objects in vagina" (Friedrich 2003).

Friedrich constructed a parent report measure of the sexual behavior of their children called the Child Sexual Behavior Inventory (CSBI; Friedrich 1997). He attempted to develop norms for the instrument from an initial validation sample of 880 2- to 12-year-old predominantly white children from middle-class families without a history of sexual abuse. They had no reported developmental disability and had not received mental health counseling in the previous six months. To his surprise he found that sexual behavior was nearly ubiquitous within this sample of children, with more than 20% of them endorsing ten of the thirty-five items and at least 50% endorsing four of the items. It quickly became clear to him that distinguishing sexually abused from non-sexually abused children on the basis of their display of sexual behavior was not going to be a straightforward matter. "Consequently," he admitted, "I began to increasingly consider the normative aspects of children's sexual behavior" (Friedrich 2003, 111). As discussed previously, further validation of the instrument revealed that parental attitudes about sex influenced the manifestation of a child's sexual behavior

Sexual behavior in children was a more complex and multifaceted phenomenon than Friedrich had anticipated. The simplistic assumption of a one-to-one correspondence between sexual behavior in children and sexual abuse needed to be revised. Sexual behavior is not unique to sexually abused children. The idea that sexual behavior in children must be caused by sexual abuse was based on the assumption that children are sexually pure and innocent and that they must have been contaminated by sexual abuse if they were displaying such behavior. Sex is not a part of childhood, the assumption reads, and if it shows up it must have been put there by someone—a version of Mary Douglas's "dirt is matter out of place" idea. Subsequent research by Friedrich (1997) demonstrated that sexually abused children often exhibited greater frequency and diversity of sexual behavior but that sexual behavior was not exclusively manifested by them. Moreover, nonabused children with psychiatric problems manifested as great a level and diversity of sexual behavior as did sexually abused children, suggesting that high rates of sexual behavior may be a nonspecific factor indicative of general emotional distress and not an exclusive sign of sexual abuse. Elevated displays of sexual behavior seem to be just like any other behavioral problem, like aggression, oppositionality, or defiance. It is just another way children manifest or express emotional stress. The fact that the behavior is sexual does not necessarily carry any specific diagnostic meaning.

The promoters of the new category of sexualized children or children with sexual behavior problems warned about the perils of the continued denial and minimization of the seriousness of this emerging population, imploring that the behavior of these child perpetrators not be ignored any longer. Consider this description of this newly established population offered by Johnson (1988):

It is now time to acknowledge the existence of another population whose sexual behavior must be taken seriously. This population is preadolescent, latency-aged, and pre-school children who sexually victimize children younger than themselves. . . . Sexual behavior between children 13 years old and younger is generally dismissed as "playing doctor" or normal childhood exploration. While this is true in the majority of cases, there is a sub-population of children whose sexual behavior is beyond what is to be expected normally and requires assessment and, possibly, intervention by the mental health system. (220)

Johnson also advocated for the criminal prosecution of child perpetrators between the ages of 4 and 12. The criteria for inclusion for this newly forged clinical category of sexual offender are broad: any sexual act with another child or a pattern of sexually overt behavior in the child's history. Coercion is expanded to include even verbal cajoling, bribes, or enticements. Johnson consistently refers to sexual behavior among the very young as abnormal without reference to baseline norms, since she admits that none exist. "While norms do not presently exist for what is normal sexual behavior of children, the behaviors exhibited . . . led us to label the behaviors as being outside the normal range of sexual activity for their age group" (Johnson 1988, 221).

The Child Sexual Behavior Checklist (CSBCL; Gil and Johnson 1993) is an expansive 150-item behavioral inventory designed by Johnson to capture sexual behavior "ranging from natural and healthy explorations to behaviors of children experiencing severe difficulty in the area of sexuality" (Gil and Johnson 1993, 329). The words "natural" and "healthy" should immediately give one pause—"natural" and "healthy" from whose point of view? Presumably the author's, as this instrument is based on clinical experience and has never been subjected to empirical validation (Okami 1992). The CSBCL is a hodge-podge of normal-seeming sexual behaviors that are relabeled as deviant and described as outside the normal range for children from preschool and kindergarten age to fourth graders: "touch/rub genitals in public after being told not to do this," "continues to ask questions about genital differences after all questions have been answered," "keeps asking people sexual questions even after parent has answered questions at age-appropriate level," "wants to be nude in public after parent says no," "interest in watching bathroom functions does not wane," "frequently plays doctor and gets caught after being told no," "sex talk gets child into trouble," "shows an interest in where babies are made," "plays doctor or hospital with other children," "talks about opposite sex in a negative way, such as girls are stupid and boys are dumb and noisy," "wants parents to stop sexual behavior like kissing or speaking romantically," and so on. These behaviors are recast as symptoms of sexual deviance despite the agreement of many development psychologists and sexologists that sexual rehearsal in children is healthy and cross-culturally consistent (Money 1993).

Carolyn Cunningham and Kee MacFarlane open their 1991 workbook of group treatment strategies for young sexual abusers, entitled *When Children Molest Children,* with the following statement in the preface:

> This book is for and about sex offenders. No, not the ones in trench coats who hang out in playgrounds. This book is for the ones who go to play-grounds to play ball and swing on the swings. It is about the young ones, the not-yet-adolescents, the kids whom none of us wants to see labeled with pejorative terms like "offender" or "perpetrator." And yet, these are the children whose behavior can be defined by these terms. (1991, v)

Like Johnson (1988) before them, the authors declare that the existence of this group has been previously overlooked. They warn that one should not be fooled by their small bodies and immature minds. Their behavior emanates from the same psychological dynamics as that of their adult counterparts: the abuse of power. The terms used to describe these children—"abuse-reactive children" or "sexualized children"—were derived to reflect the staunchly held belief that these children had been sexually abused in *some way* and are reacting to their early sexual trauma, often unrecalled by them, in sexually abusive ways. The authors adopt an addiction model for the diagnosis and treatment of these children, seeing their behavior as a form of sexual addiction or compulsion. "Certainly none of us wants to look into the eyes of young children and see the seeds of potential destructiveness" (Cunningham and MacFarlane 1991) but to avoid seeing them as such, the reader is told, is tantamount to denial.

More recent scholarly reviews have, if not challenged the validity of the category known as childhood sexual behavior problems, at least tempered its more unsupported claims. A task force assembled by the Association for the Treatment of Sexual Abusers (ATSA) concluded in a 2006 report that sexual behavior problems in children do not represent a medical/psychological syndrome or a specific diagnosable disorder but rather a pattern or set of behaviors that exist outside of normative sexual behavior for children. The report, however, is silent on the issue of where one can obtain information about normal sexual behavior against which such judgments can be made. They admit that no data exists on prevalence rates and that the etiology of the problem remains unclear, but assert that sexual abuse is no longer a necessary and sufficient cause, though it may place a child at greater risk for the problem. There is no profile or pattern of demographics that makes up the group of children displaying sexual behavior problems. There are no distinct subtypes. Most importantly, there is no longitudinal research about the developmental outcomes of these children. It is simply unknown what happens to them. Whether they grow out of their overly sexualized behavior completely, transition to some other problems, or continue on a sexually deviant pathway remains undetermined.

There have been two large, federally funded, randomized-treatment-outcome research projects on children with sexual behavior problems. The first randomly assigned 115 children with sexual behavior problems to either a relapse-prevention treatment group or an expressive therapy group (Gray, Pithers, Busconi et al. 1999; Pithers, Gray, Busconi et al. 1998). The expressive therapy group was educational, focusing primarily on teaching about sexual rules and boundaries, helping subjects understand the effects of sexual abuse, and teaching emotional management, problem solving, and social skills. The relapse-prevention treatment focused on identifying precursors to sexual behavior and enacting intervention strategies. This treatment group also assembled a prevention team consisting of members of the family's everyday life who were willing to support the family in its adoption of an abuse-prevention style of life (ATSA 2006; Pithers, Gray, Busconi et al. 1998). They found at followup that both treatment groups had significantly improved and there was no significant difference between them on their rates of sexual behavior problems. However, a more highly traumatized group did respond better to the relapse-prevention treatment.

The second study randomly assigned children with sexual behavior problems to either a 12-session group treatment where they learned various cognitive-behavioral skills or a 12-session play-therapy control group (Bonner, Walker, and Berliner 1999). The cognitive-behavioral treatment group was highly structured, using a combination of education and behavior modification principles to address the identification and acknowledgment of inappropriate sexual behavior and teaching self-control techniques. The therapists taught specific behavioral child-management skills for preventing problematic sexual behavior. The play therapy group was much less structured and minimally directive. Treatment sessions began with a discussion of a theme relating to sexual behavior problems, but rather than being directive and educational, the group consisted of an open discussion of the issue with the therapist often following the caregivers' lead. After a two-year followup, the researchers reported a reduction in sexual behavior problems in both groups, with 15-17% incurring an additional report of a sexual behavior problem. Neither approach emerged as more effective than the other. A 10-year followup of the sample, however, found a marked advantage for the cognitive-behavioral group, who had a significantly lower arrest rate, 2%, than the control group, 10% (Carpentier, Silovsky, and Chaffin 2006). Interestingly, the cognitive-behavioral group had a similar arrest rate as a clinical comparison group of children diagnosed with Attention Deficit Disorder or other behavioral problems but with no history of sexual behavior problems. The result suggests that childhood sexual behavior problems may be similar to other childhood behavioral problems. This finding argues that children labeled as having sexual behavior problems may be more similar to than different from children with other mental health diagnoses.

These studies converge to offer a few very important conclusions about children with so-called sexual behavior problems. First, there is no supporting empirical evidence that they are tomorrow's sexual offenders in the making who without intervention will move on to sexually deviant careers. According to empirical research, they are actually at low risk to reoffend in the future and there appears to be no strong evidence that they are much different from other children displaying the symptoms of psychological distress or maladjustment. Second, there seems therefore to be little support for the automatic recommendation that they be removed from their homes and placed in restrictive exclusionary treatment programs. In most cases they can remain at home with proper support and supervision.

Collective fears about the disfiguring effects of sexuality on children were probably at work in the response of the Brockton public school system to the incident of the 6-year-old boy who pulled the waistband of his female classmate. Concern extended no doubt to the "victim" but it was the "perpetrator" of this act who provoked the greatest concern. His behavior was assigned the most sinister meanings: budding sexual predator, a sex offender in the making. Why else would they expel him and refer his case to the district attorney for consideration for prosecution? The incident is emblematic, representative, of a growing fear, panic really, about the convergence of two figures, the sexualized child and the sexual offender, coming together to form the juvenile sex offender. It is new fears about this new figure, the juvenile sex offender, that are driving the increasingly punitive legal response to him —transfer to adult court for prosecution, civil commitment as a sexually dangerous person, and the requirements for registration and community notification as a sexual offender—that occupy the chapters ahead.

6

Becoming a Man

The Waiver of the Juvenile Sex
Offender to Adult Court

In 1967 a 15-year-old juvenile sex offender from Arizona caused a revolutionary change in the juvenile court with nothing more than a phone call. His case, decided by the United States Supreme Court, forever changed the juvenile court from an institution founded on the rehabilitative ideal into the more formal due process institution that it is today (*In re Gault* 387 U.S. 1, 1967). For nearly three-quarters of a century, beginning in 1899, when the charter for the first juvenile court was passed by the Illinois state legislature establishing the juvenile court in Chicago, the juvenile court was an informal institution where juveniles, often without the aid of legal counsel or other due process protections, had their cases decided on the basis, presumably, of their individual rehabilitative needs. But unrestrained discretionary power, no matter how "benevolently motivated," is often at risk for abuse and does not always translate into compassionate treatment. The juvenile court had exercised unchecked decision-making authority over the lives of juvenile offenders since its invention. The case of Gerald Gault changed that.

Gerald Gault and a friend were taken into custody by the sheriff of Gila County, Arizona, in June 1964 as a result of a complaint by a female neighbor, Mrs. Cook, regarding an obscene call made to her. Judge Abe Fortas, writing the majority opinion, described the remarks as being of the "irritatingly offensive, adolescent, sex variety" (*In re Gault* 1967, 1432). Gerald was detained by the police for this offense and placed in a detention center. At the time, he was on probation for having been in the company of another juvenile who had stolen a wallet from a woman's purse. Both of his parents were working and not at home. No effort was made to contact them and advise them that their son had been arrested. It was not until his mother arrived home at 6:00 p.m. that she discovered he was not at home. She was informed by the parents of Gerald's codefendant that he had been arrested, had been placed in a detention center, and was scheduled to be arraigned the next day in juvenile court.

A formal complaint against Gerald was filed but no one was sworn in at the hearing and no recording or transcript of the proceedings was made. At a habeas corpus hearing held about two months later, the U.S. Supreme Court had to rely on testimony from various parties at the original hearing, including the juvenile court judge, the probation officer, and Mrs. Gault. There was some discrepancy among the various parties regarding whether Gerald ever admitted making the lewd statements over the telephone. His mother's memory was that he admitted dialing the phone and handing it to his codefendant, who made the remarks. The juvenile court judge recalled that Gerald admitted uttering some of the remarks. No record of the hearing, which might have arbitrated the conflicting reports, was made. Gerald had been charged with making "lewd phone calls," and he was committed as a delinquent child to Arizona's state industrial school until age 21, a potential 6-year period of incarceration. The Arizona Criminal Code listed his offense as a misdemeanor and provided that an adult found guilty of using vulgar, abusive, or obscene language in the presence of a woman or child was subject to a fine between five and fifty dollars or imprisonment for not more than two months. The state of Arizona did not provide for the appeal of juvenile court adjudications and commitments.

The U.S. Supreme Court, reflecting on the performance of the juvenile court, concluded that

> the results have not been entirely satisfactory. Juvenile Court history has again demonstrated that unbridled discretion, however benevolently motivated, is frequently a poor substitute for principle and procedure. . . . The absence of substantive standards has not necessarily meant that children receive compassionate, individualized treatment. The absence of procedural rules based upon constitutional principles has not always produced fair, efficient, and effective procedures. Departure from established principles of due process has frequently resulted not in enlightened procedure, but in arbitrariness. (*In re Gault* 1967, 1439)

Prior to *Gault* (1967), the adolescent caught within the web of control of a juvenile court devoid of any of the due process protections naturally extended to the mature and responsible adult had virtually no protections against the juvenile court's nearly carte blanche discretion to do whatever it deemed fit, even if that meant confining the adolescent in an industrial-training or reform school for a long period of time. *Gault* (1967) tore away the closed curtain shrouding the juvenile court and looked critically at the wide gulf between its promise of rehabilitation and its actual practice. On behalf of Gerald Gault and the millions upon millions of juveniles who had stood before the juvenile court during its nearly 70-year history, Fortas wrote,

> It is of no constitutional consequence—and of limited practical mean-ing—that the institution to which he is committed is called an Industrial School. The fact of the matter is that, however euphemistic the title, a "re-ceiving home" or an "Industrial School" for juveniles, it is an institution of confinement in which the child is incarcerated for a greater or a lesser time. His world becomes "a building with whitewashed walls, regimented routine and institutional hours." Instead of mother, father, sisters and brothers, friends, and classmates, his world is peopled by guards, custo-dians, state employees, and "delinquents" confined with him for anything from waywardness to rape and homicide. (1443)

Gault brought formal procedure to the juvenile court. In the post-*Gault* juvenile court, juveniles receive formal notice of their charges, have a right to counsel, are afforded the opportunity to confront and cross-examine their accusers, have a right against self-incrimination, and have the right to be provided transcript recordings of their trial and hear-ings, as well as appellate review of their adjudications. Almost all the due process protections extended to adults are now available to juveniles, who are shielded, at least in theory, from the dubious historically humanitarian mission of the juvenile court that the *Gault* court had exposed. But what these liberating authors of *Gault* may not have contemplated was the pos-sible negative effect that granting adolescents adult-like rights might have on the juvenile court's perception of the adolescents before them. Armed with due process rights, "lawyered up" and ready to fight, the post-*Gault* juvenile begins to resemble the adult defendant. He no longer appears de-pendent and immature but more like his rational and free-acting adult counterpart, able to defend and protect himself, and as a result he may be opening himself up to receiving more adult-like forms of retributional punishment.

The Court was not unanimous in its decision. Justice Stewart Potter, in a lone dissenting opinion, raised concern about the rights-based juvenile court born from *Gault*:

> I believe the Court's decision is wholly unsound . . . and sadly unwise. . . . Juvenile proceedings are not criminal trials. . . . A juvenile proceeding's whole purpose and mission is the very opposite of the mission and purpose of a prosecution in a criminal court. The object of the one is correction of a condition. The object of the other is conviction and punishment for a criminal act. . . . To impose the Court's long catalog of requirements upon juvenile proceedings in every area of the country is to invite a long step backwards into the nineteenth century. (*In re Gault* 1967, dissenting opinion, 1470-71)

Justice Potter seemed aware of the risk of this transformative decision, and the slippery slope that it created. It would be many years before it would become clear whether he was prescient or alarmist.

The 1990s may go down as the hardest decade in the centenarian juvenile justice system. It was the decade when state legislatures across the country, in a domino-like effect, in reaction to an unprecedented juvenile crime wave, began a wide-scale further retraction of the rehabilitative ideal of the juvenile court begun by *Gault* (1967). It was the decade that nearly signaled the death knell for the juvenile court, threatening to collapse it back into the adult court from which it had emerged at the dawn of the 20th century. Justice Potter had warned that the seeds sown by *Gault* might reap this transformation.

It is difficult to pinpoint a specific cause of the "juvenile crime wave" that hit the United States in the late 1980s and early 1990s (Zimring 1998). The upturn in violent juvenile crime began in the late 1980s, and it was not until the mid-1990s that the epidemic of juvenile crime settled down to a level lower than at the start of the crime wave (Snyder and Sickmund 2006; Zimring 1998). But though these numbers receded, nearly every state, believing that the staggeringly increased rates of juvenile crime were portentous of a new era of juvenile violence that was here to stay and only going to get worse, enacted stricter laws governing the waiver—in some states it is referred to as "transfer" or "certification"—of youth from juvenile court to adult court (Zimring and Fagan 2000).

A total of forty-six states passed legislation enabling the swifter, automatic, and often permanent movement of juvenile offenders to adult criminal court for prosecution of their offenses (Feld 2000; Griffin 2003; Griffin, Torbet, and Szymanski 1998; Torbet, Gable, Hurst, et al. 1996). Most of the legislation targeted the most serious crime, homicide, by the most deadly of means, guns. But at least twenty-five states passed legislation that made it mandatory for juveniles accused of sexual offenses, most often rape, to be transferred from juvenile to adult court, where they faced the likely outcome of sentencing to adult prison facilities if found guilty (Feld 2000). These juveniles accused of sexual offenses would no longer be adjudicated within juvenile court and face commitment to juvenile justice facilities. For these states, the juvenile court would no longer have jurisdiction, and these juveniles would be tried as though they were adults and would serve time alongside adults in prison.

The waiver of juvenile offenders to criminal court is nothing new. Procedures and policies for the movement of adolescents out of the juvenile court and into adult court have existed since the invention of the juvenile court (Tanenhaus 2000, 2002). In most states, a juvenile court judge made the decision to transfer or waive a juvenile to criminal court on the basis of a set of factors such as the nature of the offense, the juvenile's delinquency history, his or her potential for rehabilitation or amenability to treatment, and the juvenile justice system's ability to provide effective rehabilitative services. This form of waiver is referred to as "judicial waiver." Zimring (2000) has emphasized the functional aspect of the judicial waiver process, likening it to a "safety value" at the bottom of the juvenile court, allowing for the siphoning out of a few corrupted, serious, older offenders so as to preserve the many younger, salvageable ones. Older, more serious, and violent juvenile offenders were viewed as existing outside and beyond the reach of the mission of the original charter of the juvenile court. They were considered to bear a closer resemblance to adults in criminal court than the younger and less serious offenders who made up the majority of the juvenile court's daily docket. Their movement out, though a decision of serious consequence, was seen as unfortunate but necessary to preserve the basic social enterprise of the juvenile court and its primary mission of rehabilitation.

During the "juvenile crime wave" of the late 1980s and early 1990s, the process of waiver in nearly every state was transformed to allow a larger portion of juvenile offenders to be moved from juvenile court jurisdiction to adult court. This was achieved by state legislatures in four major ways. First, judicial waiver—a discretionary decision by the juvenile court judge—was abolished in many states. In its place a list of offenses was designated, resulting in the automatic waiver of juveniles accused of these specified offenses to adult court. This automatic process is often termed "legislative waiver" or "statutory exclusion." Legislative waiver require-ments for specific offenses, like murder or forcible rape, were passed in many states, usurping the decision-making capacity of the juvenile court judge. Juveniles charged with offenses on a legislative waiver list had their cases automatically waived to adult court.

Second, in variants of the legislative waiver process, often referred to as "presumptive" and "mandatory" waiver procedures, certain offenses are automatically waived to adult court, but there is an evidentiary hearing in which the presumption of the waiver can be rebutted, with the possibility that the juvenile will be transferred back to juvenile court. In presump-tive waiver procedures the juvenile is automatically waived to adult court and the juvenile carries the burden of having to challenge the legal pre-sumption that his or her case belongs there and not in juvenile court. In mandatory waiver procedures, the decision to waive the juvenile to adult court rests with the prosecution, but there is still an evidentiary hearing in which the juvenile's waiver can be reversed, resulting in his or her be-ing set back to juvenile court. In about half of the states, serious sexual offenses, like forcible rape, are on the list of presumptively or mandatorily waived offenses (Feld 2000).

Third, direct file procedures placed the waiver procedure under the ex-ecutive control of the prosecutor. In direct file procedures the decision to waive a juvenile to adult court is at the discretion of the prosecutor, and there is no evidentiary hearing for possible reversal back to juvenile court as in the case of mandatory waiver. The case is beyond the reach of the juvenile court and the defense. Control rests solely in the hands of the prosecutor.

A fourth mechanism takes the form of blended sentencing schemes. Blended sentencing provisions vary widely, with some occurring in juve-nile court and granting the juvenile court judge the power to sentence juveniles to adult correctional settings and some occurring in adult court where the judge has the power to sentence to either adult or juvenile jus-tice settings. In most blended sentencing schemes, a dual juvenile and adult sentence is issued, often with the adult sentence suspended and only brought into play if the juvenile is rearrested, violates the terms of his or her juvenile sentence or probation, or is later declared fit for an adult sentence because of his or her lack of progress in rehabilitative treatment.

The transfer of a juvenile from juvenile court to adult court jurisdiction, even though it has been made easier to achieve in recent years, is still a statistically rare event. Less than 1% of the total cases of delinquency in juvenile court were waived to criminal court in 2003 and 2004 (Stahl, Puzzanchera, Sladky et al. 2007). While the total number of juveniles waived increased 70% from 1985 to 1994, this occurred largely because the number of delinquency arraignments increased by about that proportion within that decade. During this same time frame, the percentage of juveniles waived as a proportion of the total number of juveniles arraigned never went above 2%, even during the height of the so-called juvenile crime wave.

Though rare, the waiver has deep symbolic meaning and, more importantly, significant practical effects on the affected juvenile. Zimring (1982, 2000) has referred to juvenile waiver as the exception to the rule in juvenile court jurisdiction, comparing it to capital punishment for the adolescent. The waiver of a juvenile is a transformative decision for the life of a juvenile offender, representing a total foreclosure of the hope of rehabilitation. Within the legal arena, it is a boundary decision, marking the end of childhood and the solicitous care and concern extended to children, and the opening up of what Zimring describes as "the disfiguring punishment" of sentencing to adult correctional institutions. The juvenile is exposed to sentencing in strict proportionality to his or her offense, like an adult, and is placed at risk for long-term incarceration with all the potential attendant harm that may be a byproduct of that legal fate. Waiver decisions constitute the borderland of juvenile justice. Beyond its borders are cast youth considered irredeemable. Those expelled are no longer children. The transfer decision defines the end of legal childhood for those still of minority age.

The waiver of a juvenile is an example of a "successful degradation ceremony" (Garfinkel 1956) whereby the public identity of the juvenile offender as a child suitable for juvenile court processing is transformed into that of a hardened adult offender beyond the reach and hope of rehabilitation. It is the destruction of one identity and the constitution of another; the child has been replaced by the adult. In this total identity overhaul, "the former identity stands as accidental; the new identity is the (new) 'basic reality'" (Garfinkel 1956, 422). The juvenile offender is not regarded as being transformed by some action on the part of the juvenile court. It is not the juvenile court that brings about the transformation as much as it unmasks the degraded identity that lurked behind the childish appearance all along. In the waiver hearing, the juvenile offender is cast out, placed outside of the juvenile justice system and made strange.

The U.S. Supreme Court has acknowledged the enormous significance of the waiver process and has found the informality of the hearing to be constitutionally deficient. In *Kent v. U.S.* (1966), the U.S. Supreme Court held that "there is no place in our system of laws for reaching a result of such tremendous consequence without ceremony" (*Kent v. U.S.* 383 U.S. 541, 554). The Court in *Kent* set forth the terms of that ceremony. It even went as far as to suggest, though it did not require, a set of factors, often referred to as the "*Kent* factors," to arbitrate the waiver ceremony.

The juvenile at the center of this case, Morris Kent, like Gerald Gault, was a juvenile sex offender. In 1961, Kent, a 16-year-old adolescent, was detained by the police in the District of Columbia and taken into juvenile custody for allegedly entering a woman's home, taking her purse, and raping her. He had a prior juvenile record and had been placed on probation in 1959 at the age of 14 for housebreaking and purse snatching. At the scene of the 1961 crime, police found latent fingerprints and processed them. They were later matched to Kent, whose fingerprints were on file for the 1959 case. During a seven-hour police interrogation, Kent confessed to the offense and to several other prior offenses. His mother was not aware that he was in police custody until the day after his arrest.

The prosecution filed a motion to waive juvenile jurisdiction and to transfer Kent to the United States District Court for prosecution as an adult. Kent opposed the transfer, asking for a hearing on the matter and attaching an affidavit from a psychiatrist attesting that he was mentally ill, suffered from a psychosis, and met civil commitment standards as a mentally ill person. Counsel for Kent also petitioned the court for access to the social service file that had been accumulated by the staff at the juvenile court during his probation period. Counsel argued that access to this file was essential to provide effective assistance to the petitioner.

The juvenile court did not rule on Kent's motion. It did not hold a formal hearing and did not confer with Kent, his mother, or his counsel. A week after his arrest, the juvenile court simply transferred him, stating that after "a full investigation" it was moving to place him within the district court for trial as an adult. No findings of fact or recitation of reasons was entered in the decision, and there was no reference to the motions filed on behalf of Kent.

In district court Kent was subsequently indicted as an adult on three counts of housebreaking, three counts of robbery, and two counts of rape.

A competency to stand trial evaluation was ordered, and he was committed to the psychiatric division of the D.C. General Hospital for a 60-day evaluation. The hospital, in a report to the court, concluded that he was severely mentally ill and not competent to stand trial. The prosecution opposed this finding, and at its request the district court committed him to St. Elizabeth's Hospital in Washington, D.C., for another evaluation. In a letter to the district court the superintendent of St. Elizabeth's wrote that Morris Kent suffered from a psychosis—a Schizophrenic Reaction, Undifferentiated Type—that he had been suffering from this mental disorder at the time of the alleged offense, and that if the crimes were committed by him they were the product of this disease. Yet they concluded that he was competent to stand trial.

A jury convicted Kent of housebreaking and robbery but found him not guilty by reason of insanity for rape. The district court sentenced him to thirty to ninety years with credit for the time he spent as an involuntarily committed mental patient at St. Elizabeth's Hospital in Washington, D.C. He was returned to St. Elizabeth's Hospital on an order of commitment for the two counts of rape for which the jury had found him not guilty by reason of insanity. Had he been retained and tried in the juvenile court, his maximum time of commitment within the juvenile justice system would have been five years, until he turned 21.

Kent appealed the transfer decision to the district court of appeals, which affirmed the opinion of the juvenile court, rejecting his argument that the juvenile court had failed to comply with the statutory requirement of a full investigation, had failed to state its reasons for the transfer, and had failed to comply with the constitutional requirements of fundamental fairness. Kent appealed again, this time to the United States Court of Appeals for the District of Columbia, which once again affirmed the lower court's decision. A vigorously worded dissent was written by Chief Justice David Bazelon (*Kent*, 343 F. 2d 247, 264, 1964, Bazelon, *dissenting*). Bazelon (1988) later wrote in an essay that the decision to transfer a mentally ill juvenile was improper, particularly since one of the justifications presented by the court of appeals was that the juvenile court lacked the facilities to treat him. According to Bazelon (1988),

> When the Juvenile Court washes it hands of a child, it throws him on the scrap heap of a prison, it gains nothing by employing euphemisms to describe this tragedy. . . . As long as the Juvenile Court practices self-deception that allows it to believe in the existence of facilities "elsewhere,"

it will not face squarely the need to develop for itself the tools it requires to care for these children. (131)

The United States Supreme Court, describing the case as raising "a number of disturbing questions," reversed the convictions of Kent citing lack of due process protections afforded him at his transfer hearing. The Court agreed that "the juvenile court should have considerable latitude within which to determine whether it should retain jurisdiction over a child. . . . But this latitude is not complete" (553) The Court established the necessity of holding a formal transfer hearing in juvenile court, where defense counsel is given access to records and reports that will be considered by the juvenile court in its decision making, and of the juvenile court supporting its decision regarding transfer with a statement of reasons.

The Court listed in an appendix the criteria that the juvenile court of the District of Columbia had set forth in a policy on transfer hearings issued in 1959, the same year as the arrest of Morris Kent. Among the criteria listed were the seriousness of the offense, the prosecutorial merit of the complaint, the sophistication and maturity of the juvenile, the delinquency history of the juvenile, the prospects for adequate protection of the public, and the likelihood of reasonable rehabilitation of the juvenile through the means available by the juvenile court. As we have seen, these factors, along with others noted by the Court, have become known as the "*Kent* factors" and have come to govern judicial decisions regarding transfer across the country. Although the specific *Kent* factors were not constitutionally mandated by the Court, about three-fourths of the states utilize *Kent*-style criteria to guide judicial decisions about waiver (Dawson 1992).

In a final indictment of the juvenile court, Justice Abe Fortas raised suspicion about the foundational jurisprudential doctrine of the juvenile court as a worthy aspirational institution, stating,

> While there can be no doubt of the original laudable purpose of the juvenile courts studies and critiques in recent years raise serious questions as to whether actual performance measures well enough against theoretical purpose. . . . There is evidence, in fact, that there may be grounds for concern that the child receives the worst of both worlds; that he gets neither the protections accorded to adults nor the solicitous care and regenerative treatment postulated for children. (556)

With this statement, the due-process-rights movement of the juvenile court was underway. The next year, in the case of *Gault* (1967), the U.S. Supreme Court picked up the dangling due process thread left by *Kent* (1966) and pulled it, unraveling the fabric of the rehabilitative juvenile court established in Cook County in 1899. The case of Gerald Gault was very different than that of Morris Kent. They represent different ends of the spectrum of juvenile sex offenders. Kent was charged with breaking into the home of a woman and forcibly raping her while Gault was charged with making an obscene phone call to his female next-door neighbor. Despite their differences, however, they share an important historical fate: together these two juvenile sex offenders rehabilitated a juvenile court that had disregarded their due process rights and generally held a dim view of their prospects for rehabilitation. Juvenile sex offenders are hard cases for the juvenile court, which is why two juvenile sex offenders played the transformative role of the foil to the juvenile court's history of unchecked powers.

These two landmark U.S. Supreme Court cases, *Kent* (1966) and *Gault* (1967), are considered by most legal scholars as the two most significant cases in the jurisprudential history of juvenile justice, bringing about the transformation of the juvenile court, making it a more formal legal process requiring many of the due process protections extended to adult defendants. A key aspect of these cases is that both defendants were juvenile sex offenders. The significance of this occurrence is made all the more forceful by the relative rarity of sexual offending within the delinquency docket of juvenile courts across the nation. The transformation of the juvenile court into the rights-based institution it is today was carried forward by the cases of two juvenile sex offenders in the 1960s.

It was nearly twenty-five years after the *Kent* and *Gault* courts before the waiver laws underwent the drastic overhaul in reaction to the juvenile crime wave of the late 1980s and early 1990s. Between 1990 and 1996, forty states passed legislation altering the criteria of waiver, and in some cases creating new pathways for the transfer of adolescents to criminal court (Feld 2000; Griffin, Torbet, and Szymanski 1998). In every case, the intent of the legislative changes was to expand the number and types of juveniles eligible for waiver. Sexual offenses figured heavily in many of the statutory revisions of the waiver laws. Age and emotional maturity or level of psychological sophistication have always been primary considerations in judicial decisions regarding waiver. Older, more mature and sophisticated adolescents are more adult-like and, therefore, judged as more appropriate for waiver. Maturity and sophistication are among the original *Kent* factors. Juvenile sex offenders may be particularly prone to be viewed by the juvenile court as more mature and psychologically sophisticated than nonjuvenile sex offenders. Sex is an activity reserved for adults. Minors engaging in sex may appear less innocent and child-like, unlike adolescents who are sexually unknowing or uninitiated. Sexual experience carries within it the idea of the loss of innocence and the end of childhood, an initiation to one of the great mysteries of life from which children have been judiciously protected from sexually knowing adults. Once they cross the threshold, they leave a vital aspect of their childhood behind.

The jurisprudential principle of proportionality calculates justice and punishment in relation to the seriousness of the offense and the blameworthiness of the offender. Younger and less mature offenders are considered less blameworthy than older and more mature offenders and are, therefore, regarded as deserving of less punishment. But sexual offenses, whether forcible rape as in the case of Morris Kent or lewd comments uttered over the phone line as in the case of Gerald Gault, may act as an intervening variable in this equation, casting the offending adolescent in a mix of shadow and light reflecting a more mature profile.

The commission of a sexual offense by an adolescent may make waiver more likely by altering the view of the adolescent's status on essential *Kent* factors. Sexually knowledgeable adolescents may appear more sophisticated and mature. They may also be viewed as more dangerous and more likely to repeat their sexual transgression once they have crossed over the forbidden sexual threshold. Finally, adolescent sex offenders may appear less amenable to treatment and rehabilitation since sexual behavior may make them appear more adult-like and less amenable or open to change.

Zimring (2000) describes amenability to rehabilitation, another of the *Kent* factors, as an amorphous standard—a retrofitted rationale designed to account for legal decisions that are little more than foredrawn conclusions. The finding of a lack of amenability, for Zimring, functions as a "counterfeit account," a justification for the real reason for the waiver decision, namely, sophistication/maturity (culpability) and dangerousness (seriousness of the offense), the other two primary *Kent* factors. Amenability to treatment is not a factor that is independently weighed but is heavily determined by a juvenile's perceived sophistication and dangerousness. A recent survey of juvenile court judges found that while they endorsed the view that amenability to treatment was the most useful construct in their decisions about transfer, they typically placed greater weight on dangerousness and sophistication/maturity when asked to make transfer decisions in hypothetical case presentations (Brannen, Salekin, Zapf et al. 2006). This finding lends some limited empirical support to the idea that dangerousness and sophistication/maturity are the primary bases for legal decisions for transfer and that amenability is a less relevant consideration that may be determined by the juvenile's status on these former factors.

The exclusion of juvenile sex offenders from juvenile court jurisdiction is as old as the juvenile court, and many states have long included rape among the excluded offenses (Tanenhaus 2000). There is a long-standing view, evident at the very outset of the juvenile court, that rape is not a fit crime for the juvenile court and more properly belongs in the adult court. Historically, judicial waiver of juveniles to adult court through the discretionary decision-making authority of the juvenile court judge has been the main mechanism by which juveniles were expelled from juvenile court jurisdiction. This is the process reformed in *Kent*. Recently, however, other mechanisms, like statutory or legislative exclusion, presumptive and mandatory waiver, prosecutorial direct filing, and blended sentencing, have gained ascendancy.

Dawson (2000) provided an analysis of judicial waiver laws in the United States. He reported that as of 1997 forty-six states had judicial waiver available. Seventeen of these states were what he referred to as "purist" states, offering only judicial waiver without legislative or statutory exclusion and direct filing. Legislative exclusion and direct filing dispense with the ceremonious procedures of the *Kent* Court, replacing them with the primacy of the offense. It is the offense and no longer the offender behind the offense that determines the waiver. The ceremony of the waiver hearing, in which the juvenile court judge weighs the cost of transfer against the benefits of retention using factors like amenability to rehabilitation, the maturity and sophistication of the offender, the seriousness of the offense, and the ability of the juvenile justice agency to provide services, is usurped by the principle of the offense (Feld 1987), which automatically arbitrates who is a child and who is an adult. It is a retributional or "just desserts" model of jurisprudence operating within juvenile court.

Three of the "purist" states identified by Dawson (2000)—Rhode Island, Texas, and Kansas—had blended sentencing in addition to judicial waiver, allowing for adult sentences to be attached to dispositions in juvenile court. Six states in Dawson's analysis had mandatory waiver laws

TABLE 6.1   *States with Judicial Waiver and no Statutory Exclusion and Direct Filing*

State	Mandatory Waiver	Mandatory Waiver for Sexual Offense	Presumptive Waiver for Sexual Offense	Blended Sentences
California			X	
Hawaii				
Kansas				X
Kentucky	X			
Maine				
Missouri				
New Hampshire			X	
New Jersey			X	
North Carolina	X	X		
North Dakota	X	X		
Ohio	X	X		
Rhode Island				X
South Carolina	X	X		
South Dakota				
Tennessee				
Texas				X
West Virginia	X	X		

Source: Dawson 2000.

along with their judicial waiver provisions: Ohio, South Carolina, North Carolina, West Virginia, North Dakota, and Kentucky. Three of these had specific provisions for the waiver of juvenile sex offenders. In Ohio, waiver is mandatory for a child 16 years or older charged with rape who was previously committed to a training school or who used or exhibited a firearm during the commission of an offense (Ohio rev. Code Ann. 2151.26). In West Virginia waiver is mandatory if a juvenile is age 14 or older and charged with a first-degree sexual assault (W.V. Code 49-5-10(d)). In North Dakota waiver is mandatory for all juveniles 14 years or older when there is probable cause for the commission of or the attempt to commit gross sexual imposition by force or threat (N.D. Cent. Code 27-30-34.1). In North and South Carolina juveniles are subjected to mandatory waiver when charged with a class of serious felonies that may include sexual offenses. In Kentucky only juveniles who are charged with a felony while using a firearm are at risk of mandatory waiver. Three states—California, New Hampshire, and New Jersey—have presumptive waiver for some categories of sexual offenses.

This leaves only five of the "purist" states—Hawaii, Maine, Missouri, South Dakota, and Tennessee—that had judicial waiver absent mandatory and presumptive juvenile waiver, making them the "purest" of the pure. Table 6.1 lists the states with judicial waiver without legislative or statutory exclusion.

Most of the recent legislative changes in waiver laws have been expansions of statutory or legislative waiver laws to include more offenses, like sexual offenses, and direct filing provisions. The U.S. Congress has supported state legislation favoring increased statutory exclusion and prosecutorial direct filing over judicial waiver. In fiscal years 1998 and 1999 this support included making federal grants to states through the Office of Juvenile Justice and Delinquency Prevention conditional upon states enacting statutory exclusions or prosecutorial direct filing for juveniles fifteen years or older charged with murder, aggravated sexual assault, or assault with a firearm (Dawson 2000). Legislative exclusion laws are the least discretionary, allowing little room for judicial and prosecutorial influence and control. Prosecutors can still alter facts or reduce or undercharge a juvenile, often as part of a plea agreement, such as charging a juvenile with indecent assault and battery instead of rape or with simple assault instead of indecent assault and battery. The only discretion afforded the judge is after the fact, during sentencing, when discretionary decision making can still occur.

In his review of the history of legislative exclusion, Feld (2000) concluded that states have always made limited use of the seriousness of the offense to determine waiver decisions. He views *Kent* as having cleared the way for legislative exclusion and direct filing by including seriousness of the offense as among the *Kent* factors. A few states had long excluded youth charged with serious offenses such as rape and other sexual assaults, but recent get-tough policies have lengthened the list of states and offenses. According to Feld (1987, 2000) in 1970, probably in response to *Kent*, Congress excluded youth aged 16 and over charged with rape, among other offenses, from juvenile court jurisdiction in the District of Columbia. By 1975, four states did the same, and by 1980 the number climbed to nine. The juvenile crime wave of the late 1980s and early 1990s exponentially expanded this number. Feld (2000) identified a total of thirty-four states with some form of legislative or statutory exclusion at the time of his review. Among these, twenty-four had statutory exclusion laws that banished from juvenile court jurisdiction youth charged with a sexual offense. He further found that six of the nine states with prosecutorial direct filing included sexual offenses among the list of offenses allowing for its application.

A total of thirty-one states made substantive changes in their laws governing waiver in the 5-year period from 1998 to 2003 (Griffin 2003), the time period after Feld's review (2000). Overall, the pace of legislative

change in the realm of transfer has slackened but the waiver net generally has widened and deepened over the past quarter-century. Yet some
states are beginning to move in the other direction, retracting some offenses from legislative waiver. Louisiana, for instance, removed aggravated
oral sexual battery from the list of offenses subject to statutory exclusion
(Griffin 2003).

The National Center for Juvenile Justice identifies a total of seventeen
states with presumptive transfer provisions (Griffin 2005). Among these,
eight specifically include a sexual offense as one of the offenses subject
to a presumptive transfer. Thirteen states have mandatory transfer provisions and among them, a total of six specifically mention a sexual offense
within the list of offenses. One state, Ohio, requires that the sexual offense
be committed with a gun. Statutory exclusion was found in twenty-eight
states, with fifteen of them specifically listing a sex offense as among the
offenses automatically excluded. Direct filing is used in fourteen states,
twelve of which list a sexual offense as being one of the offenses for which
a prosecutor can directly move to have the juvenile transferred to adult
court. Twenty-six states have blended sentencing provisions, and in most
instances a postadjudication hearing determines whether an adult sentence will be applied. Eight of these states specifically reference a sexual
offense among the offenses eligible for a blended sentence.

Taken together, over two-thirds (thirty-five of fifty-one) of the states
and the District of Columbia specifically include sexual offenses among
their lists of offenses eligible for waiver through these newly enacted non-
judicial waiver procedures. If the category "Certain Felonies" is assumed
to include serious sexual offenses like forcible rape, then forty-five states
and the District of Columbia allow for the waiver of juvenile sexual offenders to adult court without the benefit of judicial waiver. In eight of
these states a judge can waive the juvenile sex offender back to juvenile
court. This means that in nearly 90% of the states, juveniles can be automatically transferred for certain sexual offenses, presumably serious
felony offenses, without consideration of any of the *Kent* factors like maturity and sophistication of the juvenile, dangerousness, or amenability to
treatment. They can end up in criminal court without the ceremony of a
juvenile court hearing presided over by a juvenile court judge making a
discretionary decision about their transfer. In many of these states, such
as those with presumptive waiver provisions, the juvenile sex offender
can be waived back to juvenile court, or, in those states with blended
sentencing provisions, they can be sentenced by a juvenile court judge to

a juvenile sentence. But nevertheless, in a vast majority of the states the decision to transfer certain juvenile sex offenders is automatic. Table 6.2 summarizes the analysis by the National Center for Juvenile Justice (Griffin 2005) highlighting where states specifically provide for the waiver of juvenile sex offenders.

The six remaining states without any of these provisions—North Carolina, Tennessee, Kentucky, Missouri, Wisconsin, and Hawaii—can still waive juvenile sex offenders to criminal court, but they must do so through the old-fashioned method outlined by *Kent*: by way of the ceremony of the transfer hearing and judicial discretion. In Hawaii and Tennessee, judicial transfer is the only mechanism available for transfer. These states do not have presumptive, mandatory, or statutory waiver, direct filing, or blended sentencing. In Kentucky judicial waiver is available for certain felonies and mandatory waiver only for felonies committed with a gun. Kentucky also has blended sentencing provisions determined by way of a hearing. Missouri has only judicial waiver and blended sentencing determined through a juvenile court hearing. North Carolina has judicial waiver and the mandatory transfer of capital crimes. Wisconsin has judicial waiver, specifically including sexual offenses among the list of offenses eligible for waiver through a discretionary decision by the judge; statutory exclusion of murder and assaults against police officers and agents of the state; and blended sentencing through a discretionary hearing.

There exists virtually no empirical research about the waiver of juvenile sex offenders to adult court. Zimring (2004), in his review of the current state of the research literature on juvenile sex offenders, concluded that "the remarkable thing about contemporary writing on juvenile sex offenders by academic specialists in juvenile justice . . . is that there isn't any. . . . What one encounters is not so much a paucity of scholarly literature on juvenile sexual offenders by juvenile court experts as a void" (112).

The Office of Juvenile Justice and Delinquency Prevention compiles statistics for judicially waived cases but does not break down its analysis for specific categories of crime, such as rape or indecent sexual assault (Snyder and Sickmund 2006). It has not published national data about the number of judicially waived juvenile sex offenders. Moreover, national reporting data only includes judicial waivers, not waiver by other means such as statutory exclusion, direct filing, or blended sentencing. This makes analysis of trends in the waiver of juveniles difficult to track over time since more recent data will not capture those juveniles increasingly

TABLE 6.2 *The Waiver of Juvenile Sex Offenders to Criminal Court in the 50 States and the District of Columbia*

State	Discretionary	Presumptive	Mandatory	Statutory	Direct	Blended
Alabama	Any criminal			Certain felonies		Person offense*
Alaska	Any criminal	Person offense		Person offense		
Arizona	Certain felonies			Person offense	Certain felony*	Person offense*
Arkansas	Person offense*				Person offense*	Person offense*
California	Any criminal	Person offense*		Person Offense*	Person offense*	
Colorado	Person offense*				Person offense*	Person offense*
Connecticut			Certain felonies			
Delaware	Any criminal		Person offense*			
District of Columbia	Any felony	Person offense*		Certain felonies		Person offense*
Florida	Any criminal			Person offense*	Person offense*	
Georgia	Any criminal		Person offense	Person offense*		
Hawaii	Any felony					
Idaho	Person offense*			Person offense*		
Illinois	Any criminal	Certain felonies	Certain felonies	Person offense		Certain felonies
Indiana	Certain felonies		Certain felonies	Person offense*		
Iowa	Any criminal			Certain felonies		
Kansas	Any criminal	Person offense				Any criminal
Kentucky	Certain felonies		Certain felonies			
Louisiana	Person offense*	Person offense*	Person offense*	Person offense*	Person offense*	
Maine	Certain felonies	Person offense*				
Maryland	Any criminal			Person offense*		
Massachusetts				Murder		Person offense
Michigan	Certain felonies			Murder	Person offense*	Person offense*
Minnesota	Certain felonies	Certain felonies			Person offense*	Certain felonies
Mississippi	Any criminal			Certain felonies		
Missouri	Certain felonies				Person offense*	
Montana				Person offense*	Person offense*	Person offense*

State	Discretionary	Presumptive	Mandatory	Statutory	Direct	Blended
Nebraska					Any criminal	
Nevada	Certain felonies	Person offense*		Person offense*		
New Hampshire	Person offense*	Person offense*				
New Jersey	Any criminal*	Person offense*	Person offense*			Person offense*
New Mexico				Murder		
New York				Person offense*		
North Carolina	Certain felonies		Capital crimes			
North Dakota	Any criminal	Person offense	Person offense*			
Ohio	Certain felonies		Person offense*			Certain felonies
Oklahoma	Certain felonies			Murder	Person offense*	
Oregon	Person offense*	Person offense*		Person offense*		
Pennsylvania	Certain felonies			Person offense*		Certain felonies
Rhode Island	Certain felonies	Person offense*	Person offense*			
South Carolina	Person offense*		Certain felonies	Certain felonies		
South Dakota	Certain felonies			Certain felonies		Certain felonies
Tennessee	Person offense*					
Texas	Certain felonies			Certain felonies		Person offense*
Utah	Certain felonies	Person offense*		Person offense*	Any criminal	
Vermont	Person offense*			Person offense*	Person offense*	
Virginia	Certain felonies		Person offense	Person offense*		
Washington	Any criminal			Person offense*		
West Virginia	Person offense*		Person offense*		Person offense*	
Wisconsin	Person offense*			Person offense		
Wyoming	Any Criminal				Person offense*	

Source: Griffin 2005.
* Statute specifically identifies a sexual offense among the list of offenses eligible for waiver to criminal court.

transferred by means other than judicial waiver. It is likely that a greater number of juveniles are being transferred through more automatic, non-discretionary means as these laws have proliferated across the country over the past two decades. There exists, therefore, no national data on the number of juvenile sexual offenders transferred by the nondiscretionary means of statutory exclusion, presumptive waiver, mandatory waiver, direct filing, and blended sentencing. Recent research indicates that judicial waiver may not be the primary method of transfer and that statutory exclusion and direct filing have become increasingly the main method used to transfer juveniles to criminal court (Bishop and Frazier 2000).

There are only a few studies focusing on the judicial waiver of juvenile sex offenders for specific states. Dawson (1992), in an empirical study of judicial transfer in the Texas juvenile court system in 1987-1988, reported that for a total of fourteen thousand "delinquency petitions"—the term the juvenile court uses instead of "criminal charges"—only about 380 (2.7%) were for sexual assault. Waiver motions were filed in only eleven (2.9%) of the sexual assault cases, and eight of these were aggravated sexual assaults. Juvenile sex offenders represented 9.8% of the total motions for waiver filed, a more than threefold overrepresentation compared to their total representation among delinquency petitions (2.7%). Eight of the eleven (72.7%) petitioned sexual assault cases were waived to adult court. These eight accounted for 9.2% of the total cases waived. Overall, the results indicate that while juvenile sex offenders comprised a low percentage of delinquency petitions within the juvenile court, about 3%, they appear overrepresented among cases where a waiver motion is filed (9.8%) and among the total number of cases transferred (9.2%).

As reported by Bishop and Frazier (2000), Brown and Langan (1998), using national data on convictions in criminal court on cases transferred, estimate that twelve thousand transferred youth were convicted of felony offenses in 1994, representing 1.4% of all felony convictions in criminal court. Of these twelve thousand transferred youth, about 2% were charged and convicted of rape. Approximately 84% of transferred youth convicted of rape were sentenced to prison, while 97% of transferred youth convicted of murder, 75% convicted of robbery, and 74% convicted of aggravated assault were sentenced to a similar fate. Transferred youth convicted of rape and sentenced to prison were sentenced to an average of 200 months of prison compared to an average of 287 months for those convicted of murder, 139 months for those convicted of robbery, and 75 months for those convicted of aggravated assault.

The data provided by Brown and Langan (1998) dismisses the notion that transferred youth, at least in this sample, were beneficiaries of any leniency effect, as they were subjected to penalties often far beyond those that would have been imposed by the juvenile court. Transferred youth convicted of rape are sentenced to an average of nearly seventeen years in adult correctional facilities. A total of 85% of youth aged 16 and 17 convicted for rape in states where they were adults by definition and automatically waived to adult court were sentenced to significantly shorter prison sentences, nearly ten years.

The legal impetus behind the wave of legislative reform surrounding juvenile transfer statutes that swept through the nation in the wake of the temporary juvenile crime wave was undoubtedly a solution aimed at curbing youth violence and protecting the public by making transfer easier and more assured. Based on the research that has been conducted to date, this goal has been achieved, as evidenced by the increased rates of transfer through the more automatic means, like statutory exclusion, mandatory waiver, presumptive waiver, and prosecutorial direct file. It was also hoped that the widening of the transfer net would act as a deterrent to juveniles. Deterrence can be achieved in two ways: a general effect and a specific effect. General deterrence aims to reduce crime by lowering the rate of offending in the general population. The expectation is that the increased likelihood of negative consequences for offending, such as adult conviction and incarceration, will act as a disincentive to crime, thereby generally deterring youth in the community from engaging in violent behavior. Specific deterrence aims to reduce crime by lowering the rate of recidivism among existing offenders by means of increasing the cost of engaging in future acts of violent criminality.

There has been limited research on whether the recent legislative reform of waiver processes has been associated with any deterrent effect, and no research has directly examined whether harsher transfer processes, which carry the possibility of stricter punishment, have translated into lower rates of juvenile sex offending. One study on general deterrence examined the effect of New York's passage of the Juvenile Offender Law of 1978, also referred to as the Willie Bosket Law, named after the juvenile offender who prompted the state legislature to pass the law when he committed two murders on the New York City subway following his release from a secure juvenile treatment program (Singer 1996; Singer and McDowall 1988). The law lowered the age of criminal court jurisdiction for murder and other selected felony offenses, like rape, to age 13. The researchers examined the arrest rate of juveniles for murder and other designated felony offenses, including rape, in the 4-year period before enactment of the law and then for the 6-year period directly following passage of the law. They compared the effects for juveniles aged 13-15 who were charged with murder and designated felonies in New York City and in jurisdictions in upstate New York with the effects on a control group of older offenders aged 16-19 who were not affected by the law and were from Philadelphia, where no such legal intervention had been implemented in the time period of analysis.

Overall, researchers found no significant deterrent effect associated with the enactment of the legislation, leading them to conclude that the increased likelihood of criminal punishment did not dissuade juveniles from engaging in serious felony offenses. The researchers uncovered a significant drop in the rate of rape arrests for the target group of 13-15-year-olds, but a similar drop was also observed in the older control group from Philadelphia, suggesting a generalized reduction in juvenile sex offending across age groups and jurisdictions, probably not associated with the specific legislative intervention. The argument against a deterrent effect of the legislation is further strengthened by the finding that the rate of arrest for rape began to fall most precipitously before the law was passed, indicating that the drop in the rate of rape arrests was independent of the change in the law.

Another study testing the general deterrent effect of a mandatory transfer statute, passed in Idaho in 1981, used a similar methodological design as that employed in the New York study (Jensen and Metsger 1994). The new legislation mandated the waiver of juvenile offenders, beginning at age 14, who were charged with murder and certain other felonies, including rape. The researchers compared the arrest rates for these offenses in the 4-year time period before enactment of the legislation with the 5-year time period after implementation of the law, and their findings did not support the presence of a deterrent effect. In fact, they found the opposite: the target offenses increased in Idaho after the legislation for mandatory transfer was passed. By comparison, the rate of arrest for target offenses decreased in two states serving as control groups that were considered demographically and economically similar to Idaho.

The specific deterrence effect of waiver has been tested by examining the differential recidivism rate of matched samples of youth transferred to adult court with a sample of youth retained in the juvenile court (Bishop, Frazier, Lanza-Kaduce et al. 1996; Fagan 1995, 1996). Generally, these studies not only failed to find a specific deterrent effect but have often found the opposite, an aggravating effect. Youth transferred to adult court and potentially exposed to Zimring's "disfiguring punishment" in adult correctional settings were found to be significantly more likely to recidivate than those youth retained in the juvenile court and exposed to the rehabilitation efforts of the juvenile justice system. Fagan (1995, 1996) did not include juvenile sex offenders in his study, but Bishop and colleagues (1996) did, though they only comprised 3.2% of the sample. Bishop and colleagues (1996) did not provide separate analysis for juvenile sex offenders.

Bishop and Frazier (2000) reviewed the research literature examining the variety of negative effects on juveniles incarcerated in adult correctional institutions compared to the effects on those placed in juvenile rehabilitation programs. They report that youth placed in juvenile justice settings are more likely to be offered educational and therapeutic programming, including counseling. Youth in adult correctional settings are more likely to be exposed to criminal socialization and to be the victim of violence. Forst, Fagan, and Vivona (1989) compared the experiences of youth incarcerated in adult settings with those of youth in juvenile training schools and found that the former were more likely to report victimization by other inmates and staff, including a fourfold increase (2% vs. 9%) in the rate of sexual victimization—experiences that may be detrimental to future adjustment and socialization and may increase the likelihood of future offending and, more specifically, sexual offending.

Two juvenile sex offenders were at the center of two landmark U.S. Supreme Court cases, *Kent* (1966) and *Gault* (1967), which revolutionized the juvenile court and ushered in the rights-based institution that it is today. Though *Kent* (1966) and *Gault* (1967) were intended to protect juveniles from the "unbridled power" of a juvenile court whose seemingly "benevolently motivated" interventions may have contained the potential to do more harm than good to juvenile offenders awaiting disposition, these two watershed decisions may have unwittingly opened the door for more punitive forms of juvenile justice to follow. In the decades after *Kent* and *Gault*, there were significant changes in the waiver statutes across the country in response to the temporary juvenile crime wave of the late 1980s and early 1990s. The retraction of judicial waiver and the advent of a number of automatic waiver provisions, such as legislative or statutory exclusion, mandatory waiver, presumptive waiver, direct filing, and blended sentencing, have resulted in a generalized net-widening effect, dramatically increasing the number of juveniles waived to adult court. Juvenile sex offenders may not have been the specific target of these legal strategies, but they have clearly been among the recipients of its effects. A total of thirty-five states specifically include sexual offenses among the offenses that can be waived through the more direct and automatic provisions that bypass judicial discretion and decision making. The number of states that provide for the automatic waiver or adult sentencing of juveniles rises to forty-five if sexual offenses are assumed to be included within the "certain felonies" category eligible for these newly devised waiver and sentencing schemas. Juvenile sex offenders comprise only about 1% or 2% of the cases of delinquents arraigned in juvenile court, but they are disproportionately represented among the juveniles transferred to adult court. There is a lack of national statistical data about the numbers of juvenile sex offenders waived to adult court and very limited research regarding the characteristics of juvenile sex offenders waived from juvenile to adult court.

Transfer to adult court is only one of the serious legal fates confronting juvenile sex offenders. The following chapters examine other serious possible legal fates awaiting the juvenile sex offenders, including civil commitment as sexually dangerous persons or sexually violent predators and the expansion of collateral consequences for the juvenile sex offender in the community.

7

Making Monsters
*The Civil Commitment of
Juvenile Sex Offenders*

In 1994 Kansas quickly passed legislation to prevent the impending release of Leroy Hendricks, an inmate within the Kansas prison system with a 30-year history of child molestation. In what the U.S Supreme Court described as a "chilling history of child sexual molestation and abuse," Hendricks had sexually molested as many as twelve boys and girls—one girl was as young as age 7—beginning in 1955 when he exposed his genitals to two young girls (*Kansas v. Hendricks* 1997). Two of his victims were his own step-son and step-daughter. He had participated in a number of sex offender treatment programs while incarcerated, and at one point was declared by one program as "safe to be at large." Hendricks's most recent incarceration began in 1984 when he was convicted and sentenced to serve ten years for taking "indecent liberties" with two 13-year-old boys.

Near the end of this sentence the Kansas legislature stepped in and created the Sexually Violent Predator Act of 1994 to stop Hendricks and a similar class of sexual offenders in the Kansas criminal justice system from returning to the community. The Sexually Violent Predator Act of 1994 defined a sexually violent predator as "any person who has been convicted or charged with a sexually violent offense and who suffers from a mental abnormality or personality disorder which makes the person likely to engage in the predatory acts of sexual violence" (Kan Stat. Ann.§ 59-29a02 [Supp 1996]). It further defined a "mental abnormality" as "a congenital or acquired condition affecting the emotional or volitional capacity which predisposes the person to commit sexually violent offenses in a degree constituting such a person a menace to the health and safety of others" (Kan Stat. Ann.§ 59-29a02 [Supp 1996]).

Hendricks admitted he was at risk to further sexually abuse children, declaring that when "I get stressed out, I can't control the urge to molest a child." He endorsed the state's diagnosis of him as a pedophile, agreeing that treatment was not effective and that the only sure cure for him was "to die."

The state moved to civilly commit him as a sexually violent predator under the new statute, finding that Pedophilia met the statutory definition of mental abnormality. Hendricks appealed the decision to the Kansas Supreme Court, which found that the state had violated his substantive due process rights because the act's definition of mental abnormality did not satisfy the definition required for the civil commitment of the mentally ill.

In 1997 the U.S. Supreme Court, in a majority opinion written by Justice Thomas, reversed the Kansas Supreme Court and agreed with the state of Kansas that "mental abnormality" satisfied substantive due process requirements. The Court agreed that while freedom from physical restraint has always been an essential feature of liberty, liberty is not absolute, tracing the history of civil commitment of the mentally ill to the time of the nation's founding. States, they argued, have always had the narrow power to involuntarily confine citizens unable to control their behavior who thereby present a danger to their fellow citizens. As long as such state actions take place according to proper procedures and evidentiary standards, the confinement of a certain defined and delimited class of citizens, like the mentally ill or mentally abnormal sexual offenders, is not contradictory to an "ordered liberty."

The Court found nothing unconstitutional about the confinement of certain dangerous persons as long as the finding of dangerousness was linked with some other quality or condition of the person, such as a mental illness in the context of the involuntary civil commitment of the mentally ill or a mental abnormality in the case of sexual offenders, as in that of Hendricks. The Court emphasized the necessity that the civil commitment establish a connection between the dangerousness and some specific condition, like a "mental abnormality" or "personality disorder," so that the class of persons subject to its procedures was clearly narrowed to those unable to control their behavior. The Court was unconvinced by Hendricks's argument that since "mental abnormality" was not the equivalent of "mental illness" and was a definition fashioned by a legislative body and not mental health professionals, it was not a proper definition to govern a civil commitment procedure. The Court noted that even psychiatrists continue to disagree on the definition of mental illness, and that states have been constructing definitions of mental illness for centuries for the purpose of civil commitment. Often there is not correspondence between psychiatric nomenclature and statutory definitions crafted by state legislatures. Since "the term 'mental illness' is devoid of any talismanic significance," Justice Thomas and the majority argued, there is no reason to bar states from setting forth definitions for the civil commitment of certain violent sexual predators.

The Court was equally not persuaded by Hendricks's claim that the Kansas Sexually Violent Predator Act of 1994 amounted to double jeopardy, or being punished twice for the same offense, once by way of his criminal sentence and the other by way of his civil commitment to the same or similar correctional facility for treatment. The Court argued that the procedure was a civil action by a state against a dangerous person and was not a criminal penalty. Thus it did not constitute punishment and, therefore, Hendricks was not being punished twice for the same crime. The original conviction resulting in his confinement to state prison was a criminal procedure and constituted punishment. But his civil commitment before his impending release from criminal confinement was not punishment but an act predicated on his inability to control his sexual urges, making him a danger to the public. The purpose of the civil commitment was not to punish him again for the same crime but to protect society and provide him treatment for his lack of control of his dangerous sexual urges. The Court even went as far as to state that the civil commitment is permissible even if Hendricks and the class of sexual predators like him were beyond the effective reach of treatment or if the treatment technologies available were unproven. What the state was doing to Hendricks—civilly detaining him—was permissible even if there was not effective treatment for what ailed him. In fact, the Kansas legislature was very candid about the fact that the primary motivation to civilly commit Hendricks was to restrict his liberty through confinement, not to treat him. Treatment was an ancillary consideration.

Notwithstanding the long dissent of Justice Breyer, who cautioned the majority about the Kansas practice of waiting until after Hendricks completed his criminal sentence to civilly commit him, which looked to him as though it harbored a punitive legislative purpose, the civil commitment of Hendricks by the state of Kansas passed constitutional muster. While a number of states already had sexually violent predator statutes on their books—the state of Washington was the first in 1990—and were no doubt relieved to hear that they could remain there, a number of other states were in the wings waiting to see if it would be constitutionally permissible to enact similar sexually violent predator legislation in their states. And many soon did.

Sexually violent predator statutes or sexually dangerous person statutes, as they are referred to in some states, have proliferated since *Kansas v. Hendricks* (1997). A total of nineteen states and the District of Columbia currently have civil commitment procedures for sexually dangerous or sexually predatory offenders, with New York and New Hampshire being the latest to join their ranks and with some others, like Vermont, looking to do so in the near future. Texas provides for the civil commitment to outpatient treatment rather than confinement to institutions. Pennsylvania permits only the civil commitment of juvenile offenders "aging out" of the juvenile justice system at age 20. As of December 2004, a total of 3,493 persons had been held awaiting evaluation or had been civilly committed for treatment as sexually dangerous or violent persons at a cost of about $224 million annually (Lieb and Gookin 2005).

Most of these states have set up procedures for commitment similar to the Kansas model whereby some time is designated—usually six months prior to the discharge of the sexual offender from his criminal sentence—during which the attorney general or the district attorney within the county or jurisdiction where the offender's conviction originated has the option to file for a probable cause hearing to determine whether there is enough evidence to meet this lower standard or threshold before proceeding to a more formal trial on the question of whether or not the individual meets the legal criteria as a sexually dangerous person or sexually violent predator. If probable cause is found, the inmate is held beyond the scheduled release date of his criminal conviction, and is often transferred to a mental health facility or specialized secure treatment facility for sexual offenders, often operated by the state Department of Correction or Department of Mental Health.

He often remains detained there for as long as a year as the state prepares its civil case for commitment against him and as his attorney—he is entitled to legal counsel—prepares his defense. He will probably be visited by a parade of evaluating psychologists and psychiatrists from each side tasked to determine if he has the prerequisite "mental abnormality" or "personality disorder" and if he has sufficient difficulty controlling his deviant sexual urges. During this precommitment period he is often offered sexual offender treatment services in the facility. The decision to take up the state's offer of treatment is no easy choice, resembling a sort of "catch-22" for the inmate. If he refuses treatment, it may appear that he is treatment resistant, is avoiding responsibility for his prior sexual transgressions, and is not motivated to change. If he accepts treatment, he must take heed that everything he discusses with his therapist or in group therapy and every written homework assignment that finds its way into his treatment file is discoverable and could end up as fodder for the state to use to substantiate its claim that he is indeed a dangerous sexual offender.

At the trial there is presentation of evidence to a judge or a jury, which often involves the testimony of multiple expert witnesses, often psychologists and psychiatrists, where it is not unusual to have at least two and sometimes more mental health professionals arguing each side of the case. If the petitioner is found to be not sexually dangerous, he is released from his confinement and is a free citizen unencumbered by physical restraints on his liberty, unless he is on parole or has probation to serve and is still under some degree of state control. But he undoubtedly will need to register as a sexual offender and provide notification of his residence and activities in the community. If he is found to meet the legal criteria as a sexually violent predator, he is committed essentially for life, or until the state either decides that he no longer meets the criteria for commitment or he can prevail at a legal appeal of his commitment.

While many of the state statutes governing the civil commitment of sexual offenders include juvenile sex offenders within their scope, there has been little empirical research regarding the application of sexually dangerous person and sexually violent predator laws to juvenile sex offenders. It seems unlikely that many adolescents would have been the main the target of these laws. Legislators more than likely had the Leroy Hendrickses of the world—adult repetitive pedophiles—or violent adult rapists in the forefront of their minds when they passed these legislative schemes. Nonetheless, most states, even though they already had other forms of indeterminate sentencing mechanisms available to them within their juvenile justice statutes, did include in those statutes juvenile sex offenders and adults whose only sexual offense occurred when they were juveniles. Most states have procedures in place that can extend jurisdiction of juveniles considered to be at risk for future harm, including juvenile sexual offenders, beyond the age of majority, often until they are 21 years old. Moreover, as discussed in the previous chapter, all of the states have at least one of a variety of mechanisms available to them to transfer juvenile sex offenders out of the juvenile justice system.

There is no systematic national data maintained about how many adolescents are subjected to civil commitment procedures as sexually dangerous persons. Likewise, there is no national data available about how many of the committed sexual offenders perpetrated their only known sexual offense or offenses as adolescents, never having sexually offended as adults. A review of state statutes for sexually dangerous persons and sexually violent predators reveals, however, that many legislatures included within the scope of these laws juvenile sex offenders and adults whose only sex offense occurred when they were juveniles. They specifically wrote the law to include both of these groups.

An examination of the nineteen states and the District of Columbia with statutes providing for the civil commitment of sexual offenders indicates that thirteen of them, about two-thirds, specifically state that a delinquency adjudication of a sexual offense constitutes a conviction or that the state's juvenile justice system can be considered an agency of jurisdiction with the authority to give notice to the attorney general or district attorney that a juvenile sex offender in their custody is scheduled for release and is eligible for the filing of a petition to have him found sexually dangerous. The other seven are silent on the issue of the civil commitment of juvenile sexual offenders or the commitment of adults whose only sexual offense occurred while they were juveniles. They are also silent on the issue of whether the state's juvenile justice authority is considered an agency with jurisdiction over a person convicted of a sexually violent offense. Only California requires that only one of the two prior convictions that are required for a person to be considered for civil commitment be a delinquency adjudication. At least one of the two prior convictions must be committed while the person was an adult.

A necessary condition for civil commitment as a sexual offender is prior conviction for a sexual offense. The laws are applicable only to convicted sexual offenders. Those without a prior conviction are not subject to their reach and scope. California requires more than one prior conviction, but the others require only one prior conviction for a sexual offense. "Conviction" as the outcome of a criminal trial is not a term used in juvenile court proceedings, however. Historically, the juvenile court, based on a foundation in rehabilitation and treatment as opposed to retribution and punishment, has avoided many of the traditional terms and phrases of the criminal court. In an attempt to avoid the potential negative effects associated with the application of terms and labels used for adult felons, the juvenile court developed its own lexicon for juvenile offenders.

Instead of "criminal convictions" it has substituted "delinquency adjudications"; instead of "arrest" it refers to the "detainment" of a juvenile by the police; instead of "criminal charges" adolescents have "delinquency complaints"; and instead of "sentencing," juveniles face "dispositions" where they can be "committed" to a juvenile correctional or training facility.

Many state legislatures in their sexually dangerous person laws circumvent the problem posed by the requirement of a prior "conviction" for a sexual offense by specifically declaring that a delinquency adjudication for a sexual offense constitutes a conviction for the purpose of categorizing a juvenile as a sexually dangerous person in civil commitment proceedings. For example, Arizona defines a conviction as including "any finding of guilt at any time for a sexually violent offense or an order of the juvenile court adjudicating the person delinquent for any sexually violent offense" (Ariz. Rev. Stat.§§ 36-3701). In the District of Columbia,

> whenever it shall appear to the United States Attorney for the District of Columbia that any defendant in any criminal proceeding . . . is a sexual psychopath, such attorney may file with the clerk of the court in which such proceeding is pending a statement in writing setting forth the facts tending to show that such a defendant is a sexual psychopath. (DC ST § 22-3804)

The statute goes on to state that a "criminal proceeding" means a proceeding in any court, even the juvenile court, and includes juveniles charged with a delinquent act (DC ST § 22-3803). In Wisconsin, a "sexually violent person" includes "a person who has been . . . adjudicated delinquent for a sexually violent offense" (Wis. Stats. Chapter 980.01 [7]).

In most states with civil commitment for sexual offenders, it is the attorney general or the district attorney in the originating county or jurisdiction where the person was initially convicted who has the authority to file a petition to have someone legally declared a sexually dangerous person or a sexually violent predator. Typically, notice to the attorney general or the district attorney about the impending release from custody of a person convicted of a sexual offense is made by a custodial agency, like a jail or prison, where sexual offenders are serving criminal sentences. However, the term "agency of jurisdiction" has been defined broadly within civil commitment statutes for sexual offenders to include the state's juvenile justice authority that provides custodial care of juveniles adjudicated delinquent for a sexual offense. For instance, in Florida, the "agency of jurisdiction" is statutorily defined as including "the agency that releases . . . a person who was adjudicated delinquent and is committed to the custody of the Department of Juvenile Justice" (FLA Stat 394.913 [1]). Civil commitment laws for sexual offenders rarely specify whether adolescents younger than 17 or 18 are eligible to be declared sexually dangerous persons or sexually violent predators. The vast majority of juvenile sexual offenders are probably being released or discharged from youth corrections agencies at the age of majority, typically age 18 or, in some states, age 21, the upper end of juvenile jurisdiction. In these instances they are legally adults when the state or district attorneys are considering them for civil commitment. In Massachusetts, for instance, juvenile sex offenders can be civilly committed as sexually dangerous persons but must remain within the Department of Youth Services until they reach their twenty-first birthday, at which time they are transferred to the Massachusetts Treatment Center for Sexually Dangerous Persons—a Department of Correction facility—for an indeterminate period of between a minimum of one day and a maximum of the person's natural life (Massachusetts G.L. Chapter 123a, section 14d). Similarly, within North Dakota's civil commitment statutes, a juvenile sex offender who is of minor age may have a guardian ad litem appointed to make decisions on his behalf, indicating that minor-age respondents are indeed subject to civil commitment. In contrast, New Jersey requires that a person be 18 years or older to be subject to civil commitment as a sexually violent predator.

Table 7.1 provides an overview of the nineteen states and the District of Columbia that have civil commitment procedures for sexual offenders, specifying which explicitly include delinquency adjudications as convictions and designate juvenile or youth corrections as a designated agency of jurisdiction. The table also reviews which states explicitly permit the release of juvenile justice records for the purpose of civil commitment as a sexually dangerous person.

A prior conviction for a sexual offense is the first of the four elements that Janus (2000) identified as necessary to be proven in order for a person to be civilly committed as a sexually dangerous person. The other three are a current mental abnormality or personality disorder, a nexus between the mental abnormality or personality disorder and a volitional impairment in the ability to control sexual deviant impulses, and an elevated risk for future sexually violent acts. It is not sufficient that the offender demonstrate a high risk of future offending only. It is additionally required that the dangerousness be due to the active and ongoing

TABLE 7.1   *Review of Civil Commitment Standards for Sexually Dangerous Persons or Sexually Violent Predators and Their Application to Juvenile Sex Offenders*

State	Chapter/Section	Nonconfidentiality of Juvenile Records	Juvenile Justice System as Agency of Jurisdiction	Delinquency Adjudication as Conviction
Arizona	C. 36.3701 – 36.3716			X
California	S. 6600-6609.3		X	X
D.C.	C. 38-22-3803 – 38-22-3811			X
Florida	C. 394.910 – 394.931	X	X	
Illinois	725ILCS 205-207		X	X
Iowa	C. 229.1 -229.16			
Kansas	C. 59-29a 01 – 59-29a44			
Massachusetts	C. 123a s.1 – 123.16	X	X	X
Minnesota	253B.185			
Missouri	C. 632.484 – 632.489			
New Hampshire	C. 135-E:1 – 135-E:23			
New Jersey	C.30:4-27.25 – 30:4-27.27		X	X
New York	MHY Title B Article 10.01-10.17			
North Dakota	C. 25-03.3.01- 25-03.3.24	X		
Pennsylvania	C. 64.6403ec. 6358(f)	X	X	X
South Carolina	C. 44-48-20-170		X	X
Texas	C. 841.001 - 841.150			X
Virginia	C. 37.2-900 – 37.2-919			
Washington	C. 71.09.010 – 71.09.902			X
Wisconsin	C. 980.01 – 980.12	X	X	X

presence of a mental abnormality or personality disorder. According to Janus (2000), there must be "dangerousness plus," the "plus" being dangerousness by reason of a mental abnormality or personality disorder. The presence of a mental disorder that underlies the risk of future harm comports with the necessary elements that have historically governed the civil commitment of the dangerous mentally ill to psychiatric hospitals. In *Hendricks* the Supreme Court was clear that dangerousness alone was not sufficient for a civil commitment scheme to be constitutional. The law could not target the general population of dangerous sexual offenders because to do so would too closely resemble double jeopardy or punishing twice for the same offense: once for the act itself and again because the act represented a risk that the perpetrator might do it again. But if the risk could be connected to a mental disorder that impaired the individual's volitional control and, in effect, made that person less culpable to some degree, short of complete blamelessness, then the state, the Supreme Court argued, had the ability to intervene to commit this individual to protect the community from his impaired ability to control himself. The civil commitment scheme had to apply to a particular segment of sexual offenders, a distinctive group whose risk for future sexual offending was connected to a mental abnormality. In this way the new civil commitment standards for sexual offenders that were quickly seeping into state legislative sessions across the country would be consistent with the historic precedent of the involuntary confinement of the dangerous mentally ill.

But what about the case of a juvenile sexual offender adjudicated in juvenile court? Does his delinquency adjudication constitute a prior conviction? Does it make him eligible for civil commitment as a sexually dangerous person? Does a juvenile whose only sexual offense is a delinquency adjudication satisfy Janus's (2000) first criterion in his 4-part structural scheme? Historically, delinquency adjudications have been viewed as something apart from a criminal conviction. The creation of the juvenile court was predicated on the notion that juveniles should be protected from the stigmatizing effect of criminal convictions and the disfigurement of criminal sentencing. As we see in table 7.1, a number of states have explicitly included delinquency adjudications for a sexual offense within the set of offenses eligible for possible civil commitment. Juveniles with delinquency adjudications who have never been formally convicted of a sexual offense are designated as eligible for civil commitment.

The question of classifying delinquency adjudications as criminal convictions for the purpose of civil commitment of juveniles as sexually dangerous persons or sexually violent predators has been tested in a number of appellate cases across the county. In every instance, appellate reviews have found that delinquency adjudications indeed constitute convictions and can be the underlying basis or entry point for a petition as a sexually dangerous person.

In the 1998 case of Carl Leroy Anderson, the petitioner appealed his indeterminate commitment by the state of Minnesota as a sexual psychopath and a sexually dangerous person. Anderson was adjudicated delinquent for four separate sexual offenses against children (*In the matter of Carl Leroy Anderson* 1998). One of his victims was his sister. He reportedly made minimal progress in treatment in residential programming, and before his nineteenth birthday, just prior to his discharge from juvenile custody, the state filed a petition to have him committed as a sexual psychopath and a sexually dangerous person, and the trial court committed him as such. Anderson raised the substantive due process claim that the commitment laws should not have applied to him because his sexual offenses occurred while he was a juvenile. In his appeal he cited the U.S. Supreme Court case of *Thompson v. Oklahoma* (1988), in which the Court held that the execution of a juvenile for a capital offense committed when he was 15 years old was cruel and unusual punishment in violation of the protections provided by the Eighth and Fourteenth Amendments. The Minnesota Court of Appeals rejected this claim, stating that the finding in *Thompson* was not applicable to the matter at hand because it involved criminal matters that were not at issue. The commitment of Anderson was not a criminal procedure; it was a civil one, and there was no reason raised by the petitioner to argue against its being applied to him. The commitment of Anderson, and similarly situated persons, was ruled constitutionally permissible. Sexual offenses committed while the petitioner was an adolescent were not barred from the potential for civil commitment as a sex offender.

In a series of cases in Wisconsin, this same question was raised, beginning with the 1998 case of Marvel L. Eagans, Jr., in which the appellate courts denied the petitioner's contention that his delinquency adjudications for a sexual offense committed while he was an adolescent should be excluded from consideration as a basis to support a finding that he was a sexually violent person (*In re the Commitment of Marvel L. Eagans, Jr.* 1998). The state filed a petition against Eagans after he turned 18, just prior to his release from a sex offender treatment program to which he had been committed following his being adjudicated delinquent for a sexual assault against a 7-year-old girl. The offense petition alleged that he had inappropriately fondled her while she sat on his lap in a city bus. The petition further asserted that Eagans suffered from a mental disorder that predisposed him to engage in acts of sexual violence and that it was substantially probable that he would engage in future acts of sexual violence. Eagans had a previous delinquency petition that alleged he touched the breasts and buttocks of a developmentally disabled girl, but he was never adjudicated delinquent for this offense. However, he had been previously found delinquent at the age of 14 for having sexual intercourse with a 12-year-old girl. Trial counsel for Eagans filed a motion on his behalf arguing that the commitment statute as applied to Eagans was unconstitutional because the trial court had erred in accepting Eagans's prior delinquency adjudications as qualifying convictions for a sexual offense. The trial court denied his petition and Eagans was committed as a sexually violent person until such time as he no longer posed a substantial risk of sexual violence. The appeals upheld the ruling of the trial court.

A year later in *Wisconsin v. McCain* (1999), McCain attempted to appeal his civil commitment, arguing that another statute created after the laws establishing the civil commitment of sexually violent persons had specifically set forth that delinquency adjudications were not criminal convictions. The more recent statutory protection also declared that any delinquency dispositions were inadmissible as evidence against a juvenile in any case or proceeding except for a delineated set of exemptions. Civil commitment as a sexually violent person was not, however, among them. The state argued that barring delinquency adjudications for sexual offenses as a basis for civil commitment was contradictory because the civil commitment statute specifically provides for the disclosure of such offenses to the district attorney. The court of appeals agreed, citing that the legislation had previously mandated that state agencies notify the appropriate district attorney's office of the impending release of a person who may be a sexually violent person. In order to avoid a contradictory mandate, the appellate court found in favor of the state.

More recently, the court of appeals in Wisconsin, in *In re the Commitment of Tremaine Y* (2005), allowed the delinquency adjudication for a sexual offense when the petitioner was 11 years old to serve as the sole basis for his civil commitment. Tremaine was adjudicated delinquent of attempted first-degree sexual assault when he was 11 years old. In the state of Wisconsin, a first-degree sexual assault is a felony charge that involves sexual intercourse or sexual contact without consent that causes pregnancy or great bodily harm, or is accomplished by use or threat of use of a dangerous weapon or while aided and abetted by one or more persons through the use or threat of use of force or violence. He was later adjudicated delinquent for three fourth-degree sexual assaults. The last was for having sex when he was 16 with a child aged 16 or younger at a residential program for juvenile offenders. Fourth-degree sexual assault is a misdemeanor and is defined as sexual contact with a person without consent of that person. According to the Wisconsin statute governing the civil commitment of sexual offenders, only the first sexual offense, attempted first-degree sexual assault, qualified as a sexually violent offense. The other offenses for fourth-degree sexual assault were not eligible as qualifying offenses because they were considered statutory rape cases that did not involve force or violence. At the time of his original adjudication for the sexually violent offense, Tremaine was too young for placement in a secure correctional setting, which required that the youth be at least age 12. He was later moved to a more secure setting following his subsequent adjudications. Referral for petition as a sexually violent person also required placement in a secure setting. Because of his original disposition at age 11, Tremaine was not eligible for civil commitment. The court, however, argued that since he was subsequently placed in a secure correctional facility partly on the basis of his original sexual offense, this was sufficient to support the state's petition.

The use of delinquency adjudications as qualifying criminal convictions for civil commitment as a sex offender raises some other difficult due process issues arising out of the tradition of the juvenile court. The juvenile court has operated under a separate line of development than criminal court. As we have seen, from its very inception it was intended to be something different and separate from criminal court, and over the decades it has developed a tradition supported by its own procedural rules and practices. The era of juvenile court reform beginning in the 1960s with *Kent* (1966) and *Gault* (1967), which we reviewed in the last chapter, seriously questioned whether the juvenile court as it evolved over the decades had remained steadfast to its original mission. More recent revisionist historical scholarship (Tanenhaus 2000, 2002) has even questioned the purity of the initial intentions of the early juvenile court and its founders.

While decisions such as *Kent*, *Gault*, and others sought to bring the juvenile court in line with many of the due process rights of the criminal court, they never intended to collapse the juvenile court within the criminal court. The idea was to reform the court by limiting its unbridled discretion, divesting it of the powers it claimed to wield for the sake of benevolent ends by injecting it with a healthy dose of due process to protect the rights of juveniles who were often on the hard-luck end of its seemingly munificent decisions. But the Supreme Court clearly and quite consciously stopped short of equating the two systems of justice. It preserved many of the traditions of the juvenile court in order to keep it a system separate and apart from the criminal court. For instance, in *McKeiver v. Pennsylvania* (1971), a case decided by the United States Supreme Court, jury trials were declared not a fundamental right of juveniles facing adjudication in juvenile court. A trial of one's peers is a fundamental right guaranteed by the Sixth Amendment, but the Court did not in *McKeiver* extend that right to juveniles, thereby departing from a string of prior cases in which they provided due process rights to juvenile delinquents. The Court cited its concern that a right to a jury trial would transform the court into an adversarial process too closely resembling the criminal court. The Supreme Court determined that juvenile court proceedings were not criminal in nature and, therefore, that the Sixth Amendment to the United States Constitution did not apply to it. In their due-process-rights revolution, they elected to draw the line at the right to a jury trial. Though states were free to extend jury trials to the juvenile court if they wished, there would be no constitutional right to a trial by jury in juvenile court.

The absence of a constitutional right to a jury trial for juvenile offenders reveals one of several fault lines that emerge when the juvenile justice system interfaces with adult criminal and civil justice systems. The right to a jury trial in the criminal courts is fundamental. The aim of a jury trial is to increase the probability of reliable and valid outcomes since the unanimous decisions of a group are more likely to achieve such outcomes than the decisions of a single justice. A jury also protects the defendant from the abuse of power of overzealous prosecutors and judges by placing outcomes in the hands of the citizenry. In this way trials by jury offer a balance and protection against the power of the state. Decisions about guilt are removed from an abstracted legal agent and are turned over to the more sympathetic and commonsense judgment of one's community peers.

A flaw emerges, however, when adolescents who were adjudicated delinquent for a sexual offense and were not afforded the protection and fairness of a jury trial are later subjected to involuntary civil commitment as sexually dangerous persons. This protection is automatically afforded adults convicted of a sexual offense, but it is absent in the case of juvenile sex offenders adjudicated delinquent by a juvenile court judge.

There has been case law addressing the problem of the fundamental fairness of juveniles being committed as sexually dangerous persons in civil trials when the underlying conviction for their sexual offense did not include the right to a jury trial. The 1998 case of Hezzie R., a case decided by the Wisconsin Supreme Court, tested the constitutionality of the absence of a right to a jury trial in juvenile adjudications for juvenile sex offenders facing civil commitment (*In the Interest of Hezzie R.* 1998). The concern underlying the argument was that the juvenile court proceedings have become fundamentally more like criminal proceedings. Delinquency adjudications increasingly hold the potential of exposing juveniles to placements ordinarily reserved for adults. As the dividing line between these historically separated systems has dissolved, juveniles are more at risk for adult sanctions, and presumably their constitutional rights should grow accordingly to afford them the same protections extended to adults.

Hezzie R. was 14 years old when the state of Wisconsin charged him with first-degree sexual assault of a child. He requested a jury trial but was denied this by the trial court. He was found guilty by the court and was committed to the Serious Juvenile Offender Program, a specialized program in Wisconsin contained within an adult prison. Hezzie R. argued that his denial of a right to a jury trial at the time of his delinquency adjudication for a sexual offense violated his constitutional rights since this delinquency adjudication permitted possible lifetime commitment as a sexual offender.

The Wisconsin Supreme Court agreed that a juvenile does not have a fundamental right to a trial by jury in juvenile court but argued that the civil procedure for commitment as a sexually violent person, a separate civil procedure, did entitle him to a jury trial. They reasoned that the denial of a jury trial to a juvenile at a delinquency proceeding did not result in civil commitment as a sexually dangerous person without the benefit of a jury trial since he effectively had the benefit of a jury trial at his commitment hearing. The court went on to argue that commitment as a sexually violent person is not criminal punishment but is a civil action aimed at the remediation or treatment of a person's sexual-violence risk and the protection of the public and therefore the question of whether or not he had a jury trial prior to the filing of a petition against him is irrelevant to this civil issue.

In a stinging dissent, a minority of the justices on the Wisconsin Supreme Court criticized the majority's argument as a "smoke and mirror attempt to avoid the real issue" (dissent, *In the Interest of Hezzie R.* 1998). The dissenting justices pointed out that both adult and juvenile delinquents must first be found guilty or delinquent of a sexual offense before they are considered eligible for commitment as sexually violent persons, but only the juvenile is the subject of such a petition without the benefit of a jury trial.

The confidentiality of juvenile records was once a defining feature of the juvenile court. The fundamentality of confidentiality was based on the very foundational framework of the juvenile court: what adolescents needed was guidance, not punishment, assistance, not retribution. Delinquent acts committed as part of the perils of youth made no necessary stamp on the person to be. The public knowledge of these youthful transgressions should not be carried over the chasm into adulthood where they could interfere with a person's life chances. Part of the rehabilitative ideal of the juvenile court was the notion that a youth's tarnished past should not be a barrier to his or her making a productive future. The negative effects of labeling were a concern for the founders of the juvenile court, who erected strong walls against the outflow of information from juvenile court proceedings.

The confidential nature of juvenile court records—a legal structure that held fast for nearly its first century—began to be effaced during the legislative overhaul of the juvenile court that occurred in the late 1980s and early 1990s in response to the temporary "juvenile crime wave." It was during this period that state legislatures threw open the doors of the juvenile court in many states and began loosening some of the restrictions on the release of juvenile court records. But the doors that were flung open during the wave of concern about the rise in violent juvenile crime were taken off their hinges when the question of releasing records of juvenile sexual offenders was raised. Legislation governing the civil commitment of sex offenders generally permitted state prosecutors access to an offender's juvenile court records, which often contained police reports, victim statements, trial transcripts, school records, mental health records, and psychological evaluations. In a number of legal decisions across the country, appeal courts and state supreme courts rewrote the laws governing the confidential nature of juvenile court records. In many of these decisions, courts found themselves in the difficult position of having to reconcile a contradiction within the state's statutes. Where in one place—typically in those sections of the law covering the juvenile court—the legislature, in a tone reminiscent of its founding era, preserved the confidentiality of juvenile court records, in another place—either in the laws governing the civil commitment of sexual offenders or in the laws outlining the process for registration or community notification, a much more recent statutory addition—the statute provided for the availability of juvenile court records. Table 7.1 lists the states that specifically provide for the release of juvenile records for civil commitment procedures for sexual offenders.

In *In re the Commitment of Matthew A.B.* (1999), a case decided by the court of appeals in Wisconsin, the court denied the petitioner his post-commitment relief motion in which he claimed that the state had violated his constitutional rights by erroneously admitting his delinquency adjudication for a sexual offense into his civil commitment trial as a sexually violent person. The state filed its petition against Matthew when he was 16 years old, after he engaged in two consensual sexual acts with another boy who was committed to the same residential treatment program. Matthew had a long history of violent nonsexual incidents in his record, resulting in his placement in a number of residential treatment programs. He had been previously charged with disorderly conduct while armed with a knife in a gang-related school playground confrontation. He was also charged as a delinquent for using a BB gun in an attempted armed robbery of a jogger. His behavior at home was described by his parents as increasingly out of control, with reports that he had broken windows in the home, stolen various items and money, threatened to kill his parents in their sleep, and physically assaulted his mother and brother.

Matthew was placed in a residential treatment program for a long-term stay, but soon after his release he was charged with arson for burning down a garage. He was returned to the residential treatment program, where he reportedly engaged in an incident of consensual sexual contact with a 13-year-old male resident whom he plied with drugs and money in exchange for oral sex. He was later adjudicated delinquent for the sexual assault of a child. He was evaluated for possible commitment as a sexually violent person because of his new delinquency adjudication for a sexual offense, but the program decided against civilly committing him. He was charged a short time later, along with another resident, of assaulting a third resident. He was waived into adult court for this offense and convicted of an assault against an inmate. He remained at the residential treatment program, where he engaged in two incidents of consensual sexual relations with a 15-year-old boy. Matthew was 16 at the time. He was never formally charged with a sexual offense, but he was reconsidered by the program staff for civil commitment as a sexually violent person.

The state filed a petition against him and probable cause was found. At his trial, four mental health experts, including two retained by the defense, testified that he had a Conduct Disorder, a childhood behavioral disorder, but there was disagreement about whether it was substantially probable that Matthew would engage in future acts of sexual violence. His experts asserted that it was not substantially probable that he would do so while the state's experts argued that it was. The trial court agreed with the state's experts and found that it was substantially probable that Matthew would commit future acts of sexual violence due to his mental disorder. He was committed as a sexually violent person and transferred to a secure institutional facility for treatment.

Matthew appealed his commitment on the basis of a number of claims, among them that the trial court had erroneously admitted his delinquency adjudication, which he argued should have remained confidential.

The appeals court concluded that the trial court had properly admitted his prior delinquency adjudication for the consensual oral sex with the 13-year-old boy at the residential treatment facility and that its disclosure did not violate his constitutional rights. In Wisconsin there existed at the time a statute that protected juveniles from the disclosure of their juvenile delinquency records, but the court pointed out that another statute had been passed by the legislature more recently that clearly provided for the admission of delinquency adjudications in the proceedings that govern the civil commitment of sexually violent persons. The court argued that since this later expression of legislative intent was more recent and more specific, it effectively repealed the former by implication. Therefore, Matthew's juvenile records were admissible within this context.

In *Commonwealth v. Kenney* (2006), Thomas Kenney refused to admit guilt but agreed that the Commonwealth of Massachusetts had enough evidence to find him delinquent for the complaint of rape of a 6-year-old girl in 1989, when he was 14 years old. He was placed on juvenile probation and given a suspended sentence. Later, in 1990, he pled guilty to two complaints of indecent assault and battery on two different girls who were both 9 years old. He was found in violation of his probation because of the new offenses and was committed to the Massachusetts Department of Youth Services. The state extended his commitment until he was 24 years old and then referred him to the district attorney for possible commitment as a sexually dangerous person. Kenney was eventually committed and placed at the Massachusetts Treatment Center for Sexually Dangerous Persons in Bridgewater, Massachusetts.

In his appeal of his commitment, Kenney claimed that his juvenile records were confidential, protected by state statute (M.G.L. Ch. 120 § 60). The district attorney should have been prohibited from having access to them, and should have been prevented from introducing them into evidence at his civil commitment trial as a sexually dangerous person. But as was the case for Matthew A.B., this confidentiality protection contradicted another statute governing the civil commitment of sexually dangerous persons (M.G.L. Ch. 123a, § 14 [c]), which stated that juvenile records were admissible at sexually dangerous person trials. The Massachusetts Supreme Judicial Court found that the necessity of making the records available is implicit within the statute, for how else would a district attorney make a threshold decision about whether to file a motion against a soon-to-be-released sexual offender in the custody of the Department of Youth Services? The court resolved the contradiction of the two opposing statutory provisions by deciding the matter in favor of disclosure, since it was the more recent legislative construction and carried the legislature's last expression on the matter, and because it was the more specific of the two provisions, explicitly permitting the disclosure of juvenile records in matters related to the civil commitment of sexually dangerous persons.

The admissibility of juvenile records in a sexually violent predator hearing was also confirmed in *In the Matter of the Detention of Raymond Marshall* (2004), a case decided by the court of appeals in Washington. The appellate court opined that the trial court was not in error when it denied the petitioner's motion to exclude any reliance on or reference to his juvenile records in the expert witness testimony of the state's psychologist. It further concluded that the expert's use of records in her testimony was not hearsay as it constituted the kind of information that an expert would typically use to make clinical decisions and arrive at an opinion regarding his being a sexually violent predator.

The presence of some requisite mental condition, defined within most states as a mental abnormality or personality disorder, is the second necessary criterion for civil commitment as a sex offender (Janus 2000). Some states have adopted the more general term "mental disorder," bringing the requisite mental condition closer in line with DSM-IV (Doren 2002). Arizona may have the most specific criterion regarding the necessary presence of a distinguishing mental condition, listing specific diagnostic categories from the DSM-IV, such as a paraphilia, Personality Disorder, and Conduct Disorder. Arizona is the only state to identify Conduct Disorder, a mental disorder specific to children, as satisfying the necessary criterion of a mental abnormality or personality disorder. Texas may have the most general or nonspecific criterion for requisite mental disorder, requiring "a behavioral abnormality."

The presence of a mental disorder or abnormality is especially critical, according to the majority in *Hendricks*, because these laws can only be credibly considered civil in nature if they are applied to a distinct subpopulation of sexual offenders who are defined as being dangerous because of a mental disorder or abnormality. If they are being preventively detained merely because they are dangerous and nothing more, then the procedure is revealed as starkly retributional and thus unconstitutional. If, however, the state moves against the liberty of the individual because he is sexually dangerous due to some underlying abnormal mental condition, then the process can be neatly folded into the long-standing precedent of protecting the safety of the community by denying the liberty rights of the dangerous who have some impaired control over their dangerous behavior.

The two mental conditions that are typically diagnosed among civilly committed sexual offenders are the paraphilias and Antisocial Personality Disorder (Doren 2002). The paraphilias are a set of disorders ranging from the often-termed "hands-off" disorders such as Exhibitionism, Voyeurism, Fetishism, and Frotteurism (touching or rubbing against a nonconsenting person in public) to the more serious and harmful disorders such as Pedophilia and Sexual Sadism. Some have argued for the addition of a category within the paraphilias for recurrent or repetitive rapists who exhibit or report sexual arousal to forced or coerced sexual relations with a nonconsenting victim (Abel, Osborn, and Twigg 1993; Doren 2002; McConaghy 1999). Doren (2002) recommends that recurrent rapists with deviant arousal to sex with nonconsenting victims be captured within the generalized category of Paraphilia, Not Otherwise Specified. He adds the term "nonconsenting" to these mentally disordered sexual offenders, whom he describes as experiencing recurrent and powerful fantasies and urges to rape and engage in sexual contact with a nonconsenting victim. Rape as a paraphilia has yet to be accepted as a diagnostic category by the Task Force on DSM-IV (APA 2000). The reluctance may be a political concern about establishing a psychiatric category for a violent act committed largely against women and children that would foster a perception of the offender as disordered and in need of psychiatric treatment rather than as violently criminal and in need of punishment and incapacitation.

A problem immediately emerges when the application of the paraphilias and the personality disorders is considered in the case of juveniles facing possible civil commitment as sexual offenders. According to DSM-IV (APA 2000), to be diagnosed with Pedophilia, adolescents must be at least 16 years old and at least five years older than the child victim. This requirement is in addition to the presence of Criterion A: "Over the course of at least 6 months, recurrent, intense sexually arousing fantasies, sexual urges or sexual behaviors involving sexual activity with a prepubescent child or children (generally 13 years or younger)" (APA 2000, 572). The DSM-IV specifically rules out the case of a late-age adolescent involved in an ongoing relationship with a 12- or 13-year-old. Additionally, using DSM-IV criteria as a strict guide to the diagnosis of Pedophilia, a juvenile adjudicated delinquent at age 16, for instance, for the sexual abuse of a 9-year-old and 10-year-old female victim, where the abuse incidents were separated in time by more than six months, could not be diagnosed with Pedophilia absent any evidence of continued deviant urges, fantasies, or desires for younger-aged victims. This evidence may be hard to come by if the juvenile has been confined in a secure treatment program without access to younger female children. DSM-IV eschews the use of any strict criteria for the diagnosis of Pedophilia in late adolescence and recommends the use of clinical judgment, taking into account the maturity of the adolescent and the age difference between him and his child victims.

The diagnosis of Antisocial Personality Disorder in adolescence is a much less controversial matter than the diagnosis of the harm-inducing paraphilias, such as Pedophilia and Paraphilia, Not Otherwise Specified. The rule is clear: adolescents younger than 18 should not be diagnosed with Antisocial Personality Disorder (Criterion B). Instead, the diagnostic category of Conduct Disorder exists for youth who manifest a pattern of impulsivity, aggression, rule violation, and a disregard for and violation of the rights of others. While there is debate about the correspondence of Conduct Disorder to later Antisocial Personality Disorder, it is generally accepted that most Conduct Disordered adolescents will not develop full criteria for Antisocial Personality Disorder in adulthood (APA 2000).

Generally, appellate courts have accepted the criteria for Pedophilia set forth in DSM-IV. In the few cases when a juvenile sex offender or an adult whose only conviction for a sexual offense occurred in adolescence has been diagnosed with Pedophilia, appellate courts have generally allowed the diagnosis when it can be established that the juvenile was at least 16 years old when he exhibited deviant sexual arousal or behavior toward children and that the age difference between the juvenile and the child victim was at least five years or more.

In *In the Matter of the Care and Treatment of Peter E.J. Harvey* (2003), the supreme court of South Carolina specifically addressed the issue of the diagnosis of a qualifying mental disorder, in this case Pedophilia, for an adult. The offender was 20 years old at the time of his commitment hearing, and his only sexual offense occurred at 13, when he was adjudicated delinquent for having his 5-year-old brother perform oral sex on him. Harvey had a prior history of sexual offending against younger children. At the age of 10, while visiting relatives in Michigan, Harvey was involved in a sexual incident with twin 6-year-old boys involving his instructing them to take off their clothes along with him and the three of them walking naked for about twenty minutes around the family pool. The boys' parents discovered them and pressed charges against him. He was adjudicated delinquent and required by the juvenile court to attend a sexual offender treatment program.

Harvey reportedly had a significant history of sexual victimization as a child. At the age of approximately 8, he was reportedly molested by a married couple along with their daughter, who was about the same age as Harvey. The abuse was described as having been prolonged. Later Harvey was sexually abused by an older boy who forced him to perform oral sex on him.

Harvey was committed in 1994 for the sexual abuse of his brother, and in 1998, when he was 19, just prior to his release on parole, the state petitioned to have him civilly committed as a sexually violent predator. The state's psychiatrist, who evaluated him when he was 20, diagnosed him with the DSM-IV category of Pedophilia, citing that he had admitted having "some recurrent urges" since turning 16 about having sex with young children, though the psychiatrist did not report this finding in her written report. The psychiatrist concluded that he met the legal criteria as a sexually violent predator and that he was unfit for outpatient treatment. The psychiatrist did not believe that he met the criteria for "sociopathy" or Antisocial Personality Disorder.

During cross-examination, the state's psychiatrist stated that she relied upon the DSM-IV criteria in arriving at her diagnosis that Harvey suffered from Pedophilia. She noted that although Harvey's adjudicated sexual offense occurred prior to the age of 16, he had admitted having ongoing urges about having sex with children and, therefore, by the criteria set forth in DSM-IV, met the definition for Pedophilia as there was sufficient evidence that his deviant sexual desires regarding children had occurred over a course of time longer than the required six months and had persisted beyond the age of 16, although without his further acting upon his urges.

To testify on his behalf, Harvey called a forensic psychologist who had also conducted an evaluation of him. The forensic psychologist testified that Harvey did not meet the diagnostic criteria for Pedophilia as defined by DSM-IV because Harvey was only 10 years old the time of his adjudication and because the twin children in the pool incident in Michigan were 6 years old, less than the 5-year difference required by DSM-IV. He went on to testify that Harvey did not report ongoing deviant sexual urges regarding children and that the results of psychological testing did not reveal any "proclivities" toward sex with children. The type of test used to make this conclusion and its validity for such use was not detailed in the case. He opined that Harvey did not meet the legal standards for civil commitment and could be treated as an outpatient.

The trial court found beyond a reasonable doubt that Harvey suffered from Pedophilia and ordered his commitment as a sexually violent predator. The state supreme court reported that it shared Harvey's concern about the significance the trial court placed on the sexual offense that occurred prior to the age of 16 and agreed that the Michigan incident should be ruled out as evidence of Pedophilia since the age difference between him and his victims was less than five years. Nevertheless, they found that there was sufficient evidence of a mental abnormality, stating that "technically, (he) meets the definition of pedophilia" since, in accordance with the diagnostic criteria set out in DSM-IV, after the age of 16 he reported having urges to have sex with children. The court also disagreed with Harvey's assertion that the state had failed to sufficiently prove that his Pedophilia caused him to be likely to engage in acts of sexual violence. The state's psychiatrist's diagnosis of Pedophilia and her testimony that Harvey met the statutory criteria for finding him a sexually violent predator indicated that the state had not failed to provide evidence of dangerousness.

The South Carolina Supreme Court did provide Harvey with an escape hatch. They ruled that the admittance of the therapy log from the program was hearsay evidence and should not have been allowed. The log contained entries stating that Harvey had sexualized various female employees at the program and reported sexual fantasies about them. The state's expert claimed that while she read the log, these entries did not contribute to her diagnosis of him or her opinion about his risk. The Supreme Court, nevertheless, agreed with Harvey that the log contained subjective opinions and judgments and should have been ruled as inadmissible hearsay. It rejected the state's claim that admittance of the log was harmless to the outcome, stating that the state's psychiatrist had testified about its contents and the state had used information from the log to impeach the credibility of the defense expert. Therefore, they concluded that the log had figured into the trial in a significant way and was not harmless. They reversed and remanded the 1999 order that Harvey was a sexually violent predator.

The case of *In re the Commitment of Eric Pletz* (2000), decided by the Wisconsin Court of Appeals, also examined the issue of the validity of the diagnosis of Pedophilia for juvenile sex offenders. Pletz was originally adjudicated delinquent for two sexual offenses against children in 1989, when he was 14 years old. In 1992, when he was 17, he was convicted of another sexual assault against a child. At his civil commitment trial, the state's psychologist testified that Pletz suffered from requisite mental disorders, Antisocial Personality Disorder and Pedophilia, that rendered him likely to commit acts of sexual violence in the future. An interesting twist to the case was the admittance of two documents into evidence that the appeals court later ruled were hearsay and should have been excluded. At trial the state produced two letters that had been received from the DSM-IV Task Force. The letters were replies to a written inquiry addressed to the Task Force by the state's expert's clinical partner about whether an adjudication for a sexual offense committed prior to the age of 16 could be used as evidence of Pedophilia if the juvenile commits another sexual offense at age 16 or above. This was essentially the circumstance of Pletz, who had committed two of his three sexual offenses when he was 14 years old. The issue about whether these earlier offenses could be used as evidence of Pedophilia was argued at trial since DSM-IV specifically advises against making a diagnosis of Pedophilia in adolescents younger than 16.

Pletz argued that the letters, which asserted that the two earlier offenses could be used to support the diagnosis of Pedophilia, should have been disallowed, as they contained information not typically relied upon by an expert and therefore constituted hearsay. The appeals court agreed that the letters were hearsay even though they were written by members of the committee that had drafted the DSM-IV criteria for Pedophilia. The letters were not the views of the DSM-IV Committee or the American Psychiatric Association and were not contained within the DSM-IV, which is an established reference in the field, representing the consensus view of recognized experts. The letters contain the opinions of the members, or some of the members, of the committee in response to some hypothetical question and should never have been entered into evidence. However, the appeals court concluded that their admittance constituted a harmless error and that there was sufficient evidence for the jury to find Pletz a sexually violent person even without the evidence provided by the inadmissible letters.

Kansas v. Hendricks (1997) left open some key questions that needed to be answered. *Hendricks* had clearly set forth that the commitment of sexual offenders was a civil action, not a criminal one, and that states had the authority to set up procedures for the civil commitment of sexual offenders who were scheduled for release from their criminal sentences. The court was clear that these laws had to apply to a narrow group of sexual offenders who suffered from some mental abnormality or personality disorder that was related to a substantial risk of committing future acts of sexual violence. There had to be a nexus between the two: their mental abnormality or personality disorder had to be connected to their risk of future sexual offenses. The establishment of this connection between the requisite mental disorder and impaired volitional control over deviant sexual urges comprises the third criterion in Janus's (2000) 4-prong criteria.

The *Hendricks* court posited a volitional component to the standard. The sexual offender's mental abnormality or personality disorder had to produce an inability to control his urge to commit sexual offenses. This incapacity to control urges by reason of some mental abnormality or personality disorder set him apart from the run-of-the mill sexual offender who was at risk of sexual recidivism by choice or bad intention. It was the sexual offenders plagued by some mental abnormality or personality disorder that rendered them impaired to control their deviant sexual urges who were the special, narrow group of offenders who formed the proper target of involuntary commitment. By selecting them out for specialized confinement and treatment, states could maintain that their action to confine was based on the civil intentions of the therapeutic needs of the offender and the protection of the public. These offenders were being civilly committed because they could not help themselves and as a result were a threat to the community. The common sexual recidivist who plagued the community because he freely chose to commit sexual offenses was as serious a threat, but he could only be handled through criminal proceedings based on retribution and punishment. He could not properly be the subject of civil commitment proceedings.

The distinction between these two types of offenders is vague and imprecise from a diagnostic perspective. How does one distinguish between an offender who commits sexual offenses due to an inability to control his behavior and one who does not? From a legal perspective, however, the distinction was crucial, as it allowed the court to rationalize that only the civil commitment of a narrow band of sexual offenders was permissible: those who could not control their urge to commit future offenses because they suffered from some volitional impairment. But how much lack of control was necessary? Did states need to prove a complete or total lack of control or only some quantum of disability? Did a complete lack of control exist since even the worst pedophile spends the better part of his day not offending against children? If what was required was proof be-yond a reasonable doubt that a sexual offender with a mental abnormality or personality disorder lacked complete control over his deviant sexual urges, would this place states within an indefensible position, effectively rendering the civil commitment process unattainable and useless?

The United States Supreme Court returned to address this very issue in the case of *Kansas v. Crane* (2002). The state of Kansas had moved to civilly commit Michael Crane as a sexually violent predator. Crane was a sexual offender who had been diagnosed by mental health experts as having an Antisocial Personality Disorder and Exhibitionism. At trial he was ordered committed as a sexually violent predator. On appeal of his commitment, the Kansas Supreme Court reversed the decision, interpret-ing the previous *Hendricks* decision as insisting upon the finding that the defendant lacked the ability to control his sexual offending. The state disagreed that they were required to find a complete lack of control and moved to have the case reviewed by the United States Supreme Court.

The Court agreed with the state of Kansas in its view that *Hendricks* required no finding of a complete or total lack of control. Instead, they as-serted that what was required was that a mental abnormality or personal-ity disorder make it difficult, not impossible, for the person to control his dangerous behavior. The insertion of the word "difficult" in the standard indicates that a total or complete lack of control is not required. Even the worst mentally disordered sexual offenders retain some degree of control over their dangerous behavior. The requirement that the lack of control be absolute would effectively make unattainable the civil commitment of even the most dangerous sexual offenders who suffer from mental abnor-malities or personality disorders.

The Court rejected the claim that the volitional defect to control devi-ant sexual impulses must be proven to be total and absolute, but it refused to provide a mathematically precise or technical standard for the amount of lack of control needed. Instead, it concluded that

> it is enough to say that there must be proof of serious difficulty in control-ling behavior. And this, when viewed in light of such features of the case as the nature of a psychiatric diagnosis, and the severity of the mental abnormality itself, must be sufficient to distinguish the dangerous sexual offender whose serious mental illness, abnormality, or disorder subjects him to civil commitment from the dangerousness by the typical recidivist convicted in an ordinary criminal case. (*Kansas v. Crane* 2002, 414)

The Court acknowledged that a more precise standard would be preferred but argued that the Constitution's safeguarding of liberty in the area of the civil commitment of the mentally ill is not always best preserved through "bright-line rules." Rather, the Court has sought to provide guidelines that must be applied "deliberately and contextually," elaborating standards to guide specific circumstances that arise within particular cases.

The standards and objectives set up in *Crane* refine to a degree the previous ones created in *Hendricks*. A total or complete lack of control is not necessary, only serious difficulty controlling one's deviant sexual urges. What is required is not an absolute lack of volitional ability but merely a partial one. What is not settled in either *Hendricks* or *Crane*, however, is the question of how these standards or objectives are to apply to adolescents. Do adolescents have similar volitional capacities as adults when it comes to controlling their sexual urges? Are these manifested in a similar manner for adolescents as they are for adults? Do we hold adolescents to the same standard of serious difficulty controlling sexual urges as we do adults? Or does their immature developmental status require that one think about these capacities differently for them?

The formulation of a generalized link between a mental disorder and a volitional impairment is more easily established for Pedophilia, a diagnostic category that by definition provides a ready-made link to volitional impairment and risk. Conduct Disorder, however, bears no specific relationship to sexual recidivism. If a juvenile has a Conduct Disorder or Antisocial Personality Disorder and a prior delinquency adjudication for a sexual offense, and if expert witnesses testify that in his particular case the individual's disorder predisposes him to violent sexual acts, then a sufficient connection may be made between his mental disorder and his predisposition for violent sexual acts. But such a line of clinical reasoning opens the door for potential tautological thinking: a person has a Conduct Disorder or an Antisocial Personality Disorder because he has prior acts of sexual violence, and his prior acts of sexual violence provide the necessary evidence that his particular form of Conduct Disorder or Antisocial Personality Disorder results in a volitional impairment in his ability to control such acts from occurring in the future.

A number of state appellate cases have examined the issue of the nexus between a requisite mental disorder, like Antisocial Personality Disorder or Conduct Disorder, and deficits in volitional control of deviant sexual urges. In *In re the Commitment of Marvel L. Eagans* (1998), a case we examined earlier in this chapter for its finding that an adjudication of delinquency for a sex offense for a juvenile constitutes a criminal conviction for the purpose of civil commitment as a sexually dangerous person or a sexually violent predator, counsel for the defendant argued that the state of Wisconsin failed to prove that Eagans had a mental disorder that caused a substantial probability that he would engage in acts of sexual violence in the future. The state at trial had asserted that Eagans suffered from an Antisocial Personality Disorder, which was the basis for the substantial probability that he would continue to be at risk for violent sexual acts in the future. But Eagans argued that Antisocial Personality Disorder was not a sufficiently precise category of mental disorder to support his civil commitment as a sexually violent person and could not be used as the sole basis of commitment for a person who committed his sexual offense when he was a juvenile. But the court of appeals disagreed, deeming the issue an evidentiary one and not a constitutional one. They found that the diagnosis of Antisocial Personality Disorder meets the statutory criteria as a requisite mental disorder. Further, they found that there was reasonable evidence presented at trial by mental health experts that Eagans had an Antisocial Personality Disorder that made it substantially probable that he would commit sexually violent acts in the future. Defense counsel challenged this finding at trial, asserting that because he was 18 years of age and his sexual offenses all occurred when he was a juvenile, using this diagnostic term was improper since the offenses formed a part of the basis for the diagnosis, essentially arguing against the circularity of the reasoning in the state's case against him. Defense also contended that the diagnosis of Antisocial Personality Disorder does not specifically predispose one to sexually violent acts; it is not one of the diagnostic criteria for the diagnosis, for instance, according to the DSM-IV.

The court concluded that these assertions go to the weight and credibility of the evidence, not their constitutionality. This was a decision for the legal fact finder to settle, not an appellate court. An Antisocial Personality Disorder is a mental disorder that is precise enough for use in a civil commitment proceeding, according to the appellate court, provided other evidence is entered about the specificity of his propensity for future sexual violence. They found nothing constitutionally untoward about its application to an 18-year-old male whose only sexual offenses occurred when he was an adolescent.

In a previous case, *State v. Adams* (1998), Adams, as did Eagans, argued that his diagnosis of Antisocial Personality Disorder did not provide the necessary nexus to a predisposition for future sexual offenses. The court agreed that while a diagnosis of Antisocial Personality Disorder standing alone without other supporting evidence of a predisposition for future acts of sexual violence would be insufficient for commitment, it is still possible to be diagnosed with this mental disorder in combination with other evidence that would provide the nexus and support the legal finding that the person is a sexually violent person.

A challenge to the nexus between Antisocial Personality Disorder and a volitional impairment or a predisposition to commit future acts of sexual violence was also raised in *Wisconsin v. McCain* (1999), a case previously discussed for its establishment of juvenile adjudication as a criminal conviction. McCain had been adjudicated delinquent in 1994 for a set of sexual assaults. In 1996, the state filed a petition asserting that McCain was a sexually violent person and should be involuntary committed. At the probable cause hearing, a state psychologist testified that McCain met the diagnostic criteria for Antisocial Personality Disorder and that this acquired condition affected both his emotional and volitional capacity, predisposing him to commit acts of sexual violence. At trial a second psychologist for the state also diagnosed him with Antisocial Personality Disorder and seconded the view that his history of sexual aggression in combination with his mental disorder made it substantially probable that he would commit further acts of sexual violence in the future. The trial court found that the state had proved beyond a reasonable doubt that McCain was a sexually violent person and ordered him committed to a secure mental health facility.

McCain appealed the decision, arguing, as did Eagans before him, that the diagnosis of Antisocial Personality Disorder does not inherently predispose one to engage in acts of sexual violence. The diagnosis of Antisocial Personality Disorder is too imprecise to provide such specific behavioral predictions. The court of appeals rejected McCain's argument, citing once again its reasoning in *Adams* (1998) that the civil commitment statute

> does not define "mental disorder" as a condition that, generally, predisposes "people," or "persons," or the "prison population" to engage in sexual violence. It simply refers to "a person." And who is that person? . . . [T]hat person can be no one other than the specific individual—the subject of the petition—who is "the person" who meets the statutory prerequisites "and who is dangerous because he or she suffers from a mental disorder that makes it substantially probable that the person will engage in acts of sexual violence." (15-16)

Moreover, in *State v. Post* (1995) this same court held that "persons will not fall within (the civil commitment statute) unless they are diagnosed with a mental disorder that has the specific effect of predisposing them to engage in acts of sexual violence" (16). *Post* requires that the focus be on the particular individual who is the subject of the petition and on the link between this specific individual's mental disorder and volitional impairment. What is needed is an individualistic analysis of the particular case that does not require that a general link between a mental disorder and risk be empirically established in the aggregate. Such a generalized link is more easily established for Pedophilia, a diagnostic category that by definition provides an easy ready-made link to a volitional impairment and risk. The court in *Post* goes on to state that to require a general link between Antisocial Personality Disorder and a volitional impairment and risk is to conclude that the legislature intended to exclude from civil commitment all persons diagnosed with Antisocial Personality Disorder who also had histories of sexual violence.

A pattern of impulsivity is one of the diagnostic criteria for Antisocial Personality Disorder and may be the diagnostic feature of the disorder that bears the closest resemblance to a volitional impairment. Persons with Antisocial Personality Disorder often have histories of general impulsivity across behavioral domains. They are impulsive in a variety of settings and across time and their range and scope of criminal activities often serve as stark testaments to their impulsive lifestyles. They can impulsively steal or be aggressive or engage in acts of sexual violence. They are rarely impulsive in one sector of life and well managed and controlled in others. Their impulsivity runs the gamut.

The question as to whether evidence of impulsivity as a volitional impairment indicating an inability to control one's risk of future harm can be a generalized impairment that manifests in a variety of behavioral domains and situations, including sexual offending, or must be specifically and precisely linked to sexual offending was tested in *In the Matter of James D. Creighton* (1997), a case decided by the Minnesota Court of Appeals. Creighton began his sexual violence history early, at the age of 9, and continued his pattern of sexual offending, as well as a pattern of generalized delinquent behaviors, throughout his adolescence. The state of Minnesota committed Creighton indeterminately as a sexually psychopathic personality. Creighton contested the finding, raising a number of issues, among them that the trial court had failed to establish a causal nexus between his mental disorder and his volitional impairment and risk of future harm. He conceded that he had engaged in sexually aggressive acts in the past, but the evidence demonstrated that his impulsive behavior was of the "global variety" and not exclusively sexual in nature. In fact, one of the disorders he was diagnosed with at trial was Impulsive Disorder, Not Otherwise Specified because his impulsivity was determined to be pervasive in all aspects of his life. The lack of specificity of a volitional impairment for his risk of future sexual violence, he argued, made the connection or link between his volitional impairment and mental disorders too imprecise to warrant a finding that he was a sexually psychopathic personality. The appeals court disagreed, stating that the finding that Creighton's impulsivity extended to other areas of life was a demonstration of his lack of power to control himself and did not function as a factor mitigating the determination that his volitional impairment rendered him sexually dangerous to others.

Similar arguments about the lack of a specific nexus between the diagnosis of Conduct Disorder and a volitional impairment to control deviant sexual urges has been raised in appellate decisions. In *In re to the Commitment of Matthew A.B.*, the Wisconsin case discussed previously for its holdings on the issue of the confidentiality of juvenile records in civil commitment proceedings for juvenile sex offenders, Matthew A.B. objected to the use of the diagnostic category Conduct Disorder, used by the state to civilly commit him as a sexually violent person. Matthew A.B. argued that the diagnostic category of Conduct Disorder is too imprecise to provide the necessary nexus between its presence and the predisposition to commit a future act of sexual violence. The paraphilias, Pedophilia for instance, would provide the needed connection between a mental disorder and a specific risk for sexual violent acts, but Conduct Disorder bears no specific relationship to sexual recidivism.

The appeals court rejected his argument, applying the same logic used by *Adams* and *Eagans*, who tried to use a similar argument of nonspecificity of the diagnosis of Antisocial Personality Disorder. They agreed that Matthew A.B.'s diagnosis of Conduct Disorder standing alone might not fulfill the criteria for a sexually violent person. But this diagnosis, coupled with additional evidence about his propensity for sexual violence, would satisfy the criteria, and the court found that this necessary additional evidence that Matthew's conduct disorder predisposed him to sexually violent acts was provided at his trial. This evidence consisted of his previous adjudication for a sexual offense and the testimony of expert witnesses who stated that a Conduct Disorder could predispose some to commit acts of sexual violence.

In the court's view the necessary nexus between his mental disorder and his predisposition for violent sexual acts was established, and he was properly found to be a sexually violent person.

The fourth necessary criterion identified by Janus (2000) for the involuntary civil commitment of a sex offender is that the offender poses a substantial risk of committing future acts of sexual violence. The problem with this criterion in the context of the civil commitment of juvenile sex offenders or the commitment of adults whose only sexual offense occurred while they were juveniles is that the research literature has consistently reported a low sexual recidivism rate for juvenile sexual offenders—lower than for adult sexual offenders, and very much lower than for general juvenile delinquency. Two related issues emerge regarding the prediction of sexual recidivism for juveniles and for adults whose only offense occurred while they were juveniles. First, should such individuals be assessed with actuarial assessment instruments that were developed and normed on adult sex offenders? Second, given that the base rate of sexual recidivism is relatively low, hovering in most studies between 5 and 15%, as we saw in chapter 3, can a credible argument be made that a juvenile's risk to commit future sexual acts of violence is substantial enough to support his civil commitment as a sexual offender?

There have been a limited number of appellate cases that have addressed aspects of these two problems. In *In re Commitment of Matthew A.B.* (1999), Matthew A.B. argued that his commitment as a sexually violent person was unconstitutional because the state's expert relied upon research based on the recidivism rates of adult sex offenders to reach his conclusion that Matthew A.B. was predisposed to commit future acts of sexual violence. He asserted that this was improper because he was a juvenile when he committed his sexual offense. Matthew asserted that juveniles have a lower risk of reoffense than adults and that the trial court, therefore, had no reasonable basis for reaching the conclusion it did regarding his commitment.

The court admitted the inherent difficulty of predicting future dangerousness but went on to state that such predictions are an "attainable" and "essential" part of the judicial process. They conceded that the predictions, like those made about Matthew in his commitment trial, are difficult but they are not impossible, and are, in fact, essential if the state is to civilly commitment offenders as sexually violent persons.

•   •   •

In *In re the Commitment of Marvel L. Eagans* (1998), the state of Wisconsin called two psychologists to testify at the commitment trial that he posed a substantial risk of future sexual offenses. Both psychologists diagnosed Eagans with an Antisocial Personality Disorder, claiming that the disorder predisposed him to sexually violent behavior. One of the psychologists based his opinion on a "risk assessment process" that incorporated personal characteristics of Eagans gleaned from records and the clinical interview, along with "statistical risk factors" that had been demonstrated to be empirically correlated with recidivism. The defense called no expert to rebut the state's psychologists but did submit them to cross-examination regarding the reliability and scientific validity of their methods and findings.

Eagan appealed the decision of the trial court that he was a sexually violent person, claiming that "there is no definitive evidence that one who sexually offends as a juvenile is substantially probable to reoffend." He buttressed his argument with the postconviction hearing testimony of John Hunter, a psychologist with two decades of experience in the evaluation, treatment, and research of juvenile sexual offenders. Hunter testified that the statistical base rate of recidivism for adolescent sex offenders is low compared to that of adult sexual offenders.

The Wisconsin Court of Appeals found Eagans's argument flawed. First, they did not agree that "definitive evidence" is a necessary standard in a civil commitment proceeding. What the state requires is "proof beyond a reasonable doubt that recidivism is substantially probable." Second, the Wisconsin Supreme Court had previously and unequivocally found that the civil commitment of sexual offenders was constitutional in its entirety. In the case *State v. Post* (1995), the court had previously addressed the concern raised by Eagans about the uncertainly inherent in the prediction of future dangerousness. "The Court recognized that although predictions of future dangerousness may be difficult, they are still an attainable, in fact essential, part of the judicial process. Here, the Wisconsin Legislature has devised a statutory method for assessing the future danger posed by persons predisposed to sexual violence and we find it constitutionally sound" (7).

The Court cites *Eagans* for confusing evidentiary issues with constitutional ones, asserting that the commitment trial was not to determine whether Eagans, a juvenile sexual offender, was likely to reoffend but whether at the time of the trial, as an adult, he had a mental disorder that predisposed him to commit future sexually violent acts. They agreed with

the jury's view that the testimony provided by the two psychologists sufficiently supported the finding that Eagans had an Antisocial Personality
Disorder and that the disorder predisposed him to commit sexually violent offenses in the future.

As for the question of a person adjudicated delinquent for a sexual offense as a juvenile, without ever having committed a sexual offense as an
adult, the court construes the issue as an evidentiary one. The court argues that the issue is not so much what Eagans did as an adolescent but
what his status was presently with regard to the elements contained within
the civil commitment standard. This reasoning does raise a problem since
his present status—whether he suffers from a mental disorder that predisposes him to future sexual violence—is based on acts he committed
while he was an adolescent. It would be difficult to imagine that the jury
could have reached its conclusion that Eagans was a sexually violent person without taking into consideration the prior delinquency adjudication,
and this information was not barred from the hearing.

The use of actuarial assessment instruments has received mixed reviews
in appellate decisions for persons facing civil commitment proceedings
who committed their sexual offense during adolescence. In *In re the Commitment of Patterson* (2006), the Wisconsin Court of Appeals rejected his
argument that Patterson's order for commitment as a sexually violent person was invalid because the mental health experts relied on actuarial assessments that were developed for use with adult offenders to determine
his risk of reoffending. The court acknowledged that the experts did use
such instruments but noted that they testified at trial that the results have
limited value and should be viewed cautiously as they were not developed
for use with juveniles. The trial court in its decision explicitly remarked
that it gave the actuarial assessment results very little weight. The appellate court ruled that the trial court did not err in considering them because they did not attach great probative value to them. From their perspective, even though the value of adult actuarial assessment instruments
are of limited use, they are admissible, and it is the province of the judge
or the jury to determine how much weight to attach to them in their decision making.

The appellate court in New Jersey reached an opposite conclusion in its
consideration of the use of adult actuarial assessment instruments in the
case of a New Jersey inmate who had served seventeen years for a sexual
offense he committed when he was 14 and 15 years old. In *In the Matter
of the Commitment of J.P.* (2001), a case we considered in chapter 3, J.P.

appealed his commitment as a sexually violent predator, arguing that the use of adult actuarial assessment instruments on an individual who committed his sex offense when he was an adolescent was inadmissible. J.P. had attempted to rape one adult woman and raped two others when he was 14 and 15 years old. He was paroled seventeen years after his conviction, but the state interceded and petitioned to have him civilly committed as a sexual offender.

In his commitment trial the state's experts had assessed J.P. on two actuarial assessment instruments normed on adults and concluded that he was at high risk to reoffend. The trial court agreed and he was civilly committed. In his appeal J.P. challenged the admissibility of the actuarial assessment instruments, claiming that all of his offenses were committed while he was an adolescent. The court noted, "we have some doubt whether actuarial tools can be used to evaluate a sex offender's risk of recidivism under such circumstances" (455). It concluded, "thus the instruments themselves cast doubt on whether they are reliable predictors of future dangerousness when applied to a sex offender incarcerated since early childhood" (457) and found that the judge had erred in admitting testimony based on these instruments. J.P.'s commitment was reversed and the court called for an evidentiary hearing concerning the admissibility of the actuarial assessment instruments in a case of an adult whose only offense occurred as an adolescent.

There is currently no national data on how many juvenile sexual offenders or how many adults whose only sexual offense was committed as a juvenile have been civilly committed as sexually dangerous or violent persons. Nonetheless, it is clear from a review of state statutes for the civil commitment of sexual offenders that many state legislatures included juvenile sexual offenders within the laws governing this process. The direct interface of the juvenile justice system and the civil commitment of sexual offenders unveils some potentially unanticipated fault lines, such as whether juveniles have been properly informed of the collateral use of their delinquent pleas in civil commitment hearings prior to their tendering such pleas or whether the absence of a constitutional right to a jury trial in their juvenile court hearing later is fundamentally fair since their delinquency adjudication can be used by the state to support their civil commitment as a sexual offender.

The requisite presence of a mental abnormality or personality disorder is deeply problematized in the case of juvenile sexual offenders. First, young adolescents are unable to be diagnosed with a paraphilia, particularly Pedophilia, prior to age 16. Moreover, other frequent diagnoses, such as Antisocial Personality Disorder and Conduct Disorder, do not provide a specific nexus to a volitional impairment or risk for future sexual offending. It is necessary that evidence for the nexus be established in the specific case through the presence of prior sexual offending, which opens the door to potential tautological reasoning: their prior sexual offense is used to support the presence of a mental disorder and the nexus of their mental disorder to a volitional impairment is the presence of a prior history of sexual offending. Finally, problems emerge when attempts are made to establish their future risk of committing sexually violent acts. First, juvenile sexual offenders have an empirically established lower recidivism rate than adult sexual offenders, making the argument about their future risk more difficult to establish. Second, it is unclear that the actuarial assessment instruments in wide use with adult sexual offenders can be employed with juvenile sexual offenders or even with adults whose only sexual offense occurred when they were juveniles. Lastly, there have been a number of actuarial assessment instruments developed over the past decade designed and normed specifically on juvenile sexual offenders. However, these instruments have yet to establish sufficient predictive validity, mostly due to the low base rates of sexual recidivism for juveniles, which have posed difficult, even insurmountable, problems for the test developers. Their use in civil commitment proceedings is, therefore, questionable.

8

Collateral Consequences
The Invisible Punishment of the
Juvenile Sex Offender

Early on Easter Sunday morning, April 16, 2006, Ralph Marshall awoke to find his pickup truck and his son, Stephen Marshall, gone. He had planned to go target shooting at a nearby range with his son later that morning, and figured Stephen had gone ahead alone without him. Unbeknownst to his father, Stephen had left earlier that morning armed with an assault rifle and two handguns.

Stephen had arrived at his father's home in Houlton, Maine, a small town near the Canadian border, three days earlier on Thursday, and planned on spending a few days visiting his father. Stephen lived in North Sydney, Nova Scotia, where he worked as a dishwasher at a local restaurant. He had told his employer about the trip but told him he would be returning to work on Saturday. When he failed to arrive for work, his employer called his cell phone, concerned that there might be some problem since Stephen had always been a prompt and reliable employee. When Stephen did not answer his cell phone, he called Stephen's mother, who told him that Stephen had had car trouble and was still at his father's house (Daniel 2006; Wangsness and Burge 2006).

Stephen Marshall murdered his first victim at about 3:00 A.M. in Milo, Maine, a small town north of Bangor about one hundred miles south of Houlton. Joseph Gray, 57, had fallen asleep on the couch. His wife had been awakened by the barking of their five dogs. Stephen fired five shots into the house, hitting Gray, who collapsed immediately. His wife, who had crawled into the kitchen to call police, was also nearly hit by a bullet that flew by her.

About five hours later in Corinth, Maine, just twenty-five miles south of Milo, William Elliot, 24, was awakened by knocking at his door while he lay asleep next to his girlfriend. He pulled on a pair of sweatpants and answered the front door. Marshall fired a couple of shots into Elliot as he opened the door, killing him. His girlfriend, Anne Campbell, found Elliot dead on the floor. She pushed open the front door and saw Marshall standing outside staring blankly back at her as though he had not expected her to be there. He turned away and walked back to his father's truck, directing an ambiguous hand gesture to her, maybe an obscenity, like the middle finger, or maybe an index finger and thumb cocked like a shooting gun. She was unable to tell. As he drove away she caught sight of his license plate number and repeated it to herself as she yelled for help. A neighbor hearing her screams called the police.

Later that same day, at about 1:45 P.M., Stephen boarded a Vermont Transit Lines bus in Bangor, Maine, scheduled to arrive at South Station in downtown Boston that evening. He boarded the bus with two concealed loaded handguns.

The Massachusetts Bay Transit Police, on the basis of information received from authorities in Maine, intercepted the bus outside of South Station and prepared to evacuate the passengers when Stephen withdrew a Colt-45 handgun and killed himself with a single gunshot to the head. The other gun was later found on his person.

The details of Stephen Marshall's history remain scanty. He had no history of criminal violence and no criminal record. He had had a longstanding interest in firearms since childhood. Friends described him as a quiet, withdrawn individual with a wry sense of humor who seemed depressed and preoccupied in the months prior to his killing spree. His life up to this point had been unfocused and directionless. Over the previous few years he had moved back and forth between the homes of his parents. More recently, however, he had seemed to recover emotionally. A renewed commitment to religion had seemed to focus him. Perhaps the day he selected for his deadly actions bore some significance. His plan about what he intended to do when he disembarked in Boston remains a mystery, as he did not leave anything in writing. He may have been improvising this last leg of the day. Also lost with his suicide was an explanation for his deadly actions early that morning.

Joseph Gray and William Elliot were both listed online on the Maine Sex Offender Registry. Police uncovered that Marshall had looked up both of them, along with thirty-two other registered sex offenders. There are a total of twenty-two hundred sex offenders listed on the website, which averages about one hundred thousand hits a month. When it was first posted five years ago, the website crashed because of the volume of visits on its first day. It was later revealed that Marshall had physically visited four other registered sex offenders during the course of the morning, but they were either not at home or had not answered the door when he knocked. The death toll could have been much higher that day.

Gray had been convicted in 1992 of indecent assault and battery of a child and rape of child in Bristol County, Massachusetts. He had been sentenced to four to six years in state prison. Elliot, at the age of 19, had pled guilty to two misdemeanor counts of sexual abuse of a minor in 1992 for sexual relations with a girl who was two weeks short of her 16th birthday. He served four months in jail for a crime that was the equivalent of statutory rape. In two weeks she would have been able to legally consent to having sex with him. Technically speaking, Elliot was not a juvenile sex offender since legally he was an adult, but he was still a teenager at the time of his offense.

Maine shut down the registry site as police searched for Marshall. It was opened again the next day. Joseph Gray and William Elliot were still included within the listing, along with their addresses and photographs.

The Jacob Wetterling Crimes Against Children and Sexually Violent Predators Act (1994) was passed by the United States Congress in September 1994. It was the first federal legislation requiring that states compel certain sexual offenders to register with their local law enforcement agency. Failure to comply would result in a 10% reduction in federal anticrime funds awarded to the state. The act established the first registry for sexual offenders, a listing of sexual offenders that would be maintained by law enforcement agencies to aid in their investigation of sexual crimes, allowing for an easy rounding up of the usual suspects and for selective distribution to the public when necessary to maintain their safety. The act was named in honor of Jacob Wetterling, an 11-year-old boy believed abducted in 1989 in Minnesota by a suspected adult with a history of child molestation. Jacob has never been found.

In 1996 Megan's Law amended the Jacob Wetterling Act, mandating that all states develop community notification procedures and requiring that they provide easily accessible information about sexual offenders to the public. Megan Kanka was 7 years old when she was abducted and murdered in New Jersey by an adult previously convicted of child molestation who was residing near her home with two other sexual offenders in a community release program. Megan's parents were unaware that a group of convicted sexual offenders was living near their home. In their testimony before the United States Congress, they asserted that they would have been more vigilant had they been informed about their presence. Megan's Law created a move from the more passive registration of sexual offenders with local law enforcement to the more active notification of the public of the existence of convicted sexual offenders living in their midst.

Community notification consists of a publicly accessible registry allowing private citizens to take precautionary steps to protect themselves. Some form of community notification has been present in all fifty states since 1997. States have structured these laws differently, however. Some states list all sex offenders at large in the community without categorizing them within various risk groups; others classify the offenders by their level of risk according to the results of some actuarial assessment instrument, often the STATIC-99. Often, a three-tier classification system is utilized, with level one reserved for the lowest-risk offenders, level two for moderately at-risk offenders, and level three for the highest-risk offenders. Universal community notification is reserved in some states for only level three sex offenders.

Also in 1996, Congress passed the Pam Lychner Sexual Offender Tracking and Identification Act, a further amendment of community notification requiring the FBI to develop a national database of names and addresses of sex offenders released from prison. This act broadened the tracking of sexual offenders beyond the state level, linking the states into a national registry. Currently there are over five hundred thousand registered sexual offenders in the United States. Pam Lychner was a 31-year-old woman who was attacked by a previously convicted sexual offender in Houston, Texas.

The most recent U.S. congressional action on the community notification of sexual offenders was the Adam Walsh Child Protection and Safety Act (2006), named after Adam Walsh, a 6-year-old boy abducted from a mall in Hollywood, Florida, in 1981. His remains were found two weeks later in a canal about a hundred miles from his home. His killer was never identified. The act, sponsored by James Sensenbrener, a Republican congressman from Wisconsin, established a comprehensive national system for the registration of sexual offenders, including juvenile sexual offenders 14 years or older convicted of aggravated sexual abuse. The act excludes consensual sexual conduct or most instances of statutory rape, except in cases when the victim is less than 13 and the offender is more than four years older than the victim. Failure to comply with the registration requirements can result in a sentence of no greater than a year. The registry is maintained by the FBI and includes a picture of the offender and his fingerprints, and DNA is made available to law enforcement agencies. Offenders are required to register for fifteen years, twenty-five years, or their lifetime, according to their risk level. In the case of juvenile sex offenders, a lifetime registration requirement can be reduced to twenty-five years if they maintain a "clean record" during that time span. Information about the registrant is available to the public on the internet. For juvenile sex offenders, information about where they attend school is exempted. States are required to be in compliance with the terms of the Adam Walsh Act by 2009 or face a loss of 10% of funding from federal anticrime grants to the state.

The wide-scale registration and community notification of a specific class of offenders is unprecedented in the history of American jurisprudence. No class of offender has been subjected to the postrelease requirements of the current sexual offender. In a span of twelve years, from 1994 to 2006, the United States Congress passed four separate acts pertaining to the registration and community notification of sexual offenders, each building on the establishments of the prior one. Congress's repeated revisiting of this issue bespeaks the huge public support for the registration and community notification of sexual offenders. What makes the establishment of such procedures puzzling, however, is that these legislative acts sailed through Congress with near unanimity on the basis of the untested premise that informed community members can and will act to protect themselves.

The political popularity of these acts is largely due to the use of specific rhetorical techniques that activate strong emotional reactions on the part of politicians and the public alike (Hiller 1998). First, the acts are all named in honor of victims whose stories had been widely covered in the media. In the case of three of the laws, they are named after murdered children. All of the acts are attached to detailed narratives about a particular victim that shocks and horrifies. The cases of the abducted and murdered children function as signal crimes, a representational warning to people about the widespread distribution of risk throughout society, setting off an outraged call for new forms of crime control (Innes 2004). A story about a murdered child is easier to remember or understand than any logical argument based on statistics or empirical evidence about the effectiveness of or need for such community protections. Stories are more effective than statistics, and more likely to induce strong emotional reactions. The laws are defined as being aimed at the protection of the most vulnerable members of our society: children. A vote against the legislation is a vote against the protection of children, a perception that any elected official will avoid at any cost, even if he or she suspects that the law may lack any real public safety benefit or may come with a host of unintended negative consequences for the offender and the public.

Second, the legislative arguments are often supported by unfounded, sometimes grossly exaggerated statistical claims about the danger present in society. Distorted and overbloated statistics about the number of child abductions that occur on an annual basis or the number of children sexually abused by strangers contribute to the construction of a "mean-world" perception. Suspect statistical evidence about "stranger danger" is often presented in support of the legislation when in fact most of the child abductions and cases of child sexual abuse are committed by perpetrators known to the child, often close family members. Registration and community notification laws are unlikely to have any incremental public safety benefit in these cases since the family is already aware of the risk that the family member or friend poses to them.

Third, the targets of these laws are often depicted in dehumanizing terms, as "wolves among lambs," monsters, or sexual predators. These subhuman labels will often be attached to inflated statistical myths about the recidivism risk of sexual offenders. In the cases of Jesse Wetterling, Megan Kanka, and Adam Walsh, the offenders are arguably fittingly described by these negative labels. But these offenders are exceptional and statistically rare; the sex offenses of the vast majority of registrants bear little resemblance to them.

The use of these various rhetorical devices protects the legislation from external attack, making it seem that any resistance to or reluctance about their passage is a failure to act for the protection of vulnerable children in the community. The result in the case of Megan's Law was a unanimous congressional vote for its passage.

The threats represented by the leper and the plague victim were managed through distinct but related preventative strategies in 17th-century Europe (Foucault 1975). The leper was dealt with through the techniques of exclusion, a spatial separation from the community, banishment, and observation from a distance. The plague and its victim posed a more complex set of problems. The plague was not contained within an identifiable set of individuals or readily observable upon immediate visual inspection. It was something in the air itself—a miasma—that hung over the populace and required a different form of surveillance and containment. A "spatial partitioning" of the entire city was required, a ceaseless inspection of the entire space with strict rules regarding movement, contact, and travel. A new set of disciplinary techniques was needed that allowed for plague victims to coexist within the populace, albeit with careful tabs placed on their movements and interactions. According to Foucault, "The exile of the leper and the arrest of the plague (victim) do not bring with them the same political dream. The first is that of a pure community, the second that of a disciplined society" (Foucault 1975, 198).

The strategies used to manage the leper and the plague victim are two separate and distinct ways of exercising control over the bodies of contaminated people. Foucault identifies that the exclusionary tactics directed at the leper were replaced by a web of surveillance aimed at the plague victim. The transition created a new population, a new status of lower citizenry, the exiled among us, the stigmatized in our midst— marked but not expelled; branded but not separated; disciplined, watched, and restricted but not removed.

The architectural manifestation of the organizing technology used to manage the threat of the plague is contained within Jeremy Bentham's Panopticon, a utilitarian architectural feat of precision and efficiency designed for the modern prison. It was a central tower with a ring of windows at the top, darkened so that no one could see the sentinel figure located inside, who could take in a 360-degree panoramic view with a simple turning of his body. Along the periphery of the tower, a building forms a concentric ring around it. The periphery building was composed of honeycomb-like cells, in the formation of multiple vertical tiers, lit from the back so that the obscured figure within the central tower could visually inspect the entire cell and its occupant with a single broad, sweeping view. From the command post within the central tower, the supervising figure could view all of the cells from one pivotal vantage point. He could see everything at once, as omniscient as God, while the prisoners within their cells could never be sure if they were being watched since the figure was obscured in darkness.

The ingenuity of the Panopticon was its ability to make the prisoners feel as though they were being continuously watched when they were not. Constant surveillance is impossible. Even when the tower was properly staffed, the inspecting figure could not view every cell at the same time. The trick was to keep the prisoners in the dark about whether they were under surveillance at any given moment—to make them feel as though they were under visual scrutiny at all times. The invisibility of the observer to the observed was the power of the device—a constant threat of invisible inspection. The appearance of continuous surveillance was enough to deter. The prisoners would discipline themselves. The primary purpose of the Panopticon was not detection but prevention. The Panopticon allowed for the observation and control of the many by the few.

For Bentham the Panopticon was a utilitarian invention that promoted the establishment of an efficient operation for the prison institution. A smooth-running facility was now possible with the employment of only a few workers. A vast number of prisoners could be managed by the invisible inspection of a few supervising agents. It served humanitarian ends since it effectively eliminated the necessity of brute force and the show of violence to establish order and compliance. It was a correcting device that taught self-discipline and personal responsibility. It promoted docility and compliance in the unruly prisoner. It was an invention that in the mind of Enlightenment thinkers advanced a social good: compliance without violence or physical force.

For Foucault, the Panopticon represented something else entirely. For Foucault the Panopticon, that "cruel, ingenious cage," was a technology that spread and infiltrated its way into various social institutions. The technology of the Panopticon migrated outside of the walls of the prison, making its way into the insane asylum, the classroom, the military barracks, and the factory floor. It became a generalized model—he referred to it as the "panoptic schema"—useful "whenever one is dealing with a multiplicity of individuals on whom a task or particular form of behavior must be imposed" (205). It was a disciplinary technique for creating useful, docile people. The Panopticon was more than an architectural design; the panoptic schema was a technology for making disciplined people. The Panopticon was more than the solving of a practical problem. It led to the emergence of an entirely newly ordered society. This age, the late modern age, our age, is the panoptical age, the age of surveillance.

Community notification of sex offenders is a panoptical device with a twist: the observation of the many by the few shifts to the observation of the few by the many. Community notification turns the panoptic schema inside out, dispersing the central observing tower, the omniscient eye, and turning it into a multiplicity of eyes, diffused throughout the community. It relocates the responsibility for surveillance from the state to the public, and the site of surveillance from the prison to the community (Powers 2004). It is now the community that will manage and monitor the sexual offender.

The goals of registration and community notification are twofold: protection and prevention. An informed police force armed with knowledge about whom to watch can protect a community; offenders in the community who believe they are under continuous surveillance will be deterred from future offending. But is there any evidence that either of these goals is achieved?

There have been few empirical studies regarding the effectiveness of registration and community notification laws for adult sexual offenders and virtually no research to date about their effectiveness for juvenile sex offenders. In one of the few studies of the deterrent effect of registration and community notification, Schram and Milloy (1995) compared the rate of reoffense for a group of adult and juvenile sex offenders prior to the passage of registration and community notification laws with that of a matched group that was subjected to these procedures in the state of Washington. They report no evidence that community notification reduced recidivism during a followup period of nearly five years in the community. They did find, however, that registrants who recidivated were rearrested at a faster rate than a cohort of sexual offenders with similarly indexed offenses who were released prior to the enactment of these laws. Zevitz (2006), in a more recent study, also found that adult sexual offenders subjected to registration and community notification did not have a lower rate of recidivism than sexual offenders not subjected to these requirements.

Registration and community notification laws may be built upon a set of faulty assumptions that undermine their effectiveness. These laws are popular among politicians and the public for the appearance of safety they provide. They allow people to feel safe, as though they are armed with information that will ultimately protect them. But there is little evidence to support the claim that the procedures in fact deliver on their promise of making the community a safer place. As we have seen, the motivating force driving the swift and nearly unanimous legislative passage of these laws is often the shocking cases for which the legislative acts are often named. The individual cases behind the acts come to stand for a class of offenders at which the legislation is directed. The laws are provoked by a case but are devised for application to a class. Cases are about individuals; laws are about classes. Problems emerge when laws designed to deal with a particular case are applied to an entire class. The murders of Jacob Wetterling, Megan Kanka, and Adam Walsh were extraordinarily heinous, but they were also extraordinarily rare. The enactment of laws aimed at protecting the public from the likes of these perpetrators is certainly justifiable. A problem arises, however, when these perpetrators become the face for an entire class of offenders. These extraordinary offenders bear little resemblance to the general class of adult sexual offenders, and they bear even less resemblance to the majority of juvenile sex offenders.

A fault line emerges when laws are devised in response to extraordinary cases and are then applied to an entire class of offenders who bear little resemblance to them. The offender in the case of Megan Kanka, as was probably the case for Jacob Wetterling and Adam Walsh, was a stranger to her. A primary purpose of the registration and community notification laws is alerting the public to the presence of sexual offenders who are unknown to their neighbors so that they can be made aware of the offenders and take whatever action they deem necessary to protect themselves and their families. But the vast majority of sexual offenders have victims who are known to them. In the case of child molestation, often the perpetrator and victim are in the same family. This is even more often the case for juvenile sex offenders. Registration and community notification in these instances would add little new information since the family presumably already knows that the family member, friend, or acquaintance is a sexual offender.

The laws could have an unintended net-widening effect. While legislatures, when designing these registration and community notification laws, may have only been interested in applying them to moderate- or high-risk offenders, the laws may be netting low-risk offenders as well. Low-risk offenders who previously would have been placed only on probation in the past may now also end up on sex offender registries and community notification websites. The result is a diluted mixture of lower-risk and higher-risk offenders rather than a more targeted pool of higher-risk offenders.

The deterrent effect of registration and community notification laws may be weaker in the case of juvenile sex offenders because adolescents may be less able, due to developmental immaturity, to assess the consequences of reoffense than adults. In many instances it is not entirely clear whether they understand the consequences of community notification or whether they are even informed of them at the time of adjudication. The deterrent effect for which these laws aim may in the end be lost on juvenile sex offenders. The application of these laws to such offenders fails to take into account their unique offense characteristics. They have a substantially lower recidivism rate than adult sexual offenders and are arguably less culpable in a developmental sense than adult offenders. If their risk of recidivism is accepted as hovering around 10%, as indicated by the research, the false positive rate for community notification can be assumed to be about 90% (Trivits and Reppucci 2002). But it is typically the fear of false negatives, the missed recidivist, that directs public policy. The broadly drawn registration and community notification laws often fail to take into account the severity of the offense, so that it is entirely possible that alongside a juvenile convicted of multiple counts of child rape, an adolescent adjudicated delinquent for an age-of-consent statute would also be made to register, as was the case for William Elliot in Maine, who was shot and killed in 2006 by vigilante killer Stephen Marshall. A recent case in Michigan of an adolescent male required to submit to community notification for twenty-five years for mooning the high school principal points to the levels of absurdity to which these laws may occasionally rise (Leversee 2001).

Despite the absence of research support for the effectiveness of community notification laws, many states, though not all, have applied Megan's Law to juvenile offenders and have required that they be subjected to community notification just like adult sexual offenders (Caldwell 2002; Garfinkle 2003; Trivits and Reppucci 2002). Often the state statutes that apply to juveniles are carbon copies of the laws that apply to adults, simply with the word "juvenile" added before the phrase "sexual offender" (Zimring 2004). The same exact criteria used in the case of adult sexual offenders is applied to juveniles without any consideration of the developmental issues facing them or the more negative impact that such community labeling may have on them. Many of these registration and community notification laws were passed during a time when the rate of juvenile sex offending was declining.

There is some variation in the way these laws are applied to juveniles, with some using replicate versions of the adult laws, others setting up separate registries and criteria, some using a single registry but different criteria, and others requiring registration but not community notification. Some states have reserved judicial discretion for juvenile sex offenders, allowing juvenile court judges on a case-by-case basis to decide whether a particular juvenile should be required to register or not. It may soon come to pass that registration and community notification will be universal across all the states if they pass laws to be in compliance with the

Adam Walsh Act of 2006, and there is an incentive to do so in order to avoid the forfeit of 10% of their crime-prevention budget from the federal government.

Arguably, mandatory registration and community notification are in conflict with the historic principle of rehabilitation upon which the juvenile court was founded. The notion of labeling and making public the delinquency record of a juvenile offender was anathema within the original juvenile court. Such information was strictly protected because of concern that such labels could prove to be self-fulfilling prophecies for juvenile offenders. The labeling of youth as deviant could reduce their ability to be reintegrated within the community, increasing their likelihood of continuing along deviant pathways in the future. The laws are ostensibly not intended as punishment, but they may have this unintended effect.

There have been a number of failed attempts to legally challenge the constitutionality of registration and community notification laws on the basis that they represent double jeopardy or violate the Ex Post Facto Clause (punishing somebody under a new law for a crime that was committed before its enactment) (*Doe v. Poritz*, 662 A 2d. 367, 422 NJ 1995; Trivits and Reppucci 2002). Appellate courts have consistently interpreted these laws not as punitive measures but as regulatory ones designed not to deprive offenders of their liberty but as a means for society to protect itself. Any resulting punitive effects are an indirect result of the superseding right of the community to look out for its own safety. However, this interpretation does not address the problem that juvenile offenders are not afforded the same due process protections of adult offenders. For instance, as is the case in the civil commitment of juvenile offenders, discussed in the previous chapter, they are not constitutionally afforded the right to a trial by jury, yet community notification is still required of them. They get the same consequences as those directed at adults without the same due process protections.

A psychiatrist concluded after an hour-long meeting with J.W. and his parents that the 12-year-old boy from South Elgin, Illinois, was a danger to others (*In re J.W.* 2003). J.W. had told the psychiatrist about five instances in which he convinced two 7-year-old boys in his neighborhood to perform oral sex with each other and with him. Physical coercion and force were not used, but he did admit to applying verbal pressure on the victims. An investigator from the State's Attorney's Office had interviewed both victims. He testified at J.W.'s sentencing hearing that J.W. had instructed one victim to put his mouth on his penis and to allow J.W. to do the same to his. The incidents, numbering between five and ten, occurred under the deck of a neighbor's house and at J.W.'s house. The second victim told the investigator a similar story. At some later point in time, the step-mother of the second victim told the investigator that J.W. had anally raped her step-son. During a later interview with the same investigator, both boys admitted that J.W. had anally raped them. Then, a week before the sentencing date, the investigator met again with the first victim, who told him that J.W. had his dog lick the penises of both boys. They also said that he asked both victims to penetrate the dog's anus with their penises, but they were unable to do so. But they said that they had observed J.W. penetrate his dog's anus with his penis. This all allegedly took place at J.W.'s house. They were also directed by J.W. to penetrate each other anally, but they were unable to do so.

J.W.'s parents also told the doctor about a past incident when J.W. had exposed himself to a 5-year-old boy. J.W. denied any history of sexual abuse but did own up to having viewed his father's pornographic magazines. The psychiatrist thought it was clinically significant that J.W. had not disclosed the incident of exposure to him, and thought that J.W. had minimized much of his history of sexual offending. He diagnosed him with a Paraphilia Not Otherwise Specified, from the *Diagnostic and Statistical Manual of Mental Disorders, Text Revision, 4th edition* (APA 2000). This category of paraphilia is used for sexual perversions that do not meet criteria for any of the specific categories of paraphilia. The psychiatrist testified that he would have diagnosed him with Pedophilia, but J.W. was not yet 16, the minimum age for this diagnosis, according to the DSM-IV. The psychiatrist testified that J.W. needed comprehensive treatment for his paraphilia, including residential treatment, medication, and cognitive-behavioral therapy. He also testified that J.W. would be at risk to relapse if he did not get treatment in a residential program.

A therapist with ten years of experience in the treatment of sexually abusive youth began seeing J.W. in therapy in once-weekly sessions prior to his sentencing hearing. She testified that he was a danger "to a certain degree" and recommended probation, stating the "longer the better." She believed that J.W. had "groomed" his victims for abuse and that he experienced no guilt. She further testified that he needed a course of treatment for sexual aggression and required 24-hour monitoring and supervision by a person who understood the nature and seriousness of his problem. She also believed that his school should be notified about his sexual offenses so that school officials could protect other students from him. She believed that he should never be around other children, even children his own age, without the presence of an adult aware of his problem. Finally, she recommended that given the negative publicity surrounding his case, it would be in his best interests to move from his home in South Elgin.

At the sentencing hearing, J.W.'s parents told the judge that they were willing to place J.W. in a treatment program. They also intended to sell their house in South Elgin and move to another town. In the meantime, there was an aunt who would take J.W. into her home in an adjacent town.

J.W. apologized for his sexual offenses at his sentencing. The trial court noted that it could not sentence him to the adult Department of Correction because he was under 13 years of age. He was sentenced to five years' probation instead, and was required to attend a residential treatment program. He was also ordered to register as a sex offender for the rest of his life and to comply with AIDS/HIV testing. When he completed treatment he was required to move back with his aunt and never reside in or enter South Elgin again.

J.W. appealed the order for him to register as a sexual offender and the prohibition against his entering South Elgin. The appellate court rejected his claim that lifelong registration as a sexual offender violated constitutional prohibitions against double jeopardy. He further argued that it constituted cruel and inhuman punishment because he was improperly classified as a sexual predator under the state's Sex Offender Registration Act. They rejected this claim as well and also rejected his argument that the trial court had overstepped its authority by banning him from residing in South Elgin.

The supreme court of Illinois agreed with the appellate court that J.W. clearly and unambiguously met the statute defining sexual predators and that he was properly required to register for the rest of his natural life as sexual predators are statutorily required to do. The court reaffirmed an early position in favor of the state enacting legislation to protect children against sexual predators and did not view such procedures as infringing on the constitutional rights of the registrant. The case of a 12-year-old boy did not change their analysis. The public interest in protecting itself does not change, according to the court, when confronted by an adult or a 12-year-old sexual offender. J.W. argued that the lifetime registration of a 12-year-old runs counter to the original purpose of the juvenile court: rehabilitation and the protection of minors. However, the Supreme Court reminded J.W. that in 1999—ironically, exactly one hundred years after the first juvenile court in the United States was established in the state of Illinois—the legislature had amended the Juvenile Court Act to give priority to the mission of protecting the community above that of rehabilitating the juvenile. The change represented a fundamental shift from the overarching goal of rehabilitation to the primary function of protecting the community from dangerous juveniles.

In what amounted to a pyrrhic victory for J.W., the court found that the residency restriction may have been too broadly drawn and declared it an unconstitutional condition. A judge dissenting from the majority finding that juvenile sex offenders are required to register reminded his opposing jurists that juveniles convicted of murder do not have to register in the state of Illinois but a 12-year-old convicted of sexually abusing two 7-year-old children would need to do so for the rest of his life as a result of this decision.

There is a cascading set of collateral consequences that flow from sex offender registration and community notification laws, many of which are completely unintended or not contemplated when the laws are drafted and passed. These unintended negative effects have been referred to by a variety of phrases: "civil death," "civil disability," "invisible punishment," "internal exile," "noncitizenship," or "the mark of Cain" (Travis 2002). They represent a broad array of consequences that radiate from criminal sentences but are often separate from them. These invisible punishments result in the effacing of the rights and privileges of citizenship. It is often difficult for the offender to take in their depth and breadth because they often are applied outside of the sentencing court. They are often legislative actions that do not emerge directly from criminal sentencing by the court but are extensions of punishment that attach to the civil rights of the subject. Civil commitment of sexual offenders after they have served their criminal sentence is an example of one of the more severe collateral consequences. The requirement to register as a sex offender and be subjected to community notification is an example of a lesser one. These collateral consequences function as instruments of social exclusion, reducing and diminishing the offender, setting up boundaries between him and the rest of the citizenry (Travis 2002). These laws are not intended to rehabilitate. They are simply preventative and retributive, with these aims being achieved through selective incapacitation, such as keeping certain juvenile sex offenders from certain neighborhoods or out of certain schools. They relegate offenders who have served their time to the margins of society.

Often collateral consequences emanate from civil penalties passed by the federal or state government that place limits or restrictions on an offender's citizenship and liberty in the community: ineligibility for public benefits or educational grants, loss of voter rights, employment restrictions, housing and residential restrictions, school notification and exclusion, deportation, inability to serve in the military, and denial of professional licensure. Some of these invisible punishments do not make much sense on their face. For example, some convicted felons are ineligible to obtain a license for certain professions even if the profession has no relation to their prior criminal history, rendering some vocational training programs in prison, such as barbering, useless. The list is so broadly dispersed in federal and state statutes that it would be nearly impossible for an attorney to advise clients of the statutes' applicability and impact on them prior to their tendering a negotiated plea. In fact, an attorney may not be obligated to disclose them since they are civil penalties often imposed by agencies outside of the criminal justice system (Pinard 2006). Often the collateral consequences continue long after the direct consequences of criminal sentencing have ended. In many cases they do not begin to take effect until the direct consequences have faded.

In the case of the juvenile sex offender, his confrontation with the prospects of collateral consequences raises questions about his ability to understand their implications and to competently take them into account as he makes rational decisions about a plea or a course of defense. Many of these penalties are more abstract, longer term, more indirect, and harder to conceptualize (Pinard 2006). The consequences are complicated, and defendants may need the assistance of parents or some interested third party to help sort them out. The consequences often spread to the family—as in the case of juvenile sex offenders being unable to live in certain towns, as was the case for J.W. in South Elgin, Illinois—creating a conflict for the family. Families of juvenile sex offenders may often find themselves in the untenable position of having to decide what is in the best interests of their child versus what is in the best interest of the family as a whole. Do they remain connected to and supportive of their sex-offending child or do they cut ties with him so that they can remain in the community for the sake of the other children in the family? This was exactly the kind of "Sophie's Choice" position in which the parents of J.W. found themselves.

• • •

Surveys of adult sex offenders who have been subjected to registration and community notification have identified a variety of collateral consequences that typically befall them after their conviction or after they gain their way back into the community after having served their sentence. Thirty sex offenders from Wisconsin were interviewed in 1998 regarding their experience with registration and community notification as sexual offenders (Zevitz and Farkas 2000). The overwhelming majority of them reported a variety of collateral consequences resulting from the requirement to register. Over three-quarters reported being excluded from residences, ostracized by neighbors, and subjected to harassment and threats; two-thirds reported emotional harm befalling their family; over half reported the loss of employment; a third experienced added pressure from probation or parole; and 3% reported a vigilante attack. Vigilante attacks were rare, but the fear of them is pervasive among these men since often—as in the case of Stephen Marshall's victims—sex offenders' names, addresses, and photographs are made publicly available on websites as part of their registration.

In a similar survey of registered sex offenders in Florida, the majority of respondents reported feeling shame, anxiety, social isolation, loss of relationships, embarrassment, and hopelessness (Levenson and Cotter, 2005a and b). A survey of registered sexual offenders in Kentucky reported that over half had been harassed, nearly a third had received harassing or threatening phone calls or mail, and 16% reported being assaulted (Tewksbury 2005). The unavoidable conclusion of this research is that registry and community notification have significantly interfered with the establishment of a stable residence and employment for those registered and that the negative effects often spread to family members, disrupting the sex offender's ability to gain support from a family or social network. Often the social taint of the sex offense spreads to family members in a process Erving Goffman (1963) referred to as a "courtesy stigma," resulting in family members rejecting or cutting themselves off from the offender in an effort to avoid the contaminating effects of being linked to the sexual offender—a stigma by association.

Many communities have begun to pass residential zoning ordinances that bar sex offenders from living within a designated distance from schools, daycare centers, or playgrounds. The National Conference of State Legislatures reports that at least twenty-three states have passed residency restrictions for sex offenders (Elton 2007). In 2002 the Iowa legislature passed a bill that prohibited child molesters from residing within two thousand feet of a school or registered child care facility. A group of convicted child molesters brought a class action appeal and a district court agreed with them that the law was unconstitutional, but the Eighth Circuit United States Court of Appeals in 2004 reversed the district court, finding that the residence restrictions were constitutional and declaring that the infringement on the liberties of sex offenders was superseded by the community's compelling interest in protecting itself (*Doe v. Miller* 405 F. 3rd 700 2005).

Since the passage of the restriction, the number of unregistered sex offenders has doubled in Iowa (Elton 2007). In an effort to avoid the stigmatization of registration, sex offenders instead go underground, taking on a shadow existence. The destabilizing effect of the housing restrictions can lead to social isolation, stress, and financial burdens, the very things that may precipitate a relapse. The residential restrictions aimed at protecting the community could paradoxically bring about the very event that the community fears most: a stressed out, socially isolated sexual offender leading a nomadic lifestyle, devoid of stability and the binding responsibilities of home, job, and social relationships. They stigmatize the sexual offender, branding him an outcast, setting up an itinerant class of offenders wandering from place to place, job to job, rootless and isolated, the very conditions that promote recidivism.

Erving Goffman (1963) described two types of stigmatized individuals: the discredited and the discreditable. The stigma of the discredited individual is readily apparent upon encountering him. He or she bears some outward physical sign— blindness, a physical disability, a facial disfigurement—that is immediately recognized and responded to by the perceiver. The individual bearing a discreditable stigma carries his mark on the inside as part of a hidden identity; it is not something that can be seen but is something that is revealed, often by stigmatized people themselves when they feel ready or prepared to do so. Discreditable stigmas are possessed by former mental patients, recovering drug addicts, and released prison inmates. Often they reveal their hidden stigma, if they reveal it at all, at a time when they feel some trust has been established between themselves and another person. The other person can respond to the revelation in multiple ways. He or she can revise his or her entire perception of the other, exchanging the previous nonstigmatizing identity with a discrediting, stigmatizing one. Or the other person can choose to ignore the new data or integrate it in a way that does not call for a total revising of the previous social perception. A prior sex offense, like any prior serious felony, functions as a discreditable stigma— something not seen or readily apparent on first encounter but only later discovered either by way of self-disclosure from the offender or through a bit of social gossip or the uncovering of some record or dossier. The registration and community notification laws act to convert what was formerly a discreditable stigma into something that more closely resembles a discrediting stigma, a revelation outside the control of the individual, a reputation that now precedes rather than follows behind him or her. The process is a public shaming technique, a public degradation ceremony (Garfinkel 1956) in which the sexual offender is branded through various iterations of social exclusions: he may not live here or there, he cannot work here or there, he must not walk within a certain distance of this or that child-populated public place, he must report in periodically and wear a bracelet that lets the authorities know of his location at every instance. He has becomes Foucault's carrier of the plague in the community, a plague victim living among us, an internal exile in the community.

Residency restriction laws continue to proliferate despite the lack of empirical evidence that they protect the public. The continued proliferation of residency restrictions on sex offenders seems unavoidable as adjacent states quickly enact laws preventing sex offenders from migrating within their borders as they flee from a neighboring state from which they have been warned out.

There has not been any published research examining the collateral consequences of registration and community notification for juvenile sex offenders, but as we have seen, they are often subjected to the same sorts of social and civil disabilities. In 1996 California passed a bill requiring courts to notify school officials when an enrolled student has been convicted of a sex offense (Lowe 1997). In a recent delinquency case in Massachusetts, a 17-year-old adolescent boy diagnosed with Asperberger's Disorder, a form of Childhood Autism, was placed on probation after being adjudicated delinquent for exposing himself to a 5-year-old girl and asking her to do the same in a small private room of a local church during a party. He was required to register as part of his sentence and his high school was notified of the charge. He was immediately excluded from the school even though the sexual offense did not occur on school grounds and he probably represented no major risk of harm to his fellow high school students.

Many states are passing interagency collaboration initiatives that promote communication of information about juvenile offenders, including juvenile sex offenders, among law enforcement, school, juvenile court, and public housing officials (Henning 2004). These initiatives have the stated goals of sharing information about high-risk adolescents so that they can better serve this population. But the good intentions of these procedures may backfire if these adolescents are branded as high risk and subjected to higher levels of surveillance and even some exclusionary practices like expulsion from school or forced vacancy from public housing. Public housing authorities have no explicit statutory right to juvenile records, but they may get them through less formal channels such as forced disclosure on public housing applications or prescreening processes that allow the public housing authority to conduct criminal background checks. Families may feel compelled to reject the offending member, eschewing the "courtesy stigma" that he carries with him, leaving him bereft of home and family support.

There is no evidence that such procedures have contributed in any way to increased public safety, yet they continue to operate without any check. Colorado has passed residential zoning ordinances for juvenile sex offenders that apply to foster homes, group homes, and residential facilities (Leversee 2001). In some instances specialized residential treatment facilities may be required to exclude juvenile sex offenders from entering their programs. The widespread passage of such restrictions could interfere with the treatment of juvenile sex offenders, limiting the programs and placements that they will be eligible to enter. The most successful treatment programs for juvenile sex offenders promote family and community support with full participation in school and other pro-social activities, but the collateral consequences of registration and community notification may disrupt these supportive social networks of relationships and limit youths' ability to transition to more adaptive and healthy pathways and lifestyles.

Epilogue

The role of the finger-wagging critic can be very alluring. Critique is easy compared to the heavy lifting necessary for solving problems. To tear down a flawed structure without erecting a new and improved one in its place is a deeply cynical position leaving the reader feeling left out in the cold. Finding the gaps, soft spots, and warps in the science, clinical practice, and legal policies of juvenile sex offenders is one thing; building a better way to think and respond to them is entirely another.

In the previous eight chapters I have played the role of critic, exerting restraint to tone down any signs of moral indignation, although I fear that some of these sentiments may have seeped in now and again. In this epilogue, I want to leave the security of the role of critic and assume the more difficult role of problem solver, keeping in mind the warning of Lionel Trilling from the opening chapter about the seeds of new problems that any solution carries within it. In this final section I want to build from the demolition left by the previous eight chapters a more reasoned way of thinking about and acting toward juvenile sex offenders—a mode of thinking and acting that is informed by what is empirically known about them, devoid of any "moral passions" that tend to distort our vision of them and harden our actions toward them.

The arguments presented throughout this book herald good news about juvenile sex offenders, a hopeful message that the problem is not so much them but how they have been conceptualized. The problem is not that the majority of juvenile sexual offenders are sexually deviant and at high risk for reoffense as much as that they have been tagged as such, framed within a discourse of deviance that portrays them as sexual perverts in the making in need of specialized clinical classification and assessment, treatment that focuses on them as deviant, and legal strategies that label and stigmatize them. There is very little empirical research to support the exclusion of juvenile sex offenders into a specialized category of youthful offender in need of specialized schemes of assessment, treatment, and legal management strategies such as civil commitment or community registration or notification. There is little empirical support for the legal course that has been charted for juvenile sex offenders over the past two decades. The decided balance of empirical research has consistently characterized juvenile sex offenders as a heterogeneous group varying widely on demographic, family history, early childhood, mental health, and delinquency factors. Juvenile sex offenders are as varied on these dimensions as are delinquents in general, or even "normal adolescents" for that matter. Often the only thing they hold in common with each other is that they have committed a sexual offense, a legal designation that is insufficient to support the conceptualization of them as a distinct clinical category.

Consider the following hypothetical demonstration, a study that could be easily conducted and written up for publication as a research article for a peer-reviewed journal. A sample of juvenile sex offenders is randomly drawn from a larger population of juvenile sex offenders. A brief narrative description of each member of the sample is written up in a brief paragraph or two. The paragraphs contain the kind of descriptive information that would be found in the concluding section of a psychological assessment report. Demographic information, information about family background, early developmental history, and delinquency history, data about mental health and psychological functioning, and the results of psychological testing are extracted from their case file or from a preexisting psychological assessment report and placed within a narrative description about them. All this information is included, but their identity as juvenile sex offenders is omitted. There is no information in the case descriptions that would indicate that they have been adjudicated delinquent for a sexual offense.

Next, the same procedure is conducted for a sample of juvenile nonsex offenders. Similar descriptive paragraphs are constructed from their files or from a preexisting psychological assessment report minus any information about their adjudicated delinquent offense.

Once the case descriptions have been constructed and sanitized of information about adjudicated delinquent offense, they are presented to a small sample of mental health professionals with expertise in the assessment and treatment of juvenile sex offenders, blind to the methodology of the study and its underlying hypothesis. They are asked to sort the cases into two piles: one pile for those cases that describe a juvenile sex offender and a second pile for cases that describe juvenile nonsex offenders. After they sort all the cases into these two piles, their accuracy, or the percentage of correctly sorted cases, is calculated. How would they do? This procedure has never been conducted and published, but a review of the empirical literature about juvenile sex offenders suggests that the sample of mental health professionals would probably perform at about a chance level of accuracy; that is, they would probably classify about 50% of the cases correctly. Why? Because the empirical literature indicates that the descriptions contained within these constructed narratives would read about the same for juvenile sex offenders and juvenile nonsex offenders. With information about the type of offense removed from the descriptions, there would be little that distinguishes one from the other. Other than the categorizing sexual offense, these cases would be about the same.

The fact that the empirical literature reveals strong similarities between juvenile sex offenders and the general delinquent is a strong argument for summoning them back to rejoin their delinquent brethren, for shepherding them back into the fold of "children-at-risk" or "children-in-need." According to the accumulated empirical evidence, it is no longer viable to see them as a specialized group, standing apart from the large population of adolescents who commit delinquent acts for all sorts of reasons and who then go on to desist from such conduct for all sorts of reasons when they emerge into adulthood. The existence of a sexually deviant few among the nondeviant many is not a good enough reason to continue to conceptualize the entire legal category of juvenile sex offenders as different and apart from that of the general juvenile delinquent. It seems that the commission of a sex offense by an adolescent is not necessarily a "red flag" about a sexually deviant identity that is fixed or necessarily telling. For an exceptional few it may be, but for the majority it is not, and what might be true for the rare few is not sufficient support for its application to the many.

At a recent academic conference, I attended a session in which was presented a collection of research papers about juvenile sex offenders. One of the presentations detailed the results of a study about the predictive ability of a set of actuarial assessment instruments for juvenile sex offenders: the J-SOAP-II, the ERASOR, the JSORAT-II, and the STATIC-99, instruments reviewed in chapter 3. The results of the study were consistent with the review of these instruments discussed in this book: these instruments had poor predictive validity for sexual recidivism for the sample of juvenile sex offenders studied. The problem should be a familiar one to the reader by now: the overall base rate of reoffense for the study sample was low and these instruments could not outperform an automatic decision of "no reoffense." The study was impeccably designed, an exemplar of how validity studies should be conducted. Yet despite its superior design quality, the study could not support the validation of these instruments for the prediction of sexual recidivism.

In the postsession discussion, a member of the audience lamented that "there was a problem with these tools," implying that perhaps with superior instruments assessing some other domain of characteristics with better precision and greater depth, the science could overcome this humbling experience and provide mental health clinicians in the field with a better predictive instrument of risk of sexual reoffense. But maybe the problem isn't the tools. Perhaps the problem has more to do with a misguided and ill-informed research mission and agenda. If it is the case that locating the juvenile sexual recidivist is a bit like finding the proverbial needle in a haystack, and that committing a sexual offense as an adolescent is just not a strong predictor of doing so in adulthood, we need to revise the meaning of a juvenile sex offense from its construal as indicative of a sexually deviant pathway to its construal as a more generalized index of a nonspecific problem in that particular adolescent's life.

In most cases it would seem that the commission of a juvenile sex offense functions like any other form of delinquent activity: it is a sign of some generalized behavioral problem, not necessarily a sign of a specific problem of sexual deviancy. If this is the case, then it would make better sense to assess juvenile sex offenders with the same validated instruments and procedures with which we assess the general delinquent. The problem is not the design of the tools specific for juvenile sex offenders but the fact that they have been created in the first place with the idea that they are capturing a stable and fixed behavioral pattern that is destined to repeat itself over time, a pattern that does not appear to hold true for the vast majority of juvenile sex offenders. What seems significant is not whether they commit a sex offense but only the mere fact that they committed some delinquent act. And though the characteristics of the act—whether it is sexual or not sexual—may provide telling details about the unique idiom of the youthful perpetrator, they do not seem particularly telling about whether the perpetrator will continue committing these same sorts of acts in the future.

To be clear, this is not to say that there does not exist the rare and exceptional juvenile sex offender who is sexually deviant—research estimates indicate that such offenders may comprise about 5% to 15% of the population of juvenile sex offenders—and suffers from some significant deficit in self-control and is therefore prone to repetitive sexual offenses through his life course. While these cases undoubtedly exist, it does not appear that specialized actuarial assessment instruments have demonstrated an ability to identify them with sufficient precision.

Research on existing juvenile sex offender assessment instruments will undoubtedly continue in the future and there will undoubtedly be continued development of new instruments promising better predictive validity. Research and development in this area should continue. The problem is that these instruments are not confined within the researcher's laboratory and are not restricted to discussion and debate at professional conferences or within the pages of peer-reviewed academic journals. These instruments are utilized in the field. They are being used in residential and community-based programs across the country. They are being used every day to make decisions about the lives of adolescents. They are presented in juvenile court where decisions are being made about transfer to adult court or civil commitment or community registration and notification. But until they can consistently demonstrate predictive validity, a wide-scale moratorium on the use of these instruments to predict recidivism is in order. In the meantime, juvenile sex offenders should be assessed with the same instruments and procedures that are available for the general juvenile delinquent.

A similar argument can be made regarding sex offender–specific treatment for juveniles: the empirical support, in the form of randomized controlled studies, is lacking. Yet thousands of adolescents who have committed sexual offenses are confined within residential treatment programs—many of them secure, prison-like facilities—with other similarly situated adolescents, where they are required to construct sexually deviant cycles, relapse prevention plans, and sexually deviant fantasy logs and to restructure cognitive distortions—all on the basis of the slimmest of empirical support regarding the efficacy of these methods.

Based simply on the rather robust research finding that most juvenile sex offenders will desist from further sexual offending due to nothing more than maturation, a reasonable argument for "doing nothing" could be made. But a "do nothing" approach is not acceptable. Something needs to be done even if it does not involve working from the unsupported presumption that the sexual offense is rooted in the deeply entrenched operation of a deviant sexual desire that is improperly controlled and managed. Juveniles who commit a sexual offense, even though the offense is not connected to fixed deviant arousal, are probably exhibiting some form of developmental, social, or emotional dysfunction that has manifested itself within the sexual offense, and these problems need addressing. The point of contention here, however, is that it does not seem to be the case, in the majority of instances, that the sexual offense has to be conceptualized and addressed as an instance of deviant sexuality. Nonetheless, an intervention of sufficient intensity and duration is in order.

It is striking that the only empirically supported efficacious treatment for juvenile sex offenders, consisting of randomized controlled studies, is a form of treatment that was not designed to treat juvenile sex offenders and in no direct way addresses sexual deviancy itself: Multisystemic Treatment (MST). The effectiveness of MST for juvenile sex offenders may be the best empirical support to date that deviant sexuality is not what ails most juvenile sex offenders. MST is effective even though it does not directly focus on deviant arousal. There are no fantasy logs, relapse prevention plans, or deviant cycles. Rather, the treatment focuses on the various systems of support that the juvenile exists within and targets interventions at these sites. The effectiveness of MST with juvenile sex offenders is another supporting argument that sexual offending among juveniles is often nothing more than just a particular form of delinquency that has manifested along a sexual pathway. Its effectiveness with juvenile sex offenders, an effectiveness that has been found for even violent juvenile offenders, is another reason why juvenile sex offenders should no longer be excluded from the larger heterogeneous population of juvenile offenders and cordoned off within a specialized class of juvenile offenders who are considered to be sexually deviant.

MST is a community-based intervention that is not only more effective but also less expensive. It is not conducted in the sterile confines of a secure treatment program over many months, even years. It does not take the juvenile out of his home, school, or community, separating him from the world and then looking to reintegrate him later, if the program works on reintegration at all. Since the offender is not excluded or confined and not made to work on sex offender issues, MST is less likely to result in negative labeling or stigmatization and more likely to promote a healthy, positive attitude and regard for sexuality, free from shame and humiliation.

The success of MST may have spurred the more recent development of other nondeviant treatment models and approaches such as Ward's Good Lives Model and the Holistic or Well-Being Approach of Longo. These approaches, in a near complete reversal of the relapse-prevention approach for the treatment of sexual offenders, place primary focus on the therapeutic relationship and the establishment of a supportive alliance between client and therapist. The focus is decidedly on the nondeviant aspects of sexual offending, on conceptualizing sexual offenses as motivated by some unmet emotional or psychological needs. The task of treatment is not to address sexual deviancy but to focus on client strengths and the promotion of emotional coping—on encouraging the offender to develop more appropriate, socially acceptable, and ultimately more rewarding ways to meet interpersonal needs. These approaches are particularly well suited for juvenile sex offenders, whose sexual offenses for the most part stem not from deviant desires but from underdeveloped social skills, emotional neediness, and reliance on overly rigid and narrow sexual scripts that view sexual conquests as indices of masculine affirmation. These newly developed models have not as yet been empirically validated, but theoretically they appear to be a better match for what is empirically known about juvenile sex offenders.

The nondeviant treatment models like MST, the Good Lives Model, and the Holistic and Well-Being Approach will not be suited for the rare and exceptional sexually deviant juvenile sex offender. The repetitive aggressive rapist and the fixated pedophilic offender will probably need exclusionary treatment in secure settings where they will be subject to the legally mandated management strategies of transfer, civil commitment, and community monitoring and notification, and to the deviancy-centered treatment focus of relapse-prevention training and other cognitive-behavioral interventions. But for the vast majority of juvenile sex offenders, such strict treatment and legal interventions are not necessary. Again, the high-intensity treatment needs of these deviant few should not dictate the treatment regimes for the nondeviant many. This is all the more true when such deviant-focused treatment strategies may cause real and lasting harm to those so treated, without advancing the protection of society in any measurable way. The exposure of juvenile sex offenders to "disfiguring" forms of legal intervention and treatment may facilitate the stabilization of a deviant identity, placing juveniles on a deviant pathway that may unwittingly exclude them from nondeviant outlets of development, effectively narrowing their life chances and expectations for themselves.

Psychological and legal intervention that focuses on normalization and healthy development appears to be the better solution for the vast majority of juvenile sex offenders. Hopefully it will be this frame that will assume ascendancy, informing the empirical research, clinical practice, and legal strategies for future juvenile sex offenders.

References

Abel, G.G. 1995. *Abel Screening System Manual.* Atlanta, GA: Abel Screening.

Abel, G.G., J.V. Becker, M.S. Mittelman, J. Cunningham-Rathner, J.L. Rouleau, and W.D. Murthy. 1987. Self-reported sex crimes of nonincarcerated paraphiliacs. *Journal of Interpersonal Violence* 2: 3–25.

Abel, G.G., A. Jordan, J.L. Rouleau, R. Emerick, S. Barboza-Whitehead, and C. Osborn. 2004. Use of visual reaction time to assess male adolescents who molest children. *Sexual Abuse: A Journal of Research and Treatment* 16: 255–65.

Abel, G.G., M.S. Mittelman, and J.V. Becker. 1985. Sexual offenders: Results of assessment and recommendations for treatment. In *Clinical Criminology: The Assessment and Treatment of Criminal Behavior,* ed. M.H. Ben-Aron, S.J. Hucker, and C.D. Webster. Toronto, Ontario: M & M Graphics.

Abel, G.G., and C.A. Osborn. 1992. The paraphilias: The extent and nature of sexually deviant and criminal behavior. *Clinical Forensic Psychiatry* 15: 675–87.

Abel, G.G., C.A. Osborn, and D.A. Twigg. 1993. Sexual assault through the life span: Adult offenders with juvenile histories. In *The Juvenile Sexual Offender,* ed. H.E. Barbaree, W.L. Marshall, and S.M. Hudson. New York: Guilford.

Adam Walsh Child Protection and Safety Act. 2006. H.R. 4472. 109th Congress.

Ageton, S.S. 1983. *Sexual Assault among Adolescents.* Lexington, MA: Lexington Books.

Alexander, M.A. 1999. Sexual offender treatment efficacy revisited. *Sexual Abuse: A Journal of Research and Treatment* 11: 101–16.

Alexander, R.M. 1995. *The "Girl Problem": Female Sexual Delinquency in New York, 1900–1930.* Ithaca, NY: Cornell University Press.

Allan, A., M.A. Allan, P. Marshall, and K. Kraszlan. 2002. Juvenile sexual offenders compared to juvenile offenders in general in Western Australia. *Psychiatry, Psychology, and Law* 9: 214–34.

American Academy of Child and Adolescent Psychiatry. 1999. Practice parameters for the assessment and treatment of children and adolescents who are sexually abusive of others. *Journal of the American Academy of Child and Adolescent Psychiatry* 38 Supplement: 55S–76S.

American Psychiatric Association. 1994. *Diagnostic and Statistical Manual of Mental Disorders. 4th Edition.* Washington, DC: American Psychiatric Association.

American Psychiatric Association. 2000. *Diagnostic and Statistical Manual of Mental Disorders. Text Revision. 4th Edition*. Washington, DC: American Psychiatric Association.

American Psychological Association. 2005. *Roper v. Simmons*, Brief for the American Psychological Association and the Missouri Psychological Association as *Amici Curiae* Supporting Respondent, July 19, 2004.

Ariès, P. 1962. *Centuries of Childhood*. New York: Knopf.

Arizona Rev. Stat. Ann.§§ 36-3701.

Arnett, J.J. 2006. G. Stanley Hall's *Adolescence*: Brilliance and nonsense. *History of Psychology* 9: 186–97.

Association for the Treatment of Sexual Abusers. 2000. The effective legal management of juvenile sexual offenders. Retrieved January 12, 2008 from http://www.atsa.com/ppjuvenile.html.

———. 2006. Report of the Task Force on Children with Sexual Behavior Problems. Retrieved October 5, 2007 from http://www.atsa.com.

Atcheson, J.D., and D.C. Williams. 1954. A study of juvenile sex offenders. *American Journal of Psychiatry* 111: 366–70.

Awad, G.A., and E.B. Saunders. 1984. A clinical study of male adolescent sexual offenders. *International Journal of Offender Therapy and Comparative Criminology* 28: 105–16.

———. 1991. Male adolescent assaulters: Clinical observations. *Journal of Interpersonal Violence* 6: 446–60.

Bancroft, J. 2006. Normal sexual development. In *The Juvenile Sex Offender. 2nd Edition*, ed. H.E. Barbaree and W.L. Marshall. New York: Guilford.

Barbaree, H.E., and F.A. Cortoni. 1993. Treatment of the juvenile sex offender within the criminal justice and mental health system. In *The Juvenile Sexual Offender*, ed. H.E. Barbaree, W.L. Marshall, and S.M. Hudson. New York: Guilford.

Barbaree, H.E., and W.L. Marshall. 1989. Erectile responses among heterosexual child molesters, father-daughter incest offenders, and matched nonoffenders: Five distinct age preference profiles. *Canadian Journal of Behavioral Sciences* 21: 70–82.

Barbaree, H.E., and W.L. Marshall. 1998. The development of deviant sexual behaviour among adolescents and its implications for prevention and treatment. *Irish Journal of Psychology* 19: 1–31.

———. 2006. An introduction to the Juvenile Sex Offender: Terms, concepts, and definitions. In *The Juvenile Sex Offender. 2nd* Edition, ed. H.E. Barbaree and W.L. Marshall. New York: Guilford.

Barbaree, H.E., W.L. Marshall, and J. McCormick. 1998. The development of deviant sexual behavior among adolescents and its implications for prevention and treatment. *Irish Journal of Psychology* 19: 1–31.

Barbaree, H.E., M. Seto, C.M. Langton, and E.J. Peacock. 2001. Evaluating the predictive accuracy of six risk assessment instruments for adult sex offenders. *Criminal Justice and Behavior* 28: 490–521.

Bazelon, D.L. 1988. *Questioning Authority: Justice and Criminal Law*. New York: Knopf.

Becker, J.V. 1990. Treating adolescent sexual offenders. *Professional Psychology: Research and Practice* 5: 362–65

Becker, J.V., and J.A. Hunter. 1997. Understanding and treating child and adolescent sexual offenders. *Advances in Child Clinical Psychology* 19: 177–97.

Becker, J.V., M.S. Kaplan, J. Cunningham-Rathner, and R. Kavoussi. 1986. Characteristics of adolescent incest sexual perpetrators: Preliminary findings. *Journal of Family Violence* 1: 85–97.

Bengis, S., A. Brown, R.E. Freeman-Longo, B. Matsuda, J. Ross, K. Singer, and J. Thomas. 1999. *Standards of Care for Youth in Sex Offense-specific Residential Programs*. National Offense-Specific Residential Standards Task Force. Holyoke, MA: NEARI Press.

Benoit, J.L., and W.A. Kennedy. 1992. The abuse history of male adolescent sex offenders. *Journal of Interpersonal Violence* 7: 543–48.

Berliner, L. 1998. Juvenile sex offenders: Should they be treated differently? *Journal of Interpersonal Violence* 13: 645–46.

Best, J. 2001. *Damned Lies and Statistics*. Berkeley: University of California Press.

Bishop, D., and C. Frazier. 2000. Consequences of transfer. In *The Changing Borders of Juvenile Justice: Transfer of Adolescents to Criminal Court*, ed. J. Fagan and F.E. Zimring. Chicago: University of Chicago Press.

Bishop, D.M., C.E. Frazier, L. Lanza-Kaduce, and L. Winner. 1996. The transfer of juveniles to criminal court: Does it make a difference? *Crime and Delinquency* 42: 171–91.

Boer, D.P., R.J. Wilson, C.M. Gauthier, and S.D. Hart. 1997. Assessing risk of sexual violence: Guidelines for clinical practice. In *Impulsivity: Theory, Assessment, and Treatment*, ed. C.D. Webster and M.A. Jackson. New York: Guilford.

Bonner, B.L., C.E. Walker, and L. Berliner. 1999. *Children with Sexual Behavior Problems: Assessment and Treatment* (Final Report, Grant No. 90-CA-1469). Washington, DC: Administration of Children, Youth, and Families, DHHS.

Borduin, C.M., S.W. Henggler, D.M. Blaske, and R.J. Stein. 1990. Multisystemic treatment of juvenile sexual offenders. *International Journal of Offender Therapy and Comparative Criminology* 34: 105–13.

Borduin, C.M., and C.M. Schaeffer. 2001. Multisystemic treatment of juvenile sexual offenders: A progress report. *Journal of Psychology and Human Sexuality* 13: 25–42.

Brannen, D.N., R.T. Salekin, P.A. Zapf, K.L. Salekin, F. Kubak, and J. Decoster. 2006. Transfer to adult court: A national study of how juvenile court judges weigh pertinent Kent Criteria. *Psychology, Public Policy, and Law* 12: 332–55.

Bremer, J. 1992. Serious juvenile sex offenders: Treatment and long-term follow up. *Psychiatric Annals* 22: 326–32.

Briere, J., and M. Runtz. 1989. University males' sexual interest in children: Predicting potential indices of "pedophilia" in a nonforensic sample. *Child Abuse and Neglect* 13: 65–75.

Bronfenbrenner, U. 1979. *The Ecology of Human Development: Experiments by Nature and Design*. Cambridge, MA: Harvard University Press.

Brown, J.M., and P.A. Langan. 1998. *State Court Sentencing of Convicted Felons, 1994*. Washington, DC: U.S. Department of Justice, Bureau of Justice Statistics.

Bruckner, H., and P.S. Bearman. 2005. After the promise: The STD consequences of adolescent virginity pledges. *Journal of Adolescent Health* 36: 271–78.

Bullough, V. 1990. History of human sexual behavior in Western societies. In *Pedophilia: Biosocial Dimensions*, ed. J.R. Feierman. New York: Springer-Verlag.

Bumby, K. 2006. Understanding treatment for adults and juveniles who have committed sex offenses. Center for Sex Offender Management. www.csom. org. Retrieved on June 26, 2008.

Burton, D. 2008. An exploratory evaluation of the contribution of personality and childhood sexual victimization to the development of sexually abusive behavior. *Sexual Abuse: A Journal of Research and Treatment* 20: 102–15.

Burton, D.L., J. Smith-Darden, and S.J. Frankel. 2006. Research on adolescent sexual abuser treatment programs. In *The Juvenile Sex Offender. 2nd Edition*, ed. H.E. Barbaree and W.L. Marshall. New York: Guilford.

Butler, S.M., and M.C. Seto. 2002. Distinguishing two types of adolescent sex offenders. *Journal of American Academy of Child and Adolescent Psychiatry* 41: 83–90.

Caldwell, M. 2002. What do we know about juvenile sexual reoffense risk? *Child Maltreatment* 7: 291–302.

———. 2007. Sexual offense adjudication and sexual recidivism among juvenile offenders. *Sexual Abuse: A Journal of Research and Treatment* 19: 107–13.

Carpentier, M.Y., J.F. Silovsky, and M. Chaffin. 2006. Randomized trial of treatment for children with sexual behavior problems: Ten-year follow-up. *Journal of Consulting and Clinical Psychology* 74: 482–88.

Chaffin, M. 2006. Can we develop evidence-based practice with adolescent sex offenders? In *Current Perspectives: Working with Sexually Aggressive Youth and Youth with Sexual Behavior Problems*, eds. R. Longo and D.S. Prescott. Holyoke, MA: NEARI Press.

Chaffin, M., and B. Bonner. 1998. Editor's Introduction: "Don't shoot, we're your children": Have we gone too far in our response to adolescent sexual abusers and children with sexual problems? *Childhood Maltreatment* 3: 314–16.

CNN. 2007a. Wilson released after two years behind bars for teen sex conviction. CNN.com, October 26. Http://www.cnn.com/ 2007/US/law/10/26/wilson. freed/index.html#cnnSTCText.

———. 2007b. Glenarlow Wilson: Plea deal would have left me without a home. CNN.com, October 29. Http://www.cnn.com/ 2007/US/law/10/29/Wilson. released/index.html.

Cohen, S. 1972/2000. *Folk Devils and Moral Panic. 3rd Edition.* London: Routledge.

Commonwealth v. Kenney 850 N.E. 2nd (2006).

Cravens. H. 2006. The historical context of G. Stanley Hall's *Adolescence* (1904). *History of Psychology* 9: 172–85.

Crepault, C., and M. Couture. 1980. Men's erotic fantasies. *Archives of Sexual Behavior* 9: 565–81.

Cromer, W., and P. Anderson. 1970. Freud's visit to America: Newspaper coverage. *Journal of the History of the Behavioral Sciences* 6: 349–53.

Cunningham, C., and K. MacFarlane. 1991. *When Children Molest Children: Group Treatment Strategies for Young Sexual Abusers.* Brandon, VT: Safer Society Press.

Daleiden, E.L., K. Kaufman, D.R. Hilliker, and J.N. O'Neil. 1998. The sexual histories and fantasies of youthful males: A comparison of sexual offending, nonsexual offending, and non-offending groups. *Sexual Abuse: A Journal of Research and Treatment* 10: 195–209.

Daniel, M. 2006. Suspect in killings wasn't screened boarding bus. *Boston Globe,* April 18.

Dawes, R.M., D. Faust, and P.E. Meehl. 1989. Clinical versus statistical judgment. *Science* 243: 1668–74.

Dawson, R.O. 1992. An empirical study of *Kent* style juvenile transfers to criminal court. *St. Mary's Law Journal* 23: 975–1054.

———. 2000. Waiver in theory and practice. In *The Changing Borders of Juvenile Justice: Transfer of Adolescents to Criminal Court*, eds. J. Fagan and F.E. Zimring. Chicago: University of Chicago Press.

DC ST § 22-3803-3804.

Di Mauro. D. 1997. Sexuality research in the United States. In *Researching Sexual Behavior: Methodological Issues*, ed. J. Bancroft. Bloomington: Indiana University Press.

Dishion, T.J., J. McCord, and F. Poulin. 1999. When interventions harm: Peer groups and problem behavior. *American Psychologist* 54: 755–64.

Doe v. Miller 405 F. 3rd 700 2005.

Doe v. Poritz 662 A 2d. 367, 422 NJ 1995.

Doren, D. 2002. *Evaluating Sex Offenders: A Manual for Civil Commitments and Beyond.* Thousand Oaks, CA: Sage.

———. 2006. Assessing juveniles' risk within the civil commitment context. In *Risk Assessment of Youth Who Have Sexually Abused: Theory, Controversies, and Emerging Strategies*, ed. D.S. Prescott. Oklahoma City, OK: Wood & Barnes.

Doshay, L.J. 1943. *The Boy Sex Offender and His Late Career.* New York: Grune & Stratton.

Douglas, M. 1966. *Purity and Danger: An Analysis of Conceptions of Pollution and Taboo.* London: Routledge & Kegan Paul.

———. 1992. *Risk and Blame: Essays in Cultural Theory.* New York: Routledge.

Elliott, D.S., D. Huizinga, and S. Ageton. 1985. *Explaining Delinquency and Drug Use.* Beverly Hills, CA: Sage.

Elliott, D.S., D. Huizinga, and B. Morse. 1987. Self-reported violent offending: A descriptive analysis of juvenile violent offenders and their offending careers. *Journal of Interpersonal Violence* 1: 472–514.

Elton, C. 2007. Behind the picket fence. *Boston Globe Magazine*, May 6.

Epperson, D.L., J.D. Kaul, and C. Hesselton. N.d. *Minnesota Sex Offender Screening Tool-Revised (MnSOST-R): Development, Performance, and Recommended Risk Level Cut Scores.* http://129.186.143.73/faculty/epperson/mnsost_download.htm.

Epperson, D.L., C.A. Ralston, D. Fowers, J. DeWitt, and K.S. Gore. 2006. Actuarial risk assessment with juveniles who offend sexually: Development of the Juvenile Sexual Offense Recidivism Risk Assessment Tool-II (JSORRAT-II). In *Risk Assessment of Youth Who Have Sexually Abused: Theory, Controversy, and Emerging Strategies,* ed. D.S. Prescott. Oklahoma City, OK: Wood & Barnes.

Evans, R.B., and W.A. Koelsch. 1985. Psychoanalysis arrives in America: The 1909 psychology conference at Clark University. *American Psychologist* 40: 942–48.

Fagan, J. 1995. Separating the men from the boys: The comparative advantage of juvenile versus criminal court sanctions on recidivism among adolescent felony offenders. In *Serious, Violent, and Chronic Juvenile Offenders: A Sourcebook,* eds. J.C. Howell, B. Krisberg, J.D. Hawkins, and J.J. Wilson. Thousand Oaks, CA: Sage.

———. 1996. The comparative advantage of juvenile versus criminal court sanctions on recidivism among adolescent felony offenders. *Law and Policy* 18: 77.

Fagan, J., and S. Wexler. 1988. Explanations of sexual assault among violent delinquents. *Journal of Adolescent Research* 3: 363–85.

Fedora, O., J.R. Reddon, J.W. Morrison, S.K. Fedora, H. Pascoe, and L.T. Yendall. 1992. Sadism and other paraphilias in normal controls and aggressive and non-aggressive sexual offenders. *Archives of Sexual Behavior* 21: 1–15.

Fehrenbach, P.A., W. Smith, C. Monastersky, and R.W. Deisher. 1986. Adolescent sexual offenders: Offender and offense characteristics. *American Journal of Orthopsychiatry* 56: 225–33.

Feld, B.C. 1987. The juvenile court meets the principle of the offense: Legislative changes in juvenile waiver statues. *The Journal of Criminal Law and Criminology* 78: 471–533.

———. 2000. Legislative exclusion of offenses from juvenile court: A history and critique. In *The Changing Borders of Juvenile Justice: Transfer of Adolescents to Criminal Court, eds.* J. Fagan and F.E. Zimring. Chicago: University of Chicago Press.

Finkelhor, D., and L.M. Jones. 2004. *Explanations for the Decline in Child Sexual Abuse Cases*. Washington, DC: U.S. Department of Justice, Office of Juvenile Programs, Office of Juvenile Justice and Delinquency Prevention.

———. 2006. Why have child maltreatment and child victimization declined? *Journal of Social Issues* 62: 685–716.

Fla. Stat 394.913 (1).

Ford, M.E., and J.A. Linney 1995. Comparative analysis of juvenile sexual offenders, violent nonsexual offenders, and status offenders. *Journal of Interpersonal Violence* 10: 56–69.

Forst, M.A., J.A. Fagan, and T.S. Vivona. 1989. Youth in prisons and state training schools: Perceptions and consequences of the treatment-custody dichotomy for adolescents. *Juvenile and Family Court Journal* 39: 1–13.

Fortenberry, J.D., and M.C. Aalsma. 2003. Abusive sexual experiences before age 12 and adolescent sexual behaviors. In *Sexual Development in Childhood*, ed. J. Bancroft. Bloomington: Indiana University Press.

Forth, A.E., D.S. Kosson, and R.D. Hare. 2003. *The Psychopathy Checklist-Youth Version*. Toronto, Ontario, Canada: Multi-Health Systems.

Foucault, M. 1975. *Discipline and Punish*. New York: Vintage.

———. 1978. *The History of Sexuality: An Introduction, Volume 1*. New York: Vintage.

France, K., and S.M. Hudson. 1993. The conduct disorders and the juvenile sex offender. In *The Juvenile Sexual Offender*, ed. H.E. Barbaree, W.L. Marshall, and S.M. Hudson. New York: Guilford Press.

Frayser, S.G. 2003. Cultural dimensions of childhood sexuality in the United States. In *Sexual Development in Childhood*, ed. J. Bancroft. Bloomington: Indiana University Press.

Freud, S. 1910. The origin and development of psychoanalysis. Translated by H.W. Chase. *American Journal of Psychology* 21: 181–218.

Freud, S., and C.G. Jung. 1974. *The Freud/Jung Letters*, ed. W. McGuire. Princeton, NJ: Princeton University Press.

Friedman, D.M. 2001. *A Mind of Its Own: A Cultural History of the Penis*. New York: Penguin.

Friedrich, W.N. 1997. *Child Sexual Behavior Inventory: Professional Manual*. Lutz, FL: Psychological Assessment Resources.

———. 2003. Studies of the sexuality of nonabused children. In *Sexual Development in Childhood*, ed. J. Bancroft. Bloomington: Indiana University Press.

Friedrich, W.N., P. Grambsch, D. Broughton, J. Kuiper, and R.L. Beilke. 1991. Normative sexual behavior in children. *Pediatrics* 88: 456–64.

Furby, L., M.R. Weinrott, and L. Blackshaw. 1989. Sex offender recidivism: A review. *Psychological Bulletin* 105: 3–30.

Garb, H. 1998. *Studying the Clinician: Judgment Research and Psychological Assessment*. Washington, DC: American Psychological Association.

Garfinkle, E. 2003. Coming of age in America: The misapplication of sex-offender registration and community notification laws to juveniles. *California Law Review* 93: 163–208.

Garfinkel, H. 1956. Conditions of successful degradation ceremonies. *The American Journal of Sociology* 61: 420–24.

Gil, E., and T.C. Johnson. 1993. *Sexualized Children: Assessment and Treatment of Sexualized Children and Children Who Molest*. Rockville, MD: Launch Press.

Goffman, E. 1963. *Stigma: Notes on the Management of a Spoiled Identity*. New York: Touchstone Books.

Goodman, B. 2007a. Day of split outcome in teenage sex case. *New York Times*, June 1.

———. 2007b. Man convicted as a teenager in sex case is ordered free by Georgia court. *New York Times*, October 26.

Graham, C.A. 2003. Methodological issues involved in adult recall of childhood sexual experiences. In *Sexual Development in Childhood*, ed. J. Bancroft. Bloomington: Indiana University Press.

Graves, R.B., D.K. Openshaw, F.R. Ascione, and S.L. Ericksen. 1996. Demographic and parental characteristics of youthful sexual offenders. *International Journal of Offender Therapy and Comparative Criminology* 40: 300–317.

Gray, A.S., and W.D. Pithers. 1993. Relapse prevention with sexually aggressive adolescents and children: Expanding treatment and supervision. In *The Juvenile Sexual Offender*, ed. H.E. Barbaree, W.L. Marshall, and S.M. Hudson. New York: Guilford.

Gray, A., W.D. Pithers, A. Busconi, and P. Houchens. 1999. Developmental and etiological characteristics of children with sexual behavior problems: Treatment implications. *Child Abuse and Neglect* 23: 601–21.

Gretton, H.M., M. McBride, R.H. Hare, R. O'Shaughnessy, and C. Kumka. 2001. Psychopathy and recidivism in adolescent sex offenders. *Criminal Justice and Behavior* 28: 427–49.

Griffin, P. 2003. *Trying and Sentencing Juveniles as Adults: An Analysis of State Transfer and Blended Sentencing Laws*. Pittsburg, PA: National Center for Juvenile Justice.

———. 2005. *Transfer Provisions*. State Juvenile Justice Profiles. Pittsburgh, PA: National Center for Juvenile Justice. Available: http://www.ncjj.org/stateprofiles.

Griffin, P., P. Torbet, and L. Szymanski. 1998. Trying juveniles as adults in criminal court: An analysis of state transfer provisions. Washington, DC: U.S. Department of Justice, Office of Justice Programs, Office of Juvenile Justice and Delinquency Prevention.

Groth, A.N. 1977. The adolescent sexual offender and his prey. *International Journal of Offender Therapy and Comparative Criminology* 25: 249–55.

Groth, A.N., R.E. Longo, and J.B. McFaddin. 1982. Undetected recidivism among rapists and child molesters. *Crime and Delinquency* 28: 450–58.

Grove, W., and P. Meehl. 1996. Comparative efficacy of informal (subjective, impressionistic) and formal (mechanistic, algorithmic) prediction procedures: The clinical-statistical controversy. *Psychology, Public Policy, and Law* 2: 293–323.

Guttmacher Institute. 2006. Facts on American teens' sexual and reproductive health. Retrieved on September 18, 2006, from www.guttmacher.org.

H. Con. Res. 107, 106th Cong (1999).

Hacking, I. 2002. *Historical Ontology.* Cambridge, MA: Harvard University Press.

———. 2006. Making up people. *London Review of Books*, 28, August 17.

Hall, G.S. 1904. *Adolescence: Its Psychology and Its Relations to Physiology, Anthropology, Sociology, Sex, Crime, Religion, and Education., V. 1 and 2.* New York: Appleton.

Hanson, R.K. 1997. *The Development of a Brief Actuarial Risk Scale for Sexual Offense Recidivism.* User Report No. 1997-40. Ottawa, Ontario, Canada: Department of the Solicitor General of Canada.

———. 1998. What do we know about sex offender risk assessment? *Psychology, Public Policy, and Law* 4: 52–70.

———. 2002. Age and recidivism. *Journal of Interpersonal Violence* 17: 1046–62.

Hanson, R.K., and M.T. Bussière. 1998. Predicting relapse: A meta-analysis of sexual recidivism studies. *Journal of Consulting and Clinical Psychology* 66: 348–62.

Hanson, R.K., and K. Morton-Bourgon. 2004. *Predictors of Sexual Recidivism: An Updated Meta-analysis (Cat. No.: PS3-1/2004-2E-PDF).* Ottawa, Ontario, Canada: Department of the Solicitor General of Canada.

———. 2005. The characteristics of persistent sexual offenders: A meta-analysis of recidivism studies. *Journal of Consulting and Clinical Psychology* 73: 1154–63.

Hanson, R.K., and D. Thornton. 1999. *Static-99: Improving Actuarial Risk Assessments for Sex Offenders.* User Report 99-02. Ottawa, Ontario, Canada: Department of the Solicitor General of Canada.

Hare, R.D. 1991. *The Hare Psychopathy Checklist-Revised.* Toronto, Ontario, Canada: Multi-Health Systems.

Harris, A., A. Phenix, R.K. Hanson, and D. Thornton. 2003. *Static-99 Coding Rules Revised.* Ottawa, Ontario, Canada: Department of the Soliciter General of Canada. www.sga.gc.ca

Harris, G.T., M.E. Rice, and V.L. Quinsey. 1994. Psychopathy as a taxon: Evidence that psychopaths are a discrete class. *Journal of Consulting and Clinical Psychology* 62: 387–97.

Hart, S.D., D.R. Laws, and P.R. Kropp. 2003. The promise and the peril of sex offender risk assessment. In *Sexual Deviance: Issues and Controversies*, eds. T. Ward and D.R. Laws. Newbury Park, CA: Sage.

Haugaard, J.J., and C. Tilly. 1988. Characteristics predicting children's responses to sexual encounters with other children. *Child Abuse and Neglect* 12: 209–18.

Henggeler, S.W., S.K. Schoenwald, C.M. Borduin, C.L. Hanson, S.M. Wason, and J.R. Urey. 1998. *Multisystemic Treatment of Antisocial Behavior in Children and Adolescents*. New York: Guilford.

Henning, K. 2004. Eroding confidentiality in delinquency proceedings: Should schools and public housing authorities be notified? *New York University Law Review* 79: 520–611.

Hiller, S. 1998. The problem with juvenile sex offender registration: The detrimental effects of public disclosure. *Boston University Public Interest Law Journal* 7: 271–93.

Hindelang, M.J. 1979. Correlates of delinquency: The illusion of discrepancy between self-report and official measures. *American Sociological Review* 44: 995–1014.

Hindelang, M.J., T. Hirschi, and J.G. Weis. 1981. *Measuring Delinquency*. Beverly Hills, CA: Sage.

Hirschi, T., and M. Gottfredson. 1983. Age and the explanation of crime. *American Journal of Sociology* 89: 552–84.

Hoge, R.D., and D.A. Andrews. 1996. *The Youth Level of Service/Case Management Inventory and Manual*. Ottawa, Canada: Carleton University, Department of Psychology.

Huizinga, D., and D.S. Elliott. 1986. Reassessing the reliability and validity of self-report delinquent measures. *Journal of Quantitative Criminology* 2: 293–327.

Humphrey v. Wilson. 2007. Ga. Lexus 774.

Hunt, M. 1999. *The New No-Nothings: The Political Foes of the Scientific Study of Human Nature*. New Brunswick, NJ: Transaction Books.

Hunter, J.A., and J.V. Becker. 1994. The role of deviant sexual arousal in juvenile sexual offending: Etiology, evaluation, and treatment. *Criminal Justice and Behavior* 21: 132–49.

Hunter, J.A., A.J. Figueredo, N.M. Malamuth, and J.V. Becker. 2003. Juvenile sex offenders: Toward the development of a typology. *Sexual Abuse: A Journal of Research and Treatment* 15: 27–48.

Hunter, J.A., D.W. Goodwin, and J.V. Becker. 1994. The relationship between phallometrically measured deviant sexual arousal and clinical characteristics in juvenile sexual offenders. *Behaviour Research and Therapy* 32: 533–38.

Hunter, J.A., R.R. Hazelwood, and D. Slesinger. 2000. Juvenile-perpetrated sex crimes: Patterns of offending and predictors of violence. *Journal of Family Violence* 15: 81–93.

Innes, M. 2004. Crime as a signal, crime as a memory. *Journal for Crime, Conflict, and the Media* 1: 15–22.

In re Gault 387 U.S. 1 (1967).

In re J.W. 204 Ill. 3d 50 (2003).

In re to the Commitment of Eric Pletz 239 Wis. 2d 49 (2000).
In re to the Commitment of Marvel L. Eagans, Jr. 222 Wis. 2d 217 (1998).
In re to the Commitment of Matthew A.B. 231 Wis. 2d 688 (1999).
In re to the Commitment of Patterson 232 Wis. 2d 558 (2006).
In re to the Commitment of Tremaine Y 279 Wis. 2d 448 (2005).
In the Interest of Hezzie R. 219 Wis. 2d 848 (1998).
In the Matter of Carl Leroy Anderson Minn. Lexis 1171 (1998).
In the Matter of James D. Creighton Minn. App. Lexis 793 (1997).
In the Matter of the Care and Treatment of Peter E.J. Harvey 355 S.C. 53 (2003).
In the Matter of the Commitment of J.P. 772 A. 2nd 54 (2001).
In the Matter of the Detention of Raymond Marshall 122 Wn. App. 132 (2004).
Jacob Wetterling Crimes Against Children and Sexually Violent Predator Program. 1994. 42 U.S.C. § 14071.
Jacobs, W.L., W.A. Kennedy, and J.B. Meyer. 1997. A between-group comparison study of sexual and non-sexual offenders. *Sexual Abuse: A Journal of Research and Treatment* 9: 201–7.
Jan, T., and K. Burge. 2006. Case vs. Brockton boy stuns officials. *The Boston Globe*, February 9.
Janus, E. 2000. Sexual predator commitment laws: Lessons for law and the behavioral sciences. *Behavioral Sciences and the Law* 18: 5–21.
Jenkins, P. 1998. *Moral Panic*. New Haven, CT: Yale University Press.
Jensen, E.L., and L.K. Metsger. 1994. A test of the deterrent effect of legislative waiver on violent juvenile crime. *Crime and Delinquency* 40: 96–104.
Johnson, T.C. 1988. Child perpetrators—Children who molest other children: Preliminary findings. *Child Abuse and Neglect* 12: 219–29.
Kahn, T.J., and M.A. Lafond. 1988. Treatment of the adolescent sexual offender. *Child and Adolescent Social Work* 5: 135–48.
Kalmus, E., and A.R. Beech. 2005. Forensic assessment of sexual interest: A review. *Aggression and Violent Behavior* 10: 193–217.
Kan. Stat. Ann. § 59-29a02 (Supp 1996).
Kansas v. Crane 534 U.S. 407 (2002).
Kansas v. Hendricks 117 S. Ct. 2072 (1997).
Kenny, D.T., T. Keough, and K. Seidler. 2001. Predictors of recidivism in Australian juvenile sex offenders: Implications for treatment. *Sexual Abuse: A Journal of Research and Treatment* 14: 131–48.
Kent v. U.S., 343 F. 2d 247, 264 (1964).
Kent v. U.S. 383 U.S. 541, 554 (1966).
Kincaid, J. 1998. *Erotic Innocence: The Culture of Child Molesting*. Durham, NC: Duke University Press.
Kinsey, A.C., W.B. Pomeroy, and C.E. Martin. 1948. *The Sexual Behavior in the Human Male*. Philadelphia: W.B. Saunders.

Kinsey, A.C., W.B. Pomeroy, C.E. Martin, and P.H. Gebhard. 1953. *The Sexual Behavior in the Human Female*. Philadelphia: W.B. Saunders.

Knopp, F.H., R.E. Freeman-Longo, and W.F. Stevenson. 1992. *Nationwide Survey of Juvenile and Adult Sex-offender Treatment Programs and Providers: 1992*. Brandon, VT: Safer Society.

Koss, M. 1992. The underdetection of rape: Methodological choices influence incidence estimates. *Journal of Social Issues* 48: 61–75.

Lamb, S., and M. Coakley. 1993. "Normal" childhood sexual play and games: Differentiating play from abuse. *Child Abuse and Neglect* 17: 515–26.

Langevin, R., J. Bain, M.H. Ben-Aron, R. Coulthard, D. Day, L. Handy, G. Heasman, S.J. Hucker, J.E. Purins, V. Roper, A.E. Russon, C.D. Webster, and G. Wotzman. 1985. Sexual aggression: Constructing a predictive equation: A controlled pilot study. In *Erotic Preference, Gender Identity, and Aggression in Men*, ed. R.J. Langevin. Hillsdale, NJ: Lawrence Erlbaum.

Langevin, R., R.A. Lang, and S. Curnoe. 1998. The prevalence of sex offenders with deviant fantasies. *Journal of Interpersonal Violence* 13: 315–27.

Langton, C.M., H.E. Barbaree, M.C. Seto, E.J. Peacock, L. Harkins, and K.T. Hansen. 2007. Actuarial assessment of risk for reoffense among adult sex offenders. *Criminal Justice and Behavior* 34: 37–59.

Laumann, E.O., J.H. Gagnon, R.T. Michael, and S. Michaels. 1994. *The Social Organization of Sexuality: Sexual Practices in the United States*. Chicago: University of Chicago Press.

Laws, D.R. 2001. Relapse prevention: Reconceptualization and revision. In *The Handbook of Offender Assessment and Treatment*, ed. C.R. Hollin. Chichester, England: Wiley.

Leguizamo, A. 2002. The object relations and victimization histories of juvenile sex offenders. In *The Sex Offender: Current Treatment Modalities and Systems Issues, V. 4*, ed. Barbara K. Schwartz. Kingston, NJ: Civic Research Institute.

Leitenberg, H., and K. Henning. 1995. Sexual fantasies. *Psychological Bulletin* 117: 469–96.

Lerman, P. 1982. *Deinstitutionalization and the Welfare State*. New Brunswick, NJ: Rutgers University Press.

Letourneau, E.J. 2006. Legal consequences of juvenile sex offending in the United States. In *The Juvenile Sexual Offender. 2nd Edition*, eds. H.E. Barbaree and W.L. Marshall. New York: Guilford.

Letourneau, E.J., and M.H. Miner. 2005. Juvenile Sex Offenders: A case against the legal and clinical status quo. *Sexual Abuse: A Journal of Research and Treatment* 17: 293–312.

Levenson, J.S., and L.P. Cotter. 2005a. The effect of Megan's Law on sex offender registration. *Journal of Contemporary Criminal Justice* 21: 49–66.

———. 2005b. The impact of sex offender registration: 1,000 feet from danger or one step from absurd? *International Journal of Offender Therapy and Comparative Criminology* 49: 168–78.

Leversee, T. 2001. Responding to juvenile delinquency: Eliminating the pendulum effect: A balanced approach to the assessment, treatment, and management of sexually abusive youth. *The Journal of the Center for Families, Children, and the Courts* 3: 45–54.

Levine, J. 1996. A question of abuse. *Mother Jones*, 32–37, 67–70, July–August.

———. 2002. *Harmful to Minors*. Minneapolis: University of Minnesota Press.

Lieb, R., and K. Gookin. 2005. *Involuntary Commitment of Sexually Violent Predators: Comparing State Laws*. Olympia: Washington State Institute for Public Policy.

Lillienfeld, S.O. 2002. When worlds collide: Social science, politics, and the Rind et al. (1998) child sexual abuse meta-analysis. *American Psychologist* 57: 176–88.

Litwack, T.R. 2001. Actuarial versus clinical assessment of dangerousness. *Psychology, Public Policy, and Law* 7: 409–43.

Litwack, T.R, P.A. Zapf, J.L. Groscup, and S.D. Hart. 2007. Violence risk assessment: Research, legal, and clinical considerations. In *The Handbook of Forensic Psychology, 3rd Edition*, ed. I. B. Weiner and A.K. Hess. Hoboken, NJ: Wiley.

Longo, R.E. 1982. Sexual learning and experiences among adolescent sexual offenders. *International Journal of Offender Therapy and Comparative Criminology* 26: 235–41.

———. 2004. An integrated experiential approach to treating young people who sexually abuse. In *Identifying and Treating Youth Who Sexually Offend: Current Approaches, Techniques, and Research*, eds. R. Geffner, K. Crumpton Franey, T. Geffner Arnold, and R. Falconer. New York: Haworth Press.

Longo, R.E., and A.N. Groth. 1983. Juvenile sexual offenses in the histories of adult rapists and child molesters. *International Journal of Offender Therapy and Comparative Criminology* 27: 150–55.

Lowe, R.J. 1997. School notification of student's sexual offense convictions: Does it protect our children or impede quality education? *Journal of Law and Education* 26: 169–76.

Lussier, P. 2005. The criminal activity of sexual offenders in adulthood: Revisiting the specialization debate. *Sexual Abuse: A Journal of Research and Treatment* 3: 269–92.

Malamuth, N.M. 1986. Predictors of naturalistic sexual aggression. *Journal of Personality and Social Psychology* 50: 953–62.

Malamuth, N.M., and J.V.P. Check. 1983. Sexual arousal to rape depictions: Individual differences. *Journal of Abnormal Psychology* 92: 55–67.

Malamuth, N.M., T. Linz, C.L. Heavy, G. Barnes, and M. Acker. 1995. Using the confluence model of sexual aggression to predict men's conflict with women: A 10-year follow-up study. *Journal of Personality and Social Psychology* 69: 353–69.

Marlatt, G.A., and J.R. Gordon, eds. 1985. *Relapse Prevention: Maintenance Strategies in the Treatment of Addictive Disorders.* New York: Guilford.

Martinez, R., J. Flores, and B. Rosenfeld. 2007. Validity of the juvenile sex offender assessment protocol-II (J-SOAP-II) in a sample of urban minority youth. *Criminal Justice and Behavior* 34: 1284–95.

Massachusetts G.L. Ch. 120 § 60.

Massachusetts G.L. Chapter 123a, section 14c–d.

McConaghy, N. 1999. Unresolved issues in scientific sexology. *Archives of Sexual Behavior* 28: 285–302.

McGrath, R.J., G.F. Cumming, and B.L. Burchard. 2003. *Current Practices and Trends in Sexual Abuser Management: The Safer Society 2002 Nationwide Survey.* Brandon, VT: Safer Society.

McKay, A. 2004. Oral sex among teenagers: Research, discourse, and education. *Canadian Journal of Human Sexuality* 13: 201–11.

McKeiver v. Pennsylvania 403 U.S. 528, 533 (1971).

Meehl, P. 1954. *Clinical versus Statistical Prediction: A Theoretical Analysis and a Review of the Evidence.* Minneapolis: University of Minnesota Press.

———. 1986. Causes and effects of my disturbing little book. *Journal of Personality Assessment* 50: 370–75.

Meehl, P., and A. Rosen. 1955. Antecedent probability and the efficiency of psychometric signs, patterns, and cutting scores. *Psychological Bulletin* 52: 194–216.

Megan's Law (1996). 42 U.S.C. § 13701.

Melton, G.B., J. Petrila, N.G. Poythress, and C. Slobogin. 2007. *Psychological Evaluations for the Courts. 3rd Edition.* New York: Guilford.

Michael, R.T., J.H. Gagnon, E.O. Laumann, and G. Kolata. 1994. *Sex in America: A Definitive Study.* New York: Warner Books.

Milloy, C. 1998. Specialized treatment for juvenile sex offenders. *Journal of Interpersonal Violence* 13: 653–54.

Miner, M., C. Borduin, D. Prescott, H. Bovensmann, R. Scepker, R. Du Bois, J. Schladale, R. Eher, K. Schmeck, T. Langfeldt, A. Smit, and F. Pfäfflin. 2006. Standards of care for juvenile sexual offenders of the International Association for the Treatment of Sexual Offenders. *Sexual Offender Treatment* 1: 1–7.

Moffitt, T.E. 1993. Adolescent-limited and life-course-persistent antisocial behavior: A developmental taxonomy. *Psychological Review* 100: 674–701.

———. 2003. Life-course-persistent and adolescent-limited antisocial behavior: A 10-year research review and a research agenda. In *Causes of Conduct Disorder and Juvenile Delinquency,* ed. B.B. Lahey, T.E. Moffitt, and A. Caspi. New York: Guilford.

Monahan, J. 1981. *The Clinical Prediction of Violent Behavior.* Washington, DC: Government Printing Office.

Monahan, J., H.J. Steadman, E. Silver, P.S. Appelbaum, P.C. Robbins, E.P. Mulvey, L.H. Roth, T. Grisso, and S. Banks. 2001. *Rethinking Risk Assessment: The MacArthur Study of Mental Disorder and Violence.* New York: Oxford University Press.

Money, J. 1986. *Lovemaps.* Buffalo, NY: Prometheus Books.

————. 1993. *The Adam Principle: Genes, Genitals, Hormones, & Gender: Selected Readings in Sexology.* Buffalo, NY: Prometheus Books.

Money, J., and A.A. Ehrhardt. 1972. *Man and Woman, Boy and Girl: The Differentiation and Dimorphism of Gender Identity from Conception to Maturity.* Baltimore, MD: Johns Hopkins University Press.

National Adolescent Perpetrator Network. 1993. The revised report from the National Task Force of Juvenile Sexual Offending. *Juvenile and Family Court Journal* 44: 1–115.

National Institute on Drug Abuse. 1999. *Principles of Drug Addiction Treatment: A Research-based Guide* (NIH Publication No. 99-4180). Rockville, MD: U.S. Department of Health and Human Services, National Institutes of Health.

National Research Council. 2002. *The Polygraph and Lie Detection.* Washington, DC: National Academy Press.

North Dakota Cent. Code 27-30-34.1.

Ohio rev. Code Ann. 2151.26.

Okami, P. 1992. "Child perpetrators of sexual abuse": The emergence of a problematic deviant category. *The Journal of Sex Research* 29: 109–30.

Pam Lychner Sexual Offender Tracking and Identification Act. 1996. 42 U.S.C. 14072.

Papadopoulos, M. 2006a. Boy, 6, ousted for sex harassment. *The Enterprise,* February 7.

————. 2006b. Brockton boy's ability to sexually harass girl is questioned. *The Enterprise,* February 8.

Parks, G.A., and D.E. Bard. 2006. Risk factors for adolescent sex offender recidivism: Evaluation of predictive factors and comparison of three groups based upon victim type. *Sexual Abuse: A Journal of Research and Treatment* 18: 319–42.

Perry, G.P., and J. Orchard. 1992. *Assessment and Treatment of Adolescent Sex Offenders.* Sarasota, FL: Professional Resource Press.

Pinard, M. 2006. The logistical and ethical difficulties of informing juveniles about the collateral consequences of adjudications. *Nevada Law Journal* 6: 1111–26.

Pithers, W.D., A. Gray, A. Busconi, and P. Hutchens. 1998. Children with sexual behavior problems: Identification of five distinct child types and related treatment considerations. *Child Maltreatment* 3: 384–406.

Pithers, W.D., J.K. Marques, C.C. Gibat, and G.A. Marlatt. 1983. Relapse prevention with sexual aggressives: A self-control model of treatment and maintenance of change. In *The Sexual Aggressor: Current Perspectives on* Treatment, ed. J.G. Greer and I.R. Stuart. New York: Van Nostrand Reinhold.

Poole, D., D. Liedecke, and M. Marbibi. 2000. *Risk Assessment and Recidivism in Juvenile Sexual Offenders: A Validation Study of the Static-99*. Texas: Texas Youth Commission.

Powers, P.A. 2004. Making a spectacle of Panopticism: A theoretical evaluation of sex offender registration and notification. *New England Law Review* 38: 1049–86.

Prentky, R., B. Harris, K. Frizzell, and S. Righthand. 2000. An actuarial procedure for assessing risk with juvenile sex offenders. *Sexual Abuse: A Journal of Research and Treatment* 12: 71–93.

Prentky, R., and S. Righthand. 2003. *Juvenile Sex Offender Assessment Protocol-II (J-SOAP-II) Manual*. Retrieved from http://www.csom.org/pubs/jsoap.pdf.

Quinsey, V.L., G.T. Harris, M.E. Rice, and C.A. Cormier. 1998. *Violent Offenders: Appraising and Managing Risk*. Washington, DC: American Psychological Association.

Ranalli, R., and R. Mishra. 2006. Boy's suspension in harassment case outrages mother. *The Boston Globe,* February 2.

Reitzel, L.R., and J.L. Carbonell. 2006. The effectiveness of sexual offender treatment for juveniles as measured by recidivism: A meta-analysis. *Sexual Abuse: A Journal of Research and Treatment* 18: 401–18.

Remez, L. 2000. Special report: Oral sex among adolescents: Is it sex or is it abstinence? *Family Planning Perspectives* 32: 298-304.

Reynolds, M.A., D.L. Herbenick, and J. Bancroft. 2003. The nature of childhood sexual experiences: Two studies 50 years apart. In *Sexual Development in Childhood*, ed. J. Bancroft. Bloomington: Indiana University Press.

Righthand, S., R. Prentky, R. Knight, E. Carpenter, J.E. Hecker, and D. Nangle. 2005. Factor structure and validation of the Juvenile Sex Offender Assessment Protocol (J-SOAP). *Sexual Abuse: A Journal of Research and Treatment* 17: 13–30.

Righthand, S., and C. Welch. 2001. *Juveniles Who Have Sexually Offended: A Review of the Literature*. Washington, DC: Office of Juvenile Justice and Delinquency Prevention.

Rind, B., R. Bauserman, and P. Tromovitch. 2000. Science versus orthodoxy: Anatomy of the congressional condemnation of a scientific article and reflections on remedies for future ideological attacks. *Applied and Preventative Psychology* 9: 211–25.

Rind, B., P. Tromovich, and R. Bauserman. 1998. A met-analytic examination of assumed properties of child sexual abuse using college samples. *Psychological Bulletin* 124: 22–53.

———. 2000. Condemnation of a scientific article: A chronology and refutation of the attacks and a discussion of threats to the integrity of science. *Sexuality and Culture* 4: 1–62.

Rockach, A., V. Nutbrown, and G. Nexhipi. 1988. Content analysis of erotic imagery: Sex offenders and non-sex offenders. *International Journal of Offender Therapy and Comparative Criminology* 32: 107–22.

Ronis, S.T., and C.M. Borduin. 2007. Individual, family, peer, and academic characteristics of male juvenile sexual offenders. *Journal of Abnormal Child Psychology* 35: 153–63.

Roper v. Simmons. 543 U.S. 551 (2005).

Rosenzweig, S. 1942. The photoscope as an objective device for evaluating sexual interest. *Psychosomatic Medicine* 4: 150–57.

———. 1992. *Freud, Jung, and Hall, the King-maker: The Historic Expedition to America (1909).* Seattle, WA: Hogrefe & Huber Publishers.

Ross, Dorothy. 1972. *G. Stanley Hall: The Psychologist as Prophet.* Chicago: University of Chicago Press.

Rubenstein, M., C.A. Yeager, C. Goodstein, and D.O. Lewis. 1993. Sexually assaultive male juveniles: A follow-up. *American Journal of Psychiatry* 150: 262–65.

Ryan, G. 1997. The evolving response to juvenile sexual offenders. In *Juvenile Sexual Offending: Causes, Consequences, and Correction*, eds. G. Ryan and S. Lane. San Francisco: Jossey-Bass.

Ryan, G., and S. Lane. 1997. Integrating theory and method. In *Juvenile Sexual Offending: Causes, Consequences, and Correction*, eds. G. Ryan and S. Lane. San Francisco: Jossey-Bass.

Ryan, G., S. Lane, J. Davis, and C. Issac. 1987. Juvenile sexual offenders: Development and correction. *Child Abuse and Neglect: The International Journal* 3: 385–95.

Ryan, G., T.J. Miyoshi, J.L. Metzner, R.D. Krugman, and G.E. Fryer. 1996. Trends in national sample of sexually abusive youths. *Journal of the American Academy of Child and Adolescent Psychiatry* 35: 17–25.

Saldana, L., C. Swenson Cupit, and E. Letourneau. 2006. Multisystemic Therapy with juveniles who sexually abuse. In *Current Perspectives: Working with Sexually Aggressive Youth and Youth with Sexual Behavior Problems*, ed. R. Longo and D.S. Prescott. Holyoke, MA: NEARI Press.

Santelli, J., L.D. Lindberg, J. Abma, C.S. McNeely, and M. Resnick. 2000. Adolescent sexual behavior: Estimates and trends from four nationally representative surveys. *Family Planning Perspectives* 32: 156–66.

Savin-Williams, R.C., and L.M. Diamond. 2004. Sex. In *Handbook of Adolescent Psychology. 2nd Edition*, eds. R.M. Lerner and L. Steinberg. Hoboken, NJ: Wiley.

Schram, D.D., and C.D. Milloy. 1995. *Community Notification: A Study of Offender Characteristics and Recidivism.* Olympia: Washington State Institute for Public Policy.

Schram, D.D., C.D. Milloy, and W.E. Rowe. 1991. *Juvenile Sex Offenders: A Follow-up Study of Reoffense Behavior*. Olympia: Washington State Institute for Public Policy.

Schworm, P. 2005. "Two teens face charge of statutory rape of a girl." *Boston Globe*, October 19.

Scott, E.S., and T. Grisso. 1998. The evolution of adolescence: A developmental perspective on juvenile justice reform. *Journal of Criminal Law and Criminology* 88: 137–89.

Seto, M.C. 2005. Is more better? Combining actuarial risk scales to predict recidivism among adult sex offenders. *Psychological Assessment* 17: 156–67.

Seto, M.C., and M.L. Lalumière. 2006. Conduct problems and juvenile sexual offending. In *The Juvenile Sex Offender. 2nd Edition*, eds. H.E. Barbaree and W.L. Marshall. New York: Guilford.

Seto, M.C., M.L. Lalumière, and R. Blanchard. 2000. The discriminant validity of a phallometric test for pedophilic interest among adolescent sex offenders against children. *Psychological Assessment* 12: 319–27.

Seto, M.C., W.D. Murphy, J. Page, and L. Ennis. 2003. Detecting anomalous sexual interests in juvenile sex offenders. *Annuals of the New York Academy of Sciences* 989: 118–30.

Sickmund, M., T.J. Sladley, and W. Kanf. 2005. Census for juveniles in residential placement databook. Office of Juvenile Justice and Delinquency Prevention, Department of Justice. http://www.ojjdp.ncjrs.or/ ojstatbb/cjrp/div.

Simon, J. 2005. Reversal of fortune: The resurgence of individual risk assessment in criminal justice. *Annual Review of Law and Social Science* 1: 397–421.

Singer, S.I. 1996. *Recriminalizing Delinquency: Violent Juvenile Crime and Juvenile Justice Reform*. New York: Cambridge University Press.

Singer, S.I., and D. McDowall. 1988. Criminalizing delinquency: The deterrent effects of the Juvenile Offender Act. *Law and Society Review* 22: 521–35.

Smallebone, S.W. 2006. Social and psychological factors in the development of sexual deviance and aggression in males. In *The Juvenile Sex Offender. 2nd Edition*, eds. H.E. Barbaree and W.L. Marshall. New York: Guilford.

Smallebone, S.W., and R.K. Wortley. 2004. Criminal versatility and paraphilic interests among adult males convicted of sexual offenses against children. *International Journal of Offender Therapy and Comparative Criminology* 48: 175–88.

Smith, G., and L. Fischer. 1999. Assessment of juvenile sexual offenders: Reliability and validity of the Abel Assessment for Interest in Paraphilias. *Sexual Abuse: A Journal of Research and Treatment* 11: 207–16.

Smith, W.R., and C. Monastersky. 1986. Assessing juvenile sex offenders' risk of reoffending. *Criminal Justice and Behavior* 13: 115–40.

Snyder, H.N., and M. Sickmund. 2006. *Juvenile Offenders and Victims: 2006 National Report*. Washington, DC: U.S. Department of Justice, Office of Justice Programs, Office of Juvenile Justice and Delinquency Programs.

Snyder, H.N., M. Sickmund, and E. Po-Yamagata. 1996. *Juvenile Offenders and Victims: A National Report.* Washington, DC: Office of Juvenile Justice and Delinquency Prevention.

Sonenstein, F.L., L. Ku, and J.H. Pleck. 1997. Measuring sexual behavior among teenage males in the United States. In *Researching Sexual Behavior: Methodological Issues,* ed. J. Bancroft. Bloomington: Indiana University Press.

Spaccarelli, S., B. Bowden, J.D. Coatsworth, and S. Kim. 1997. Psychosocial correlates of male sexual aggression in a chronic delinquent sample. *Criminal Justice and Behavior* 24: 71–95.

Stahl, A.L., C. Puzzanchera, A. Sladky, T.A. Finnegan, N. Tierney, and H.N. Snyder. 2007. *Juvenile Court Statistics, 2003–2004.* Pittsburgh, PA: National Center for Juvenile Justice.

State v. Adams 223 Wis. 2d 60 (1998).

State v. Post 197 Wis. 2d 279 (1995).

Steadman, H., and J. Cocozza. 1974. *Careers of the Criminally Insane.* Lexington, MA: Lexington Books.

Steadman, H., J. Monahan, P. Appelbaum, T. Grisso, E. Mulvey, L. Roth, P. Robbins, and D. Klassen. 1994. Designing a new generation of risk assessment instruments. In *Violence and Mental Disorder: Developments in Risk Assessment,* eds. J. Monahan and H. Steadman. Chicago: University of Chicago Press.

Steinberg, L., and E.S. Scott. 2003. Less guilty by reason of adolescence. *American Psychologist* 58: 1009–1118.

Swenson, C.C., S.K. Schoenwald, J. Randall, S.W. Henggeler, and K.L. Kaufman. 1998. Changing the social ecologies of adolescent sexual offenders: Implications of the success of multisystemic therapy in treating serious antisocial behavior in adolescents. *Child Maltreatment* 3: 330–38.

Tanenhaus, D.S. 2000. The evolution of transfer out of the juvenile court. In *The Changing Borders of Juvenile Justice: Transfer of Adolescents to Criminal Court,* eds. J. Fagan and F.E. Zimring. Chicago: University of Chicago Press.

———. 2002. The evolution of juvenile courts in the early twentieth century: Beyond the myth of the immaculate construction. In *A Century of Juvenile Justice,* eds. M.K. Rosenheim, F.E. Zimring, D.S. Tanenhaus, and B. Dohrn. Chicago: University of Chicago Press.

Templeman, T.L., and R.D. Stinnett. 1991. Patterns of sexual arousal and history in a "normal" sample of young men. *Archives of Sexual Behavior* 20: 137–50.

Tewksbury, R. 2005. Collateral consequences of sex offender registration. *Journal of Contemporary Criminal Justice* 21: 67–81.

Thakker, J., T. Ward, P. Tidmarsh. 2006. A reevaluation of relapse prevention with adolescents who sexually offend: A Good-Lives Model. In *The Juvenile Sexual Offender. 2nd Edition,* eds. H.E. Barbaree and W.L. Marshall. New York: Guilford.

Thompson v. Oklahoma 487 U.S. 815 (1988).

Thornton, D. 2002. Constructing and testing a framework for dynamic risk assessment. *Sexual Abuse: A Journal of Research and Treatment* 14: 139–53.

Torbet, P., R. Gable, H. Hurst, I. Montgomery, and D. Thomas. 1996. State responses to serious and violent juvenile crime: Research report. Washington, DC: Office of Juvenile Justice and Delinquency Prevention.

Travis, J. 2002. Invisible punishment: An instrument of social exclusion. In *Invisible Punishment: The Collateral Consequences of Mass Imprisonment*, eds. M. Mauer and M. Chesney-Lind. New York: New Press.

Trivits, L.C., and N.D. Reppucci. 2002. Application of Megan's Law to juveniles. *American Psychologist* 57: 690–704.

Trilling, L. 1947/2000. Manners, Morals, and the Novel. In *The Moral Obligation to Be Intelligent: Selected Essays of Lionel Trilling*, ed. L. Wieseltier. New York: Farrar Straus Giroux.

Upchurch, D.M., L.A. Lillard, C.S. Aneschenel, and N.F. Li. 2002. Inconsistencies in reporting the occurrence and timing of first intercourse among adolescents. *Journal of Sex Research* 39: 197–206.

U.S. Department of Health and Human Services. 2001. *Youth Violence: A Report of the Surgeon General*. Rockville, MD: U.S. Department of Health and Human Services, Substance Abuse and Mental Health Services Administration, Center For Mental Health Services, National Institute of Health, National Institute of Mental Health.

van Wijk, A., S.R.F. Mali, and R.A.R. Bullens. 2007. The juvenile sex-only and sex-plus offenders: An exploratory study on criminal profiles. *International Journal of Offender Therapy and Comparative Criminology* 51: 407–19.

van Wijk, A., J. van Horn, R. Bullens, C. Bijleveld, and T. Doreleijers. 2005. Juvenile sex offenders: A group of its own? *International Journal of Offender Therapy and Comparative Criminology* 49: 25–36.

van Wijk, A., R. Vermeiren, R. Loeber, L. Hart-Kerkhoffs, T. Doreleijers, and R. Bullens. 2006. Juvenile sex offenders compared to non-sex offenders: A review of the literature, 1995–2005. *Trauma, Violence, & Abuse* 7: 227–43.

Viljoen, J.L., M. Scalora, L. Cuadra, S. Bader, V. Chávez, D. Ullman, and L. Lawrence. Assessing risk for violence in adolescents who have sexually offended: A comparison of the J-SOAP-II, J-SORRAT-II, and SAVRY. *Criminal Justice and Behavior* 35: 5–23.

Waite, D., A. Keller, E.L. McGarvey, E. Wieckowski, R. Pinkerton, and G.L. Brown. 2005. Juvenile sex offender re-arrest rates for sexual, violent, non-sexual, and property crimes: A 10-year follow-up. *Sexual Abuse: A journal of Research and Treatment* 17: 313–31.

Walker, C.E., and D. McCormick. 2004. Current practices in residential treatment for adolescent sex offenders: A survey. In *Identifying and Treating Youth Who Sexually Offend: Current Approaches, Techniques, and Research*, eds. R. Geffner, K. Crumpton Franey, T. Geffner Arnold, and R. Falconer. New York: Haworth Press.

Walker, D.F., S.K. McGovern, E.L. Poey, and K.E. Otis. 2004. Treatment effectiveness for male adolescent sexual offenders: A meta-analysis and review. In *Identifying and Treating Youth Who Sexually Offend: Current Approaches, Techniques, and Research,* eds. R. Geffner, K. Crumpton Franey, T. Geffner Arnold, and R. Falconer. New York: Haworth Press.

Wangsness, L., and K. Burge. 2006. Police investigate alleged gunman's motives in killings. *Boston Globe,* April 18.

Ward, T. 2002. Good lives and the rehabilitation of sex offenders: Problems and promises. *Aggression and Violent Behavior* 7: 1–17.

Weinrott, M.R. 1996. *Juvenile Sexual Aggression: A Critical Review.* Center for the Study and Prevention of Violence, Institute for the Behavioral Science, University of Colorado, Boulder.

Weithorn, L.A. 2005. Envisioning second-order change in America's response to troubled and troublesome youth. *Hofstra Law Review* 33: 1305–1506.

West Virgina Code 49-5-10(d)).

White, J.W., K.M. Kadlec, and S. Sechrist. 2006. Adolescent sexual aggression with heterosexual relationships. In *The Juvenile Sexual Offender. 2nd Edition,* eds. H.E. Barbaree and W.L. Marshall. New York: Guilford.

White, J.W., and R.M. Kowalski. 1998. Male violence toward women: An integrated perspective. In *Human Aggression: Theories, Research, and Implications for Social Policy,* eds. R.G. Green and E. Donnerstein. San Diego, CA: Academic.

Wis. Stats. Chapter 980.01 (7).

Wisconsin v. McCain 226 Wis. 2d 158 (1999).

Wollert, R. 2006. Low base rates limit expert certainty when current actuarials are used to identify sexually violent predators: An application of Bayes' Theorem. *Psychology, Public Policy, and Law* 12: 56–85.

Worling, J.R. 1995. Sexual abuse histories of adolescent male sex offenders: Differences on the basis of the age and gender of their victims. *Journal of Abnormal Psychology* 104: 610–13.

———. 2004. The Estimate of Risk of Adolescent Sexual Offense Recidivism (ERASOR): Preliminary psychometric data. *Sexual Abuse: A Journal of Research and Treatment* 16: 235–54.

———. 2006. Assessing sexual arousal with adolescent males who have offended sexually: Self-report and unobtrusively measured viewing time. *Sexual Abuse: A Journal of Research and Treatment* 18: 383–400.

Worling, J.R,. and T. Curwen. 2000. Adolescent sexual offense recidivism: Success of specialized treatment and implications for risk prediction. *Child Abuse & Neglect* 24: 965–82.

———. 2001. *Estimate of Risk of Adolescent Sexual Offense Recidivism (ERASOR; Version 2.0).* Unpublished manuscript. Toronto, Ontario: Ontario Ministry of Community and Social Services.

Worling, J., and N. Långström. 2006. Risk of sexual recidivism in adolescents who offend sexually: Correlates and assessment. In *The Juvenile Sexual Offender. 2nd Edition*, eds. H.E. Barbaree and W.L. Marshall. New York: Guilford.

Zevitz, R.G. 2006. Sex offender community notification: Its role in recidivism and offender reintegration. *Criminal Justice Studies* 19: 193–208.

Zevitz, R.G., and M.A. Farkas. 2000. Sex offender community notification: Managing high risk criminals or exacting further vengeance? *Behavioral Sciences and the Law* 18: 375–91.

Zimring, F. 1982. *The Changing Legal World of Adolescence*. New York: Free Press.

———. 1998. *American Youth Violence*. New York: Oxford University Press.

———. 2000. The punitive necessity of waiver. In *The Changing Borders of Juvenile Justice: Transfer of Adolescents to Criminal Court*, eds. J. Fagan and F.E. Zimring. Chicago: University of Chicago Press.

———. 2004. *An American Travesty: Legal Responses to Adolescent Sexual Offending*. Chicago: University of Chicago Press.

Zimring, F.E., and J. Fagan. 2000. Transfer policy and legal reform. In *The Changing Borders of Juvenile Justice: Transfer of Adolescents to Criminal Court*, eds. J. Fagan and F.E. Zimring. Chicago: University of Chicago Press.

Zimring, F.E., A.R. Piquero, and W.G. Jennings. 2007. Sexual delinquency in Racine: Does early sex offending predict later sex offending in youth and young adulthood? *Criminology & Public Policy* 3: 507–34.

Index

childhood sexuality, 109–142; adult adjustment problems, 126–127, 128–129; "adultification" of, 110–111; between ages 2 and 12, 117–118, 121, 138; as budding juvenile sex offenders, 141–142; changes over time, 120–121; child sex abuse as a scientific category, 128–129; "children with sexual behavior problems," 136; cognitive behavior therapy, 140–141; collective denial of, 133; collective fears of disfiguring effects, 141–142; concealment by children, 115–116; consent, legally informed *vs.* simple, 128–129; context of, 118; contextual nature, 116; criminalization of, 138; cultural conditioning, 119; cycle-of-abuse notion, 132; as dirt, 136, 137; expressive therapy, 140; Foucault on, Michel, 134–135; Freud and, Sigmund, 113–114; harmfulness, 125, 128–129, 130, 131–132; hysteria over, 119; in infants, 119; interdisciplinary studies, 117–118; "is" *vs.* "ought" concerns, 131–132; Kinsey and, Alfred, 118–120; masturbation, 112, 134; mean age for initiation of sexual play, 121; moral panic, 131; pathologization, 135–141; play therapy, 140–141; political views, 124, 129–131; preadolescent orgasms, 119; problematization of, 1, 135; rate of childhood sexual activities, 119; recapitulation theory, 111–112; regulation of, 135; relapse-prevention model, 140; research about, 114–132, 135–141; research about, Congressional condemnation of, 124–132; research about, negative cast of, 116, 126; research about deviant forms, 116; as result of trauma, 136, 139;

retrospective accounts of adults, 115; sexual abuse, 117–118, 125–129, 132–133, 137; sexual attraction, first appearance, 120; as sexual deviance, 138–139, 140; sexual fantasies, onset of, 120–121; sexual predators, 132–133; sexual purity and innocence, 133–134; socialization, 115–116; ubiquity of, 118, 136–137. *See also* adolescent sex

children, sexual fantasies about, 46–47

CHINS (Child in Need of Supervision), 62

civil commitment of juvenile sex offenders, 167–202; actuarial assessment instruments, 200–201, 202; of adults whose only sexual offenses occurred during adolescence, 194, 200, 201, 202; Antisocial Personality Disorder, 186, 187, 190, 192, 193–196, 200, 202; as civil rather than criminal action, 190–191; *Commonwealth v. Kenney,* 184–185; conditions for, 172–176, 174; Conduct Disorder, 185, 187, 193, 197–198, 202; confidentiality of juvenile court records, 175t, 181–185, 189; "conviction" for a sexual offense, 172–173, 174; dangerousness, 174–175, 185–186; delinquency adjudication for juvenile sex offenders, 173, 175t, 176–179, 182, 193–194, 195, 197, 200; double jeopardy, 169, 175; Exhibitionism, 192; impulsivity as a volitional impairment, 196–197; indeterminate sentencing mechanisms, 171; *In the Interest of Hezzie R.,* 180–181; jury trials for juveniles, 179–181, 201; *Kansas v. Hendricks,* 167–170, 175–176, 190–191; legal counsel, availability of, 170; *In the matter of Carl Leroy Anderson,* 176–177;

Ward, T., 100, 229

Weinrott, M. R., 79, 81, 90

Weldon, David, 129

Wetterling, Jacob, 205, 208, 212

When Children Molest Children (Cunningham and MacFarlane), 139

Williams, D. C., 80

Willie Bosket Law (New York State, 1978), 163–164

Wilson, Genarlow, 5–7, 24

Wisconsin Court of Appeals, 189–190, 199, 200

Wisconsin Supreme Court, 180–181, 199

Wisconsin v. McCain, 178, 195

Wollert, R., 84

Worling, J. R., 45, 72–73, 80

Yeager, C. A., 80–81

Youth Forensic Psychiatric Service (Vancouver), 43

Youth Level of Service Inventory/Case Management Inventory (YLS/CMI), 66

Youth Report Survey, 31

zero tolerance policies, 110

Zevitz, R. G., 211

Zimring, Franklin: adolescent mistakes, 8; adult sex offenses of boys with prior police contact, 33; amenability to rehabilitation, 154; *Changing Legal World of Adolescence,* 8; continuum notion of moral and legal accountability, 9–10; criminalization of juvenile sex, 7; juvenile compared to adult sex offenders, 79; juvenile waivers, 147, 149; literature by juvenile court experts, 159; recidivism rate of juveniles transferred to adult court, 165

About the Author

FRANK C. DICATALDO is Assistant Professor of Psychology at Roger Williams University and the Director of the Forensic Evaluation Service for the Northeast Family Institute-Massachusetts.